MONEY, POWER AND SEX

The Implication of Money, Power and Sex

In The Downfall of People

Daniel Ukadike Nwaelene, Th.D.

MONEY, POWER AND SEX
The Implication of Money, Power and Sex

In The Downfall of People

Copyright © 2025 Daniel Ukadike Nwaelene, ThD.

Daniel Nwaelene Books, LLC
190 Palisade Ave #4D
Yonkers, NY 10703, USA
www.danielnwaelenebooksllc.com
914 282-0120

Because of the dynamic nature of the Internet, any web addresses or links contained in this book may have changed since publication and may no longer be valid. The views expressed in this work are solely those of the author and do not necessarily reflect the views of the publisher, and the publisher hereby disclaims any responsibility for them.

ISBN (eBook): 979-8-9922386-4-8
ISBN (Paperback): 979-8-9922386-2-4
ISBN (Hardback): 979-8-9922386-3-1

DEDICATION

To

The Almighty GOD.

He is the Creator and Sustainer of all life and all things.

He is the Author of knowledge and wisdom.

All power, salvation and glory belong to Him, and

HE is my GOD

PREFACE

Every negative event in the life of a person is usually believed to have been caused by something extrinsic, especially when such an event involves a downfall. Some people would attribute it to hatred or envy by enemies. In parts of Africa some would attribute it to some witch or wizard in the person's hometown or family. Hardly does a fallen person look inwards to himself or herself to determine the cause of the predicament. This is not to imply that witches and wizards do not exist or have negative activities in the society, because they are mentioned (known to exist) in the Holy Bible.

This book is, therefore, aimed at analyzing some falls from ancient times till date, to relate some falls to lust for, and inability to control/manage, money, power and/or sex.

Certainly, for every effect there is a cause. Something must lead to the fall of a person from grace to grass. And it is most likely to be one or all three elements mentioned above.

Money, power and sex in themselves are good and essential for the well-being of mankind. But abuse of any of them is very likely to be inimical to well-being, likely to lead to a fall and, sometimes, death.

The aim of the author for this book is to draw the attention of people in position of power or wealth, who are at the brink of falling, to counsel themselves to prevent a shameful fall. It is also aimed at people, young and old, desiring to become rich or get into the corridors of power, to warn them of what they may face if they throw caution to the winds.

Acknowledgment of God, the Source of your power or wealth, and the natural laws guiding and controlling all such things in life, are key to living a successful life. Self-control and humility, with the fear of God and respect for others are virtues that must be imbibed at every point in life to guide you with respect to power, money and sex. I

pray that the almighty God will give you the grace to appreciate Him and imbibe the virtue and to resist the temptation that could lead to a fall.

Where you have already fallen, believe and remember that the downfall of a man is not the end of his life, according to a popular adage. Right your wrongs; repent of your sinful ways and make a fresh start.

As most of the recommendations and instances in this book are based on the Holy Bible, it is advisable to make time to also study the Bible to learn more than what is presented in this book. The Bible is the inspired Word of God. The apostle Paul wrote, "All Scripture is God-breathed and is useful for teaching, rebuking, correcting and training in righteousness, [17] so that the servant of God may be thoroughly equipped for every good work." (2 Timothy 3:16-17 NIV). Wisdom, power, help, strength, comfort and so on, can be gained from the Bible.

As in my earlier books, most Bible references are fully quoted in this book. The purpose is to enable the reader to also read the exact words of the Scriptures, because most people never go to check out references in the books they read.

May your memory and understanding be sharpened even as you read through this book. "The hardworking farmer should be the first to receive a share of the crops. [7] Reflect on what I am saying, for the Lord will give you insight into all this." (2 Timothy 2:6-7 NIV).

Rev. Daniel Ukadike Nwaelene, ThD.

April 15, 2023.

Follow me on social media:

LINKEDIN www.linkedin.com/in/rev-daniel-nwaelene-thd-34105331

INSTAGRAM: https://www.instagram.com/nwaelenedu/#

X (Twitter): @nwaelenedu

FACEBOOK: https://www.facebook.com/daniel.nwaelene

WEBSITES: www.danielnwaelenebooksllc.com

BOOKS BY THE AUTHOR

1. JESUS CHRIST: Savior, Judge and King of the World

Originally published by: WestBow Press Year: 2017.
www.westbowpress.com Tel.: +1 866 928 1240.
Re-published by: Bookside Press www.booksidepress.com –
Year: 2024.
Tel. 1 877 741 8091.
Re-published by: Daniel Nwaelene Books LLC – Year: 2026

2. ACTING MOVIE SCRIPTS OR FULFILLING PROPHECIES?

Originally Published by: Christian Faith Publishing, Inc. –
Year: 2018.
www.christianfaithpublishing.com
Re-published by: Daniel Nwaelene Books LLC – Year: 2024
https://danielnwaelenebooksllc.com/ Tel: +1 914 920 9862.

3. FAMILY STRUCTURE BY CHOICE: A Defense of Traditional Marriage Structure

Originally published by: iUniverse Publishing - Year: 2020
www.iuniverse.com Tel.: +1 800 288 4677
Re-published by: Gotham Books, Inc
https://gothambooksinc.com Year: 2022 Tel: +1 307 404
7800.

4. GOD IS INTERESTED IN YOUR MARRIAGE: Path to a Successful, Happy Christian

Marriage
Originally published by: Gotham Books, Inc. - Year: 2024
https://gothambooksinc.com Tel: +1 307 404 7800.
Re-published by: Daniel Nwaelene Books – Year: 2026

5. MONEY, POWER AND SEX: The Implication of Money, Power and Sex In The Downfall of People

Published by Daniel Nwaelene Books, LLC. – Year: 2025
https://danielnwaelenebooksllc.com/ Tel: +1 914 920 9862.

ABOUT THIS BOOK

The title of the book, as you see on the cover, is "Money, Power and Sex: The Implication of Money, Power and Sex in The Downfall of People." Its main objective is to expose the idea that money (wealth), power and sex may be major contributors to, or causes of, the downfall of many people – men and women.

Although most of the teachings in the book are based on the Holy Bible, this book is applicable or relevant to people of all faiths, because issues about money (or wealth), power and sex affect all human beings, irrespective of their religious inclinations, race or gender.

It has been observed that from time immemorial, some people appear humble, friendly, cheerful and helpful until they assume positions of authority, when pride sets in and they begin to oppress the less privileged, use the authority at their disposal to acquire more power and wealth and do many obscene things. Before long, (it might take some years) their supporters withdraw from, and desert them, and they eventually fall ignominiously.

Many powerful men, commanders of large military formations, kings, emperors and presidents of nations may remain powerful and influential until one strange woman enters their lives, and they get involved sexually. That would lead to a scandal, which may lead to the downfall of a once-powerful man.

Stories also abound of married couples who lived happily with their paycheck-to-paycheck income until a financial breakthrough came their way. Then reasons – some verbalized and others internalized) for divorce began to arise. Similarly, a couple of some church leaders were really walking and working together from inception of their churches until their church memberships grew, and money began to roll in. Then division set in until a group, including some of the leaders broke away. Money!

Some men who suddenly become wealthy, and some 'veteran wealthy' people lose control of their money, thereby allowing their money to control them, to the extent that they say and do obscene things; they can and do kill to make more money or to silence any form of opposition, and they soon go down. Such people think they are above the law because they feel they can buy justice and freedom at any cost with money. Furthermore, because there is money to spend, some rich people waste a lot of money on sex-related relationships – changing sex partners like wardrobes - which could lead to scandal, STDs (sexually transmitted diseases). Some put plenty of money into alcohol and hard drugs.

We can state in this book that money, power and sex are very good and essential to have when they are controllable and used as servants rather than masters. And the antidote to a fall due to any of these is to not lust for them, respect the Giver of these good things and see yourself as a steward of all you are and have, and accountable to the Giver of all you are and have.

In view of the educative and far-reaching topics in this book, I do not hesitate to recommend the book to people contemplating seeking or already holding public offices. It is necessary for young people as leaders of tomorrow in the secular society, and in the Christian communities of tomorrow. Afterall nobody is immune to temptations. As a reminder, the Bible admonishes to "Train up a child in the way he should go [teaching him to seek God's wisdom and will for his abilities and talents], Even when he is old, he will not depart from it." (Proverbs 22:6 AMP). It is also important or recommended for older adults such as parents, managers, teachers, pastors, in a position to counsel or educate younger people to read this book.

EDITOR'S PREVIEW
MONEY, POWER AND SEX

The Implication of Money, Power and Sex in The Downfall of Many People.

This is a clear, pastoral, and persuasive work that addresses an enduring problem with fresh urgency: why three morally neutral gifts, money, power, and sex, so often precipitate personal collapse, and how a Christ-centered lifeguards against it. The voice is confident yet caring; the argument is anchored in Scripture and pastoral experience; and the structure guides the reader from foundations (temptation, sin, and eternal destiny) to practical counsel (right use, misuse, and safeguards). The result is a **useful, teachable** book for churches, small groups, campus ministries, and emerging leaders.

The **Introduction** situates the themes in recognizable public scandals (MeToo context; U.S. political figures), then turns the lens to the heart, matching the book's thesis that sin exposed in public is first tolerated in private. The **sections on sex** handle sensitive material frankly but not gratuitously; biblical case studies (e.g., Judah/Tamar; Rahab; Samson/Delilah; the harlots before Solomon) are used to teach rather than sensationalize. The **treatment of prostitution and trafficking** balances moral clarity with social awareness, noting law and exploitation without losing the pastoral tone. Historical/political case sketches (e.g., Nigerian coups) illustrate power's distortions and the dangers of unaccountable authority.

"Clear, courageous, and deeply pastoral, *Money, Power and Sex* **names the forces that undo lives, and shows how grace, truth, and disciplined love restore them. Rev. Nwaelene writes with the authority of Scripture and the compassion of a shepherd. Every emerging leader should read this.**

August 2025.

ACKNOWLEDGMENTS

Bearing in mind the declaration that it is ". . . 'Not by might nor by power, but by my Spirit,' says the Lord Almighty." (Zechariah 4:6), I hereby give thanks to the Almighty GOD for permitting, and enabling me to write this book, and for providing for the production of the book. God is the Author of knowledge because He is omniscient. He provided, or led me to where to find, answers to questions, and materials put together to produce the book. To Him be all the glory. I also appreciate Him for wanting you and all my readers to learn from past mistakes of people in order to prevent you from falling victim of History.

Secondly, I hereby appreciate all authors of materials (books, journals, Internet websites, etc.) that were cited or quoted in this book. Such materials have been acknowledged in the book as footnotes in the chapters, and in the bibliography, but I feel constrained to appreciate the authors, who I cannot name here one-by-one, for allowing parts of their ideas and valuable works to be placed in this one. Thank you all, authors.

Oftentimes, in the process of producing this and my other books, I could not but painfully fail to give my wife the needed attention she deserved. However, she was very helpful and cooperative all the way. Pat, thank you for your understanding. May the Lord bless you again and again.

I also extend my appreciation to Ecco Press for reviewing the manuscript of this book before its publishing. Thank you, Ecco Press for the efforts and time invested to make the work a reality. Finally, I appreciate you the reader reading the book. It would have been time, money and efforts wasted if you had not spared time to read the book. I pray GOD to illumine
your heart and mind, to enable you to comprehend, and derive all the benefits He has designed for you in the book; thank you and may God bless you.

Rev. Daniel U. Nwaelene, Th.D.

April 20, 2023.

Abbreviations of Bible Versions Quoted.

ABPE Aramaic Bible in Plain English

AKJV Authorized King James Version

BSB Berean Study Bible

CEV Contemporary English Version

CSB Christian Standard Bible

DRAB Douay-Rheims 1899 American Edition

ESV English Standard Version

GNT Good News Translation

GWT God's Word Translation

HCSB Holman Christian Standard Bible

ISV International Standard Version

NETB New English Translation

NIV New International Version

NKJV New King James Version

NLT New Living Translation

NLV New Life Version

YLT Young's Literal Translation

TABLE OF CONTENT

Page

Dedication   iii

Preface   iv

Books by this Author   vii

About this Book   viii

Editor's Preview of the Book   xi

Acknowledgments   xiii

1. Introduction   1

1.1 Temptation and Trials   4

1.2 Temptations and Sin   8

2. Temptations and People's Eternal Destinies   10

2.1 Fall of Adam (Fall of Mankind)   14

2.2 Victory of Jesus Christ   20

2.3 The God of this World   31

3. Money (Wealth)   38

3.1 Characteristics of Money Power   41

3.2 Sources and Modes of Acquiring Money   47

3.3 Good Use or Application of Money   61

3.4 Misuse or Abuse of Money   66

3.5 Contribution of Money to the Downfall of a Man   75

3.6 Bible Passages Teaching about Money (Riches,   85
Wealth)

3.7 Conclusion About Money   91

4. Power   94

4.1 Greek Words Translated as Power in the English   96
Bible

4.2 Sources of Power and Methods of Acquisition of   100
Power

4.3 Good Uses or Application of Power   117

4.4 Abuse of Power   157

4.5 Instrumentality of Power to a Leader's Downfall   205

4.6 Bible Lessons on Power/Authority   212

4.7 Conclusions and Recommendations   216

5. Sex   226

5.1 Definitions   226

5.2 Modes of Access to Sex   241

5.3 Good Application of Sex   243

5.4 Abuses of Sex   247

5.5 The Role of Sex in the Fall of People   252

5.6 Bible Teachings about Sexual Relations   270

6. Relationship Between Money, Power and Sex.   278

7. Conclusions   281

8. Recommendations   286

8.1 Repentance, Restitution and the Grace of God   291

8.2 Love of Christ versus Love for Money   293

8.3 Self Control, Power of Prayer, and Dependence on 298
the Holy Spirit

Bibliography   301

General Index   305

Scripture Reference Index   318

Appendix

About the Author   343

CHAPTER ONE
INTRODUCTION

In recent times the United States of America (USA) has been experiencing a turn of events: several women have been coming out to, and through the media, to expose and accuse some men that are seeking political offices, of sexually assaulting them in different ways in times past – some in their teen years. Similarly, some business executives, senators and sitting political office holders were forced to resign their jobs sequel to accusations of unwanted advances, touching and other forms of 'sexual harassment' and escapades. These men would never have thought, in their wildest imagination when they played with the women (their employees or past friends), that their actions then would one day come to the open and become an issue. Like the Bible says, ". . . behold, ye have sinned against the Lord: and be sure your sin will find you out." (Numbers 32:23), the simple sexual relationships that the men had enjoyed many years back now began to haunt them and adversely affect their political ambitions and careers.

A past president of the USA, President Bill Clinton was in office for the two full terms, and to a great extent, did well as president. Unfortunately, he was impeached for perjury - lying under oath to a federal grand jury, and obstructing justice with regard to his extra-marital affairs with an intern in the White

House. So, each time references are made to his great services the "but" in his life follows immediately – "but he was impeached." And references are made every so often to his case in the USA each time similar issues are in the news. This is just like the Bible describes a Syrian army general, Naaman as a man of great military prowess, "but he was a leper" (2 Kings 5:1).

You cannot imagine the number of pastors of Christian churches, including even a seminary president of repute in the United States of America, and medical doctors and other professionals that have lost their pastoral and other professional jobs, licenses and reputation, all because of sex.

There are many rich people that are humble, compass-sionate and philanthropic. On the contrary, there abound very rich men that use their wealth to oppress and intimidate, but their actions may not be well known. For instance, a real estate businessman in the USA, purportedly rich, who had been using the power of money to oppress his employees, tenants, contractors, and abuse women because he had money to cover his actions using various means. He boasted of his wealth. Much of this man was not known until he acquired political power, becoming a president of the USA. This man saw himself as above the law. He did many things unusual with the USA presidency including lying, doing business underground while in office, practicing nepotism, and associating mainly with foreign autocratic leaders. It was only when he began to seek this political office that his past dirty acts began to be exposed, but all that did not seem to change anything because he had been able to silence opponents, having bought the support of members of his party that were controlling the other arms of government at the time.

In many, if not all, nations, people in positions of authority use their positions to acquire wealth and more wealth for themselves and their families at the expense of national development and to the detriment of the generality of the people. This is power at play – using power to corner for themselves alone what belongs to all. No wonder the most popular quotation of the 19th century British politician, Lord Acton, which was quoted by author George Orwell in his Animal Farm is very correct: "Power corrupts; absolute power corrupts absolutely" is true even today. Abuse of power is an age-long practice that had brought down people. Kings, emperors, presidents, governors, other leaders, corporation executives and professionals have abused power, some to the extent of ascribing divinity/deity to themselves and causing their subjects to worship them in place of the almighty God. They used the power of office to oppress their subjects. They usually fell and were removed from office. Such power abusers forget or do not know that God said, "I am the Lord: that is my name: and my glory will I not give to another, neither my praise to graven images." (Isaiah 42:8). When a man ascribes to himself the power and glory that belong to God alone, he is bound to fall before too long.

In this book, we shall see some samples of persons that fell as a result of abuse of money, power and or sex. Sometimes these three culprits go together in bringing down a man or woman, and other times it is only one or two of them. It is, therefore, advisable that people watch their relationships and pronouncements as they grow richer and as they rise to power at any level of authority.

1.1 Temptation and Trials

Many people caught doing some mischievous things have often confessed when asked, that the devil tempted them. People are always tempted to do many things they know are evil, ranging from telling "small lies" to robbery, murder and many other heinous crimes. The first question then is, what is temptation?

Webster's Dictionary defines "to tempt" as "to entice to do wrong by promise of pleasure or gain."[1] So temptation is "the act of tempting" – act of enticing someone to do wrong. Furthermore, an online dictionary suggests that temptation is "a desire to do something, especially something wrong or unwise."

---

[1] Webster's All-In-One Dictionary & Thesaurus, 2010, 650.

Generally, temptation and trial are often used interchangeably; but there appears to be a thin line of difference between temptation and trial. While trial is more of testing of someone's ability to do, be or withstand something, temptation implies enticing or suggestion, either by a third party or by the one's mind, to do or refuse to do something.

There are times when temptation and trial go together. The story of Job in the Bible is a great example of temptation accompanied by trial. Job was facing trials – a test of his integrity and loyalty to God. God permitted the devil to try Job, causing him to lose all his property, wealth and children. When the trial did not yield the kind of result the devil desired, it was extended to include loss of his good health, and he was tempted to do things he had never done in the past. His wife, for instance, suggested he curse God and die (Job 2:9): "Then said his wife unto him, Dost thou still retain thine integrity? curse God, and die." This was temptation par excellence!

All of mankind sinned by having sin[2] imputed by birth. Sin is described as an immoral act in transgression of the divine law. It can be committed in thought or by physical action. The Bible says, "For all have sinned, and come short of the glory of God;" (Romans 3:23). Similarly, the prophet Isaiah had earlier

---

[2] "Sin" means missing the mark of God or falling short of the standard of God.

described sin thus: "All we like sheep have gone astray; we have turned everyone to his own way;" (Isaiah 53:6). In addition to the original sin that is imputed, we are all tempted at all times to do things that displease God or are sinful to Him. If we do not successfully resist such temptations, then we fall into sin. In effect, temptation can lead to, or result in, sin.

It should be noted that all temptations are by the evil one. Read the caution of the apostle James thus:

"Let no man say when he is tempted, I am tempted of God: for God cannot be tempted with evil, neither tempteth he any man: [14] But every man is tempted, when he is drawn away of his own lust, and enticed. [15] Then when lust hath conceived, it bringeth forth sin: and sin, when it is finished, bringeth forth death" (James 1:13-15).

The apostle Peter wrote:

"Beloved, think it not strange concerning the fiery trial which is to try you, as though some strange thing happened unto you: [13] But rejoice, inasmuch as ye are partakers of Christ's sufferings; that, when his glory shall be revealed, ye may be glad also with exceeding joy. [14] If ye be reproached for the name of Christ, happy are ye; for the spirit of glory and of God resteth upon you: on their part he is evil spoken of, but on your part he is glorified.

[15] But let none of you suffer as a murderer, or as a thief, or as an evildoer, or as a busybody in other men's matters. [16] Yet if any

man suffer as a Christian, let him not be ashamed; but let him glorify God on this behalf. [17] For the time is come that judgment must begin at the house of God: and if it first begin at us, what shall the end be of them that obey not the gospel of God? [18] And if the righteous scarcely be saved, where shall the ungodly and the sinner appear [19] Wherefore let them that suffer according to the will of God commit the keeping of their souls to him in well doing, as unto a faithful Creator." (1 Peter 4:12-19).

The Bible says that there are benefits of trials and temptations. For instance, the Apostle James says, "Blessed is the man who endures temptation, for when he has been tested, he will receive a crown of life, which God has promised to those who love him" (James 1:12 ABPE).

Trials draw people of God closer to Him. For example, one of the effects of the massacre of Christians in Nigeria by two terrorist groups – Boko Haram and Fulani Herdsmen – is that the Christians pray more regularly, communicate more with one another and got more united than ever. Similar blessings abound amongst believers in the Middle East and other predominantly Muslim nations. Consider the following verses:

"My brethren, count it all joy when ye fall into diverse temptations; [3] Knowing this, that the trying of your faith worketh patience. [4] But let patience have her perfect work, that ye may be perfect and entire, wanting nothing." (James 1:2-4).

Romans 5:3-5 reads, "And not only so, but we glory in tribulations also: knowing that tribulation worketh patience; [4] And patience, experience; and experience, hope: [5] And hope maketh not ashamed; because the love of God is shed abroad in our hearts by the Holy Ghost which is given unto us."

1.2 Temptations and Sin.

Temptation is not sin. To be tempted is therefore, not to sin. What is sin is falling to temptation – that is failure to resist temptation. If temptation were sin, Jesus Christ would have been a sinner. Note what the Bible says of Him: "For we have not an high priest which cannot be touched with the feeling of our infirmities; but was in all points tempted like as we are, yet without sin." (Hebrews 4:15). Since temptation implies suggestion to do, or to be, something sinful, failing to successfully resist it means succumbing to being or doing evil.

If sin is transgression of God's law (and yes, it is), failing to resist temptation means accepting the suggestion of the tempter to transgress God's standards. As seen earlier temptations are generally from/by the devil. Devil (Greek) or Satan (Hebrew) means "slanderer" or 'accuser of the people of God before Him.[3]

---

[3] "And I heard a loud voice saying in heaven, Now is come salvation, and strength, and the kingdom of our God, and the power of his Christ: for the accuser of our brethren is cast down, which accused them before our God Day and night." (Revelation 12:10).

The devil has a purpose for tempting people. He does not tempt people already in his camp. Rather he concentrates on people not on his side to get them on his side, disobeying or rebelling against God like he did and has been sentenced to everlasting hell fire.[4]

The devil suggests things that make one doubt the word of God, such as asking Eve in the Garden of Eden, "And he said unto the woman, Yea, hath God said, Ye shall not eat of every tree of the garden?" (Genesis 3:1b). But the Bible says, ". . . but the people that do know their God shall be strong and do exploits." (Daniel 11:32). In effect it takes prayer and knowledge of the word and will of God to resist the devil's temptations and not falling into sin. It is clear from Scriptures that temptation is not sin, considering what it says of Jesus Christ (quoted above) – He was tempted yet without sin.

---

[4] "Then He will also say to those on the left hand, 'Depart from Me, you cursed, into the everlasting fire prepared for the devil and his angels:" (Matthew 25:41 NKJV)

CHAPTER TWO

TEMPTATIONS AND PEOPLE'S ETERNAL DESTINIES

Merriam Webster's (online) Learner's Dictionary defines destiny as "what happens in the future: the things that someone or something will experience in the future"[5]

Words that are interchangeably used with destiny include fate, lot, portion, dole, etc.

Eternal - everlasting, never-ending, permanent, etc. The two words, eternal destiny should then mean someone's everlasting future experience. There are only two possible eternal destinies open to every man and every woman, for ". . . it is appointed unto men once to die, but after this the judgment:" (Hebrews 9:27)

Everyone that passes through this life must end up either in eternal life in heaven with God, or in eternal torment in hell with the devil, for whom hell was originally designed. Jesus said, "Then shall he say also unto them on the left hand, depart from me, ye cursed, into everlasting fire, prepared for the devil and his angels:" (Matthew 25:41). Meanwhile the devil needs people with whom to populate hell, hence he continues to seek people that would obey his biddings, disobey God and end up there in hell. Each person's eternal destiny is determined in this life on earth by his choices. Some people argue that there is no life after death. In

---

[5] http://www.learnersdictionary.com/definition/destiny 7/26/2019.

other words, they claim that life ends here on earth. But the Bible teaches that there is heaven and there is hell, both at the end of this life's journey. One of the excuses given by some of the people opposed to the existence of heaven and hell claims that nobody has access to such eternity information. But Jesus Christ came from there. Read Apostle John's record of an excerpt of Jesus Christ's conversation with Nicodemus:

"Jesus answered and said unto him, Art thou a master of Israel, and knowest not these things? [11] Verily, verily, I say unto thee, we speak that we do know, and testify that we have seen; and ye receive not our witness. [12] If I have told you earthly things, and ye believe not, how shall ye believe, if I tell you of heavenly things? [13] And no man hath ascended up to heaven, but he that came down from heaven, even the Son of man which is in heaven." (John 3:10-13 emphasis added).

This same Jesus Christ told the story of the Rich man and Lazarus:

"There was a certain rich man, which was clothed in purple and fine linen, and fared sumptuously every day: [20] And there was a certain beggar named Lazarus, which was laid at his gate, full of sores, [21] And desiring to be fed with the crumbs which fell from the rich man's table: moreover, the dogs came and licked his sores. [22] And it came to pass, that the beggar died, and was carried by the angels into Abraham's bosom: the rich man also died, and was buried;

²³ And in hell he lift up his eyes, being in torments, and seeth Abraham afar off, and Lazarus in his bosom. ²⁴ And he cried and said, Father Abraham, have mercy on me, and send Lazarus, that he may dip the tip of his finger in water, and cool my tongue; for I am tormented in this flame. ²⁵ But Abraham said, Son, remember that thou in thy lifetime receivedst thy good things, and likewise Lazarus evil things: but now he is comforted, and thou art tormented. ²⁶ And beside all this, between us and you there is a great gulf fixed: so that they which would pass from hence to you cannot; neither can they pass to us, that would come from thence. ²⁷ Then he said, I pray thee therefore, father, that thou wouldest send him to my father's house: ²⁸ For I have five brethren; that he may testify unto them, lest they also come into this place of torment. ²⁹ Abraham saith unto him, They have Moses and the prophets; let them hear them. ³⁰ And he said, Nay, father Abraham: but if one went unto them from the dead, they will repent. ³¹ And he said unto him, If they hear not Moses and the prophets, neither will they be persuaded, though one rose from the dead." (Luke 16:19-31).

The Scriptures say that accepting the offer of God in Christ leads one to eternal life with God in heaven, while rejecting the offer by rejecting Christ lands the one in hell. People are tempted to disbelieve the truth for many reasons as follows:

- Some people say that the idea of being saved just by believing in Jesus Christ appears too simplistic and cheap to be true or right.
- Some others feel that it is not scientific that merely believing in a man who lived and was executed a long time ago for rebellion or insurrection should give salvation.
- Still others claim that there are many other ways by which to reach God or get to heaven such as doing good works, being morally acceptable and right before men.
- Some say that Christianity is a newer religion than many others that are more popular in many parts of the world.

Anyone tempted to believe these ideas and fails to resist it is destined for hell and walking on the way to it. "Jesus said to him, "I am the way, the truth, and the life. No one comes to the Father except through Me." (John 14:6). No one else ever made this claim.

Also, the Scriptures say, "That if thou shalt confess with thy mouth the Lord Jesus, and shalt believe in thine heart that God hath raised him from the dead, thou shalt be saved. [10] For with the heart man believeth unto righteousness; and with the mouth confession is made unto salvation. [11] For the scripture saith, whosoever believeth on him shall not be ashamed. [12] For there is no difference between the Jew and the Greek: for the same Lord over all is rich unto all that call upon him." (Romans 10:9-12).

The way to not fall into temptation is to resist the devil as counseled by the apostle James thus: "Submit yourselves therefore to God. Resist the devil, and he will flee from you." (James 4:7). Alternatively, in the case of sexual immorality, it is safer to flee the environment as Paul exhorts as follows:

"Do you not know that he who unites himself with a prostitute is one with her in body? For it is said, "The two will become one flesh." [17] But whoever is united with the Lord is one with him in spirit. [18] Flee from sexual immorality. All other sins a person commits are outside the body, but whoever sins sexually, sins against their own body." (1 Corinthians 6:16-18).

2.1 Fall of Adam (Fall of Mankind)

It is not stated in the Bible how long Adam (and Eve) lived in the Garden of Eden before God chased them out of the Garden. What is clear is that for as long as he remained innocent, faithful to God, and obedient to God's commands, he had fellowship with God. God went down in the Person of the pre-incarnate Christ and walked in the Garden; Adam had nothing to be afraid of. He named all of God's creation, enjoyed eating the fruits and vegetables as well as drink fresh water. There is no indication that Adam was ever ill or tired. God loved Adam and adjudged him good.

God gave Adam only one commandment, which would change his life and destiny forever if he failed to obey the command:

"And the Lord God commanded the man, saying, of every tree of the garden thou mayest freely eat: "[17] But of the tree of the knowledge of good and evil, thou shalt not eat of it: for in the day that thou eatest thereof thou shalt surely die." (Genesis 2:16-17).

Perhaps Adam did not understand what it means to die, because death was not yet in his vocabulary. May be that accounted for his taking lightly the command of God not to eat of the fruit of the tree of knowledge of good and evil. But it would be wrong to carry forward this argument because the omniscient God knew that Adam would understand the command, having been created in the image of God, and God spoke in a language that Adam should understand.

The entrance of the devil into the Garden of Eden made a world of difference in the life of Adam and all mankind by extension. The devil represented by the serpent was not created in the image of God, but the Bible describes him as craftier - more subtil – than every other animal that God had made (Genesis 3:1). He went to the woman, Eve rather than to Adam. Perhaps the devil felt that if he had gone with his idea to Adam, whom God directly gave the command, Adam would probably have resisted him since he was the one that received the command – to eat fruits of every tree in the Garden except of the tree of the knowledge of good and evil.

The only thing in Scripture that could give weight to this supposition is that the woman is described as the weaker sex: "Likewise, ye husbands, dwell with them according to knowledge, giving honour unto the wife, as unto the weaker vessel, and as being heirs together of the grace of life; that your prayers be not hindered." (1 Peter 3:7). Whether the weakness be of mind or physique is a different matter.

The almighty God says what He does and does what He says. He predicted/promised or ruled that in the day that man ate the forbidden fruit he would die. Although Adam and Eve did not die physically that very hour or day, yet physical death became man's portion, and man died spiritually immediately: man's relationship with God became strained.

Consequently, when Adam and his wife heard the sound of the Lord God walking in the garden in the cool of the day, instead of being excited at the presence of the Lord, they hid themselves among the trees of the garden, the creatures that they had dominion over and covered their shame and nakedness with perishable leaves. If man had not died as God said he would, God would have become a mere talker that issues empty threats. Compare this with the story in Deuteronomy 28:1-14 where God promised blessings to the Jews if they diligently kept His commands, but curses up to and including captivity and suffering for disobedience in verses 15 to 68:

Deuteronomy 28:1-14 (Blessings for Obedience)

"And it shall come to pass, if thou shalt hearken diligently unto the voice of the Lord thy God, to observe and to do all his commandments which I command thee this day, that the Lord thy God will set thee on high above all nations of the earth:

[2] And all these blessings shall come on thee, and overtake thee, if thou shalt hearken unto the voice of the Lord thy God.

[3] Blessed shalt thou be in the city, and blessed shalt thou be in the field.

[4] Blessed shall be the fruit of thy body, and the fruit of thy ground, and the fruit of thy cattle, the increase of thy kine, and the flocks of thy sheep.

[5] Blessed shall be thy basket and thy store.

[6] Blessed shalt thou be when thou comest in, and blessed shalt thou be when thou goest out.

[7] The Lord shall cause thine enemies that rise up against thee to be smitten before thy face: they shall come out against thee one way and flee before thee seven ways.

[8] The Lord shall command the blessing upon thee in thy storehouses, and in all that thou settest thine hand unto; and he shall bless thee in the land which the Lord thy God giveth thee.

[9] The Lord shall establish thee an holy people unto himself, as he hath sworn unto thee, if thou shalt keep the commandments of the Lord thy God, and walk in his ways.

[10] And all people of the earth shall see that thou art called by the name of the Lord; and they shall be afraid of thee.

[11] And the Lord shall make thee plenteous in goods, in the fruit of thy body, and in the fruit of thy cattle, and in the fruit of thy ground, in the land which the Lord sware unto thy fathers to give thee.

[12] The Lord shall open unto thee his good treasure, the heaven to give the rain unto thy land in his season, and to bless all the work of thine hand: and thou shalt lend unto many nations, and thou shalt not borrow.

[13] And the Lord shall make thee the head, and not the tail; and thou shalt be above only, and thou shalt not be beneath; if that thou hearken unto the commandments of the Lord thy God, which I command thee this day, to observe and to do them:

[14] And thou shalt not go aside from any of the words which I command thee this day, to the right hand, or to the left, to go after other gods to serve them."

Deuteronomy 28:15-68 (Curses for Disobedience)

[15] But it shall come to pass, if thou wilt not hearken unto the voice of the Lord thy God, to observe to do all his commandments and his statutes which I command thee this day; that all these curses shall come upon thee, and overtake thee: [16] Cursed shalt thou be in the city, and cursed shalt thou be in the field. ····[45] Moreover all these curses shall come upon thee, and shall pursue thee, and

overtake thee, till thou be destroyed; because thou hearkenedst not unto the voice of the Lord thy God, to keep his commandments and his statutes which he commanded thee: ⋯ [58] If thou wilt not observe to do all the words of this law that are written in this book, that thou mayest fear this glorious and fearful name, The Lord Thy God; ⋯ [68] And the Lord shall bring thee into Egypt again with ships, by the way whereof I spake unto thee, thou shalt see it no more again: and there ye shall be sold unto your enemies for bondmen and bondwomen, and no man shall buy you."[6]

Similarly, Jesus Christ said that God loved the world so much that He gave His only begotten Son, that whoever believes in Him (the Son) should not perish but have everlasting life (John 3:16). If people that do not believe in Him should also have eternal life Jesus would be said to be unserious and unfair to them that believe(d), and He would have died in vain. God is just and righteous. After all, "God is not a man, that he should lie; neither the son of man, that he should repent: hath he said, and shall he not do it? or hath he spoken, and shall he not make it good?" (Numbers 23:19); in Malachi 3:6 God said, "For I am the LORD, I change not;" There is no partiality in God. In spite of His great love for man, He punishes sin not repented of.

---

[6] Nwaelene, Daniel U. "Jesus Christ: Savior, Judge and King of The World." (Bloomington: WestBow Press, 2017), 143 – 148.

The implication of the fall of man through disobedience can be inferred from the letter of the Apostle Paul as subjection of creation to futility and bondage of corruption, causing it to groan and labor with birth pangs. The text is Romans 8:20-22 as follows: "For the creature was made subject to vanity, not willingly, but by reason of him who hath subjected the same in hope, [21] Because the creature itself also shall be delivered from the bondage of corruption into the glorious liberty of the children of God. [22] For we know that the whole creation groaneth and travaileth in pain together until now."

Mankind was chased out of the blessedness of the Garden. The fellowship that mankind had with God in the Garden of Eden had been forever broken until the intervention of the offer of God's only begotten Son, Jesus Christ. In effect, for as long as a person remains in his natural state – not born again – he is dead and doomed for hell. This will be further discussed later in this book.

2.2 Victory of Jesus Christ

Victory may be defined as defeat of an enemy in battle, an opponent in a game, not giving in to pressure or temptation, or a challenge of some sort. On a daily basis, every living person is faced by one challenge or the other. When he succumbs to, or falls under, such challenges he has been defeated, otherwise he has victory or is said to be victorious. The apostle, Paul said we are pressed down but not perplexed. In other words, we face difficulties, challenges, troubles, persecutions (as Christians), but we are not defeated – we have victory. The reference's full text is as follows:

2 Corinthians 4:8-12 (NKJV): "We are hard-pressed on every side, yet not crushed; we are perplexed, but not in despair; [9] persecuted, but not forsaken; struck down, but not destroyed— [10] always carrying about in the body the dying of the Lord Jesus, that the life of Jesus also may be manifested in our body. [11] For we who live are always delivered to death for Jesus' sake, that the life of Jesus also may be manifested in our mortal flesh. [12] So then death is working in us, but life in you."

In the last section above, we found that the devil tempted man (a.k.a. the first Adam), and the man was defeated, resulting in death for him and the entire mankind. When Jesus Christ (a.k.a. the second Adam) came into the scene, shortly before He effectively began His earthly ministry the devil also tempted Him. But Jesus Christ was victorious. In addition, at different points in His ministry and even at the point of death He was tempted and at every point He had victory as has been stated severally in Scriptures:

Isaiah 53:9 – The prophecy of Isaiah about the then expected Messiah:

"And he made his grave with the wicked, and with the rich in his death; because he had done no violence, neither was any deceit in his mouth."

Matthew 27:24 "When Pilate saw that he could prevail nothing, but that rather a tumult was made, he took water, and washed his hands before the multitude, saying, I am innocent of the blood of this just person: see ye to it."

John 8:29 "And he that sent me is with me: the Father hath not left me alone; for I do always those things that please him."

John 19:4 "Pilate therefore went forth again, and saith unto them, Behold, I bring him forth to you, that ye may know that I find no fault in him."

2 Corinthians 5:21 (ESV) "For our sake he made him to be sin who knew no sin, so that in him we might become the righteousness of God."

Hebrews 4:15 (ESV) "For we do not have a high priest who is unable to sympathize with our weaknesses, but one who in every respect has been tempted as we are, yet without sin."

Hebrews 7:26 (NASB) "For it was fitting for us to have such a high priest, holy, innocent, undefiled, separated from sinners and exalted above the heavens;"

Hebrews 9:14 "How much more shall the blood of Christ, who through the eternal Spirit offered himself without spot to God, purge your conscience from dead works to serve the living God?"

1 Peter 1:18-19 "Forasmuch as ye know that ye were not redeemed with corruptible things, as silver and gold, from your vain conversation received by tradition from your fathers; [19] But with the precious blood of Christ, as of a lamb without blemish and without spot:"

1 Peter 2:21-22 "For even hereunto were ye called: because Christ also suffered for us, leaving us an example, that ye should follow his steps: [22] Who did no sin, neither was guile found in his mouth:"

1 John 3:2-5 "Beloved, now are we the sons of God, and it doth not yet appear what we shall be: but we know that, when he shall appear, we shall be like him; for we shall see him as he is. [3] And every man that hath this hope in him purifieth himself, even as he is pure. [4] Whosoever committeth sin transgresseth also the law: for sin is the transgression of the law. [5] And ye know that he was manifested to take away our sins; and in him is no sin."

Meanwhile let us review records of some of the temptations that Jesus Christ faced at the various stages of His ministry and sojourn on earth:

At the Commencement of His Ministry:

"Then was Jesus led up of the Spirit into the wilderness to be tempted of the devil. [2] And when he had fasted forty days and forty nights, he was afterward an hungred.

[3] And when the tempter came to him, he said, if thou be the Son of God, command that these stones be made bread. [4] But he

answered and said, it is written, Man shall not live by bread alone, but by every word that proceedeth out of the mouth of God.

[5] Then the devil taketh him up into the holy city, and setteth him on a pinnacle of the temple, [6] And saith unto him, If thou be the Son of God, cast thyself down: for it is written, He shall give his angels charge concerning thee: and in their hands they shall bear thee up, lest at any time thou dash thy foot against a stone. [7] Jesus said unto him, it is written again, thou shalt not tempt the Lord thy God.

[8] Again, the devil taketh him up into an exceeding high mountain, and sheweth him all the kingdoms of the world, and the glory of them; [9] And saith unto him, all these things will I give thee, if thou wilt fall down and worship me. [10] Then saith Jesus unto him, get thee hence, Satan: for it is written, thou shalt worship the Lord thy God, and him only shalt thou serve. [11] Then the devil leaveth him, and behold, angels came and ministered unto him." (Matthew 4:1-11).

"And there came a voice from heaven, saying, thou art my beloved Son, in whom I am well pleased. [12] And immediately the spirit driveth him into the wilderness. [13] And he was there in the wilderness forty days, tempted of Satan; and was with the wild beasts; and the angels ministered unto him." (Mark 1:11-13).

"And Jesus being full of the Holy Ghost returned from Jordan, and was led by the Spirit into the wilderness, [2] Being forty days tempted of the devil. And in those days, he did eat nothing: and when they were ended, he afterward hungered. [3] And the devil said unto him, if thou be the Son of God, command this stone that it be made bread. [4] And Jesus answered him, saying, It is written, That man shall not live by bread alone, but by every word of God. [5] And the devil, taking him up into an high mountain, shewed unto him all the kingdoms of the world in a moment of time. [6] And the devil said unto him, all this power will I give thee, and the glory of them: for that is delivered unto me; and to whomsoever I will I give it. [7] If thou therefore wilt worship me, all shall be thine. [8] And Jesus answered and said unto him, Get thee behind me, Satan: for it is written, Thou shalt worship the Lord thy God, and him only shalt thou serve.

[9] And he brought him to Jerusalem, and set him on a pinnacle of the temple, and said unto him, If thou be the Son of God, cast thyself down from hence: [10] For it is written, He shall give his angels charge over thee, to keep thee: [11] And in their hands they shall bear thee up, lest at any time thou dash thy foot against a stone. [12] And Jesus answering said unto him, It is said, Thou shalt not tempt the Lord thy God. [13] And when the devil had ended all the temptation, he departed from him for a season. [14] And Jesus returned in the power of the Spirit into Galilee: and there went out a fame of him through all the region round about." (Luke 4:1-14).

Pressure from Christ's earthly family members to declare Himself King.

"After these things Jesus walked in Galilee: for he would not walk in Jewry, because the Jews sought to kill him. [2] Now the Jew's feast of tabernacles was at hand. [3] His brethren therefore said unto him, depart hence, and go into Judaea, that thy disciples also may see the works that thou doest. [4] For there is no man that doeth anything in secret, and he himself seeketh to be known openly. If thou do these things, shew thyself to the world. [5] For neither did his brethren believe in him. [6] Then Jesus said unto them, my time is not yet come: but your time is alway ready. [7] The world cannot hate you; but me it hateth, because I testify of it, that the works thereof are evil. [8] Go ye up unto this feast: I go not up yet unto this feast: for my time is not yet full come." (John 7:1-8). Through Peter, the devil wanted to stop Jesus Christ from going to Jerusalem and subsequently to the cross, and thereby not to fulfill the purpose of His coming to earth:

"From that time forth began Jesus to shew unto his disciples, how that he must go unto Jerusalem, and suffer many things of the elders and chief priests and scribes, and be killed, and be raised again the third day. [22] Then Peter took him, and began to rebuke him, saying, be it far from thee, Lord: this shall not be unto thee. [23] But he turned, and said unto Peter, get thee behind me, Satan:

thou art an offence unto me: for thou savourest not the things that be of God, but those that be of men." (Matthew 16:21-23).

At the Garden of Gethsemane Christ's humanity desired or wished that the "cup" of suffering pass Him:

"Then cometh Jesus with them unto a place called Gethsemane, and saith unto the disciples, sit ye here, while I go and pray yonder. [37] And he took with him Peter and the two sons of Zebedee, and began to be sorrowful and very heavy. [38] Then saith he unto them, my soul is exceeding sorrowful, even unto death: tarry ye here, and watch with me.[39] And he went a little farther, and fell on his face, and prayed, saying, O my Father, if it be possible, let this cup pass from me: nevertheless not as I will, but as thou wilt. [40] And he cometh unto the disciples, and findeth them asleep, and saith unto Peter, what, could ye not watch with me one hour? [41] Watch and pray, that ye enter not into temptation: the spirit indeed is willing, but the flesh is weak.

[42] He went away again the second time, and prayed, saying, O my Father, if this cup may not pass away from me, except I drink it, thy will be done. [43] And he came and found them asleep again: for their eyes were heavy. [44] And he left them, and went away again, and prayed the third time, saying the same words. [45] Then cometh he to his disciples, and saith unto them, Sleep on now, and take your rest: behold, the hour is at hand, and the Son of man is

betrayed into the hands of sinners. [46] Rise, let us be going: behold, he is at hand that doth betray me." (Matthew 26:36-46).

When Jesus was already nailed to the cross at Calvary:

"And it was the third hour, and they crucified him. [26] And the superscription of his accusation was written over, The King of The Jews. [27] And with him they crucify two thieves: the one on his right hand, and the other on his left. [28] And the scripture was fulfilled, which saith, and he was numbered with the transgressors. [29] And they that passed by railed on him, wagging their heads, and saying, ah, thou that destroyest the temple, and buildest it in three days, [30] Save thyself, and come down from the cross. [31] Likewise also the chief priests mocking said among themselves with the scribes, He saved others; himself he cannot save. [32] Let Christ the King of Israel descend now from the cross, that we may see and believe. And they that were crucified with him reviled him." (Mark 15:25-32).

Jesus Christ said He came to earth to do His Father's will. With that great determination in mind no amount of pressure from the devil was able to derail His mission, which was to redeem fallen mankind, and destroy the devil's works as per John 3:8 "He that committeth sin is of the devil; for the devil sinneth from the beginning. For this purpose, the Son of God was manifested, that he might destroy the works of the devil."

The victory of Jesus Christ in all the temptations He faced rendered Him so sinless that the sacrifice of His blood for the redemption of man was perfect. His blood was unblemished. If He had not had victory at all points of temptation, Jesus Christ would have been a sinner like us, and would have been unable and unqualified to atone for man's sin.

The Bible says that death came by one man (first Adam), but by the second Adam (Jesus Christ) eternal life became available to mankind. The reference is as follows: (Wherefore, as by one man sin entered into the world, and death by sin; and so, death passed upon all men, for that all have sinned: - Romans 5:12).

The victory of Jesus Christ and His full obedience to the Father brought reconciliation to God, of anyone that believes in Him as personal Saviour and Lord.

The victory of Jesus Christ spelt doom for Satan because as a result of His humility and obedience, God has exalted Him above every name. See the reverence below:

"Let this mind be in you, which was also in Christ Jesus, [6] who, being in the form of God, did not consider it robbery to be equal with God, [7] but made Himself of no reputation, taking the form of a bondservant, and coming in the likeness of men. [8] And being found in appearance as a man, He humbled Himself and became obedient to the point of death, even the death of the cross. [9] Therefore God also has highly exalted Him and given Him the name, which is above every name, [10] that at the name of Jesus every knee should bow, of those in heaven, and of those on earth, and of those under the earth, [11] and that every tongue should confess that Jesus Christ is Lord, to the glory of God the Father." (Philippians 2:5-11 NKJV)

By not yielding to Satan's offers of power and riches of the world, which did not really belong to him[7] but God, Jesus got all the power by yielding to the will of the Father.

That is why Jesus told His disciples at their commissioning, ". . . All power is given unto me in heaven and in earth." (Matthew 28:18).

When Jesus returns to reign with us who believe in Him, the devil shall be banished in the abyss for one thousand years and later to hell fire for the rest of eternity. Death will also be abolished and thrown into hell fire.

In total, while the fall of Adam to the schemes and craftiness of the devil so negatively impacted the destiny of mankind, the victory of Jesus changed the course of History and the destiny of mankind (especially whoever believes in Him) for good eternally.

---

[7] Psalms 24:1 – "*The earth is the Lord's, and the fulness thereof; the world, and they that dwell therein.*"

2.3 The God of This World.

The almighty God created the heavens and the earth and all that are in them. Psalms 24:1 confirms that, and it says, "The earth is the Lord's, and the fulness thereof; the world, and they that dwell therein." In his letter to the Colossians, the apostle Paul also made a similar assertion as follows:

"[Jesus Christ] is the image of the invisible God, the firstborn of every creature: [16] For by him were all things created, that are in heaven, and that are in earth, visible and invisible, whether they be thrones, or dominions, or principalities, or powers: all things were created by him, and for him: [17] And he is before all things, and by him all things consist." (Colossians 1:15-17).

One would then wonder why the same Apostle Paul referred to the devil as the god of this world when he said, "But if our gospel be hid, it is hid to them that are lost: [4] In whom the god of this world hath blinded the minds of them which believe not, lest the light of the glorious gospel of Christ, who is the image of God, should shine unto them." (2 Corinthians 4:3-4).

A confirmation of this ascription is the offer of the world and its glories to Jesus Christ by the devil if Jesus would bow and worship him. The text reads as follows:

"And the devil, taking him up into an high mountain, shewed unto him all the kingdoms of the world in a moment of time. [6] And the devil said unto him, all this power will I give thee, and the glory of them: for that is delivered unto me; and to whomsoever I will I give it. [7] If thou therefore wilt worship me, all shall be thine." (Luke 4:5-7)

Other titles by which the devil is mentioned in the Bible, some of which suggest his influence on this world and its events include the following:

Serpent - Genesis 3:1, 14

King of Babylon - Isaiah 14:4

Lucifer and son of the morning - Isaiah 14:12

Crooked serpent - Isaiah 27:1

Leviathan - Isaiah 27:1

King of Tyrus - Ezekiel 28:12

Anointed cherub that covereth - Ezekiel 28:14

Little horn - Daniel 8:9-11

Prince of the kingdom of Persia - Daniel 10:13

The tempter - Matthew 4:3

Enemy - Matthew 13:39

Wicked one - Matthew 13:38

Beelzebub - Matthew 12:24, Luke 11:15

Satan - Mark 1:13

The prince of demons - Luke 11:15

Liar - John 8:44

The Father of lies - John 8:44

Murderer - John 8:44

Thief - John 10:10

The prince of this world - John 12:31

The evil one - John 17:15

God of this world - 2 Corinthians 4:4

Belial - 2 Corinthians 6:15

Serpent - 2 Corinthians 11:3.

Angel of light - 2 Corinthians 11:14

Prince of the power of the air - Ephesians 2:2

The wicked - Ephesians 6:16, 2 Thessalonians 2:8

Rulers of the darkness - Ephesians 6:12

Power of darkness - Colossians 1:13

Son of perdition - 2 Thessalonians 2:3

Man of sin - 2 Thessalonians 2:3

Lawless one - 2 Thessalonians 2:8 (NKJV)

Seducing spirits - 1Timothy 4:1.

Adversary - 1 Peter 5:8

The spirit of antichrist - 1 John 4:3

Star fallen from heaven - Revelation 9:1

Angel of the bottomless pit - Revelation 9:11

Abaddon - Revelation 9:11

Apollyon - Revelation 9:11

Great fiery red dragon (serpent), Revelation 12:3

The great dragon, old serpent, the Devil, Satan - Revelation 12:9

Accuser of our brethren - Revelation 12:10

The beast - Revelation 14:9

Dragon, Revelation 12:7.

It is certain that from the story of creation recorded in Genesis chapters one and two, God did not transfer to Satan authority over the world. Rather God handed to man dominion over every living thing. The verse says, "And God blessed them, and God said unto them, be fruitful, and multiply, and replenish the earth, and subdue it: and have dominion over the fish of the sea, and over the fowl of the air, and over every living thing that moveth upon the earth." (Genesis 1:28). It was Adam that gave names to God's creation. The reference for this is:

"And out of the ground the Lord God formed every beast of the field, and every fowl of the air; and brought them unto Adam to see what he would call them: and whatsoever Adam called every living creature, that was the name thereof. [20] And Adam gave names to all cattle, and to the fowl of the air, and to every beast of the field; but for Adam there was not found an help meet for him." (Genesis 2:19-20).

Having dominion over the creatures also involved tending them and the Garden of Eden in which God placed the man. When man fell to the temptation of the devil and God chased him out of the Garden he lost fellowship with God, who holds and gives authority, hence he lost the authority that God had given him. Even though God did not make any explicit statement withdrawing the authority man could no longer exercise it with confidence. The devil understood the situation and began to parade himself as the owner of the world. There is no vacuum in nature.

At the pre-ministry temptation mentioned earlier Satan offered to give Jesus Christ the power and glory of this world if Jesus would bow down to worship him.[8] Though Jesus did not dispute the claim of "possession" of the world, it sounded foolish and out of place or rather absurd for a creature (the devil) to offer to its Creator the world that He created for Himself. The book of John says, "All things were made by him; and without him was not anything made that was made." (John 1:3). The apostle Paul also said,

"For by him were all things created, that are in heaven, and that are in earth, visible and invisible, whether they be thrones, or dominions, or principalities, or powers: all things were created by him, and for him: [17] And he is before all things, and by him all things consist." (Colossians 1:16-17).

Dr. Ironside suggests that what the devil was offering Jesus was his by the permissive will of God because "the most High ruleth

---

[8] "And the devil, taking him up into an high mountain, shewed unto him all the kingdoms of the world in a moment of time. [6] And the devil said unto him, all this power will I give thee, and the glory of them: for that is delivered unto me; and to whomsoever I will I give it. [7] If thou therefore wilt worship me, all shall be thine." (Luke 4:5-7).

in the kingdom of men, and giveth it to whomsoever he will."
(Daniel 4:25). He adds, "Satan had robbed Adam of the authority
given him and reigned as usurper in the hearts of wicked men; but
he had no undisputed title to the kingdoms of the world, ..."[9]
Jesus Christ simply dismissed the devil to get behind Him because
it's written that only God should be worshipped (Luke 4:8-9).

According to Jesus Christ, the devil has a three-fold agenda for
humanity: to steal, to kill and to destroy (John 10:10). He does not
give anything good. Any gift from the devil that appears good
must be a wrapper of something evil, whether it be power, money,
children, or other material wealth. For instance, Walvoord notes
that accepting the offer of Satan in the temptation mentioned
above would have made Jesus Christ his slave rather than his
Victor.[10] The devil shields people who let him from coming to the
knowledge of the saving knowledge of the Lord. Paul says, "But
if our gospel be hid, it is hid to them that are lost: [4] In whom the
god of this world hath blinded the minds of them which believe
not, lest the light of the glorious gospel of Christ, who is the image
of God, should shine unto them." (2 Corinthians 4:3-4).

"For I am jealous over you with godly jealousy: for I have
espoused you to one husband, that I may present you as a chaste

---

[9] H. A. Ironside. *An Ironside Expository Commentary. MATTHEW.* (Grand Rapids: Kregel Publications, 1976), 27.
[10] John F. Walvoord. *Matthew. Thy Kingdom Come.* (Chicago: Moody Press, 1974), 36.

virgin to Christ. [3] But I fear, lest by any means, as the serpent beguiled Eve through his subtilty, so your minds should be corrupted from the simplicity that is in Christ." (2 Corinthians 11:2-3).

Satan counterfeits and disguises with the intention of destroying. This is found in the following: "For such men are false apostles, deceitful workers, disguising themselves as apostles of Christ. [14] No wonder, for even Satan disguises himself as an angel of light." (2 Corinthians 11:13-14 NASB).

The devil in his effort to execute his three-fold agenda, does not rest but goes up and down sneakily looking for children of God to pull down. The apostle Peter says to "Be of sober spirit, be on the alert. Your adversary, the devil, prowls around like a roaring lion, seeking someone to devour." (1 Peter 5:8 NASB).

Chapter Three
Money (Wealth)

Some words or terms that are used interchangeably in everyday communications are defined differently in high school Economics. Such words include money, wealth, riches and estate. In spite of these differences in definition, however, money is generically used in this book to represent people's great possessions and all other synonyms for the following reasons:

- Money is more popularly used than the other terminologies.
- Money acquires material wealth.
- Material wealth is convertible to money.
- Material wealth is measured in terms of money these days.

In fact, money, called mammon in Matthew 6:24 also implies wealth or any material thing, which has or adds value to a person.[11] Some of the synonyms of money as used here found in different translations of the Bible include the following:

Substance: Job 1:10 (KJV) "Hast not thou made an hedge about him, and about his house, and about all that he hath on every side? thou hast blessed the work of his hands, and his substance is increased in the land."

---

[11] Practical Word Studies in the New Testament Volume 2 L-Z (Chattanooga: Leadership Ministries Worldwide, 1998), 1390

Estate: Luke 15:12 (NIV) "The younger one said to his father, 'Father, give me my share of the estate.' So he divided his property between them."

Riches: Genesis 36:7 (KJV) "For their riches were more than that they might dwell together; and the land wherein they were strangers could not bear them because of their cattle."

1 Chronicles 29:12a (KJV) "Both riches and honour come of thee, and thou reignest over all;"

2 Chronicles 32:27 (KJV) "And Hezekiah had exceeding much riches and honour: and he made himself treasuries for silver, and for gold, and for precious stones, and for spices, and for shields, and for all manner of pleasant jewels;"

Livelihood: Luke 15:12 (NKJV) "And the younger of them said to his father, 'Father, give me the portion of goods that falls to me.' So he divided to them his livelihood."

Means: 2 Corinthians 8:11 (NIV) – UK "Now finish the work, so that your eager willingness to do it may be matched by your completion of it, according to your means."

Wealth: Genesis 34:29 (KJV) "And all their wealth, and all their little ones, and their wives took they captive, and spoiled even all that was in the house."

Proverbs 10:15 (KJV) "The rich man's wealth is his strong city: the destruction of the poor is their poverty."

Proverbs 19:4 (KJV) "Wealth maketh many friends; but the poor is separated from his neighbour."

Goods: Ecclesiastes 5:11 (KJV) "When goods increase, they are increased that eat them: and what good is there to the owners thereof, saving the beholding of them with their eyes?"

Mark 3:27 (KJV) "No man can enter into a strong man's house, and spoil his goods, except he will first bind the strong man; and then he will spoil his house."

1 Corinthians 13:3 (KJV) "And though I bestow all my goods to feed the poor, and though I give my body to be burned, and have not charity, it profiteth me nothing."

However, occasionally these words may still be used interchangeably in this book. Do not be confused. We don't intend to be economist in our interpretation. So, under the heading above, the power and influence of money shall be presented to encompass positive and negative characteristics of money and the very rich. Somebody has said that you may not know the true character of a person until you put a lot of money in his possession.

In other words, money exposes the true person that poverty seems to obscure. Nobody remains exactly the same in character and demeanor when his amount of money changes upwards or downwards. Such changes also reveal a man's true relationship with God. Several people have allowed great wealth to come in between them and God, which never happened when they were poor. Conversely poverty has also driven some farther from God. No wonder the wise man said, "Remove far from me vanity and lies: give me neither poverty nor riches; feed me with food convenient for me: [9] Lest I be full, and deny thee, and say, Who is the Lord? or lest I be poor, and steal, and take the name of my God in vain." (Proverbs 30:8-9).

3.1 Characteristics of Money Power

Evidently it is not a sin or evil to be wealthy. The Scriptures say that it is God that gives you the power to get wealth (Deuteronomy 8:18). The power of money has both positive and negative characteristics. Some of the positive characteristics are as follows:
-

1) Money enables the rich and gives them the freedom or power to do what they want and like to do. Ecclesiastes 10:19 says that money answers all things.

2) Money brings around many friends (Proverbs 19:4). My late father-in-law often said that the world loves a winner and want to be associated to him. This is one of the reasons one should get married before becoming very rich as to attract the wrong person that is only interested in the one's wealth rather than in his or her person.

3) Money creates or allows options and limitless choices for the rich. When money is available a rich person has more options in life that are open to him, while options and choices open to the poor are restricted and limited – fun, vacations, food, kind and location of housing, business, etc.

4) Money gives boldness for taking risks. Even though the rich do not like to give or lose money, yet they are not afraid of losing when they invest. They easily diversify and hire help, and they can outsource tasks.

5) As like begets like, so wealth begets wealth. So, the rich get richer as they have the means to acquire more. Money also attracts gifts.

6) The rich man's money can, and does, easily procure the best healthcare and physical care.

7) Money makes some people philanthropic, as such people would like to give back some of their gains to the society . This accounts for the setting up of some foundations and not-for-profit organizations.

8) Money can drastically change one's life for the better or the worse especially as it shapes the man's attitude.

9) It leaves inheritance for children and grandchildren (Proverbs 13:22).

10) Money gives a man confidence when he speaks in society; the rich is given attention when he talks.

The negative characteristics of the power of money include the following: -

"When goods increase, they are increased that eat them: and what good is there to the owners thereof, saving the beholding of them with their eyes?" (Ecclesiastes 5:11)

"But they that will be rich fall into temptation and a snare, and into many foolish and hurtful lusts, which drown men in destruction and perdition." (1 Timothy 6:9)

"For the love of money is the root of all evil: which while some coveted after, they have erred from the faith, and pierced themselves through with many sorrows." (1 Timothy 6:10).

(i)   Money gives the rich man a false sense of security and strength (Proverbs 10:15 NIV: "The wealth of the rich is their fortified city, but poverty is the ruin of the poor.").

(ii)   Money gives a kind of boldness that makes the rich disrespectful, giving them elated ego.

(iii)   Unlike the poor laborer, the abundance of the rich causes him sleeplessness (Ecclesiastes 5:12 NIV: "The sleep of a laborer is sweet, whether they eat little or much, but as for the rich, their abundance permits them no sleep.").

(iv)   When money gets into the head it often intoxicates like alcohol.

(v)   Love of money creates insatiability by money (Ecclesiastes 5:10-11 NIV: "Whoever loves money never has enough; whoever loves wealth is never satisfied with their income. This too is meaningless. [11] As goods increase, so do those who consume them. And what benefit are they to the owners except to feast their eyes on them?").

(vi)   Money attracts favoritism and preference. It may not be sinful to be given preference, but it is to give preference to the rich over the poor (James 2:1-4 NIV: "My brothers and sisters, believers in our glorious Lord Jesus Christ must not show favoritism. [2] Suppose a man comes into your meeting wearing a gold ring and fine clothes, and a poor man in filthy old clothes also comes in. [3] If you show special attention to the man wearing fine clothes and say, "Here's a good seat for you," but say to the poor man, "You stand there" or "Sit on the floor by my feet," [4] have you not discriminated among yourselves and become judges with evil thoughts?").

(vii)   Money breeds hunger for political power mainly for the purpose of acquiring more money.

(viii)   Much money leads some people to alcohol and/or drug addiction.

(ix)   Many rich persons become less empathetic with the poor and pay less attention to them, except for the purpose of exploiting and oppressing them.

(x)   Money can become addictive, leading to the love of it, which the Bible says is the root of all evils (1 Tim. 6:10 quoted above).

(xi)   When a man allows his money to control him, he may backslide from the faith if he was a Christian.

(xii)   Money breaks friendships and fellowships as well as business relationships. Some couples break up their marriages due to money. The real underlying reason for some divorce suits is money – the desire to get a share of the wealth of the divorced spouse. Money tears families apart, especially when sharing inheritance, whether there is a will or not.

(xiii)   Money obscures genuine love. As money grows, it becomes hard to know true friendship as love may be of the man's wealth rather than the man himself.

(xiv)   The rich and their immediate family members sometimes become targets for kidnapping, robbery and blackmail for ransom, causing the rich man to live in constant fear, anxiety and suspicion. This may lead to sleeplessness and stress.

(xv)   Money does lead to, or increase, narcissism, which Webster's Dictionary has defined as "undue dwelling on one's own self or attainments."[12]

(xvi)   Money does not have the ability to procure salvation, and makes it hard (not impossible, though!) for the rich to enter heaven, according to Jesus Christ (Mark 10:23-25 NIV: "Jesus looked around and said to his disciples, "How hard it is for the rich to enter the kingdom of God!" [24] The disciples were amazed at his words. But Jesus said again, "Children, how hard it is to enter the kingdom of God! [25] It is easier for a camel to go through the eye of a needle than for someone who is rich to enter the kingdom of God.").

Note that it is not a sin to be rich. Money in itself is not evil or the root of all evils. Rather it is what you do with money that could be evil. Forsaking the Giver of money and worshipping money is sinful or idolatrous - the Bible says that you cannot serve God and mammon (Matthew 6:24 NIV: "No one can serve two masters. Either you will hate the one and love the

---

[12] Webster's All-in-one Dictionary & Thesaurus, 2008, 426.

other, or you will be devoted to the one and despise the other. You cannot serve both God and money.").

3.2 Sources and Modes of Acquiring Money

People have different ways of acquiring money. God gives wealth. Similarly, the devil does give. The difference is that while "The blessing of the LORD makes one rich, and He adds no sorrow with it" (Proverbs 10:22 NKJV); on the contrary, as mentioned earlier, the devil – the god of this world – gives wealth and gifts that hurt the recipient at the end of the day. So, every ungodly way of acquiring money is a way to sorrow.

3.2.1 Clean Means Inheritance

A popular adage says that some people are born with silver (if not golden) spoons in their mouths. This implies being born into riches. Children born into such rich families usually have some inheritance bequeathed them by their parents. The Bible says that a good man leaves inheritance for his children (Proverbs 13:22a NKJV). Such inheritance must have been genuinely and neatly acquired for it to last and remain a blessing to the children receiving it.

Hardworking

Working hard brings in money – especially if God's blessing is on the work and on the hard worker. Hard work requires investment of time, money, energy and some personal sacrifices.

Working hard may involve doing some genuine business, building up capital for investment from a good salary. It may also involve developing a product or service for sale. Hard working is recommended in Scripture. The apostle Paul said to the Thessalonians that if a man does not work, he should not eat (2 Thessalonians 3:10).

Miracle of God

There is a testimony of a Christian brother, an only son of his widowed mother. He was helped through high school and college by some close relative. He got employed for a short period of time after the mandatory one-year national service. As an only son he married early and he and his wife were struggling to survive. He incorporated a company and began to do supplies businesses. He made a vow to spend his money to serve the Lord if He would bless him.

Shortly afterwards, Charlie (as he was called) discovered that industrial salt was a major ingredient in high demand in a particular industrial group in the country. Before too long, one of the big companies in the group gave Charlie's company an order for a quantity of the salt that would last for only a few months production. The manufacturer gave some repeat orders and other manufacturers in the group also began to patronize the brother, to the extent that he began to import shiploads of the salt for them.

At a point, in partnership with his foreign suppliers, Charlie's company built a factory to package and stock the salt locally. That was a miracle! This is a confirmation of the claim of Scripture that "[God] raises the poor out of the dust, And lifts the needy out of the ash heap, That He may seat him with princes - With the princes of His people." (Psalm 113:7-8 NKJV).

All the above means of making money are effective and productive when performed in the fear of the Lord and He blesses the efforts and ideas. The Bible says, "And you shall remember the Lord your God, for it is He who gives you power to get wealth," (Deuteronomy 8:18 NKJV). "Both riches and honor come from You, And You reign over all." (1 Chronicles 29:12a NKJV). When King Solomon chose wisdom in response to God's demand for a request from him early in his reign as king of Israel, God said to him, "wisdom and knowledge are granted to you; and I will give you riches and wealth and honor, such as none of the kings have had who were before you, nor shall any after you have the like." (2 Chronicles 1:12 NKJV).

3.2.2 Crooked Means of Making Money

There are a thousand and one ways to acquire money illegally (crookedly), which are summed up under a few headings below: - Money from Inheritance.

Ill-gotten money that is not recovered before the death of the wicked man may be willed to, or simply passed down to, a son, daughter, spouse or other relative. This is cursed wealth and does not bring blessings to the one that inherits it and is likely to be lost. The Bible says, "A good man leaves an inheritance to his ch ildren's children, But the wealth of the sinner is stored up for the righteous." (Proverbs 13:22 NKJV).

Money from Stealing.

A simple, personal (non-legal) definition of stealing is taking and appropriating to oneself something that belongs to someone else. This could be done by force, without force, by tricks or various other ways. In view of this, stealing is used here to imply and include robbery (armed or unarmed), fraud, embezzlement, breaking-in, etc. Some people say that robbing a bank is not evil because the money there does not belong to any particular person. In the same vein, some claim that defrauding government is not evil. NO! Such people overlook the fact that government money belongs to the generality of the people and that such fraud reduces the ability of government to discharge its responsibilities to the community. Actually, it takes a depraved mind to plot to, and defraud a government or bank The eighth of the Ten Commandments in the Word of God is that you should not steal (Deuteronomy 5:19; Exodus 20:15).

Often times when robbery is mentioned, and as per one of its definitions, people think of someone taking something with arms from another by force. And armed robbery in many nations of the world carries long term or capital sentences. Many robberies involve carting away articles of various values – some small and others large. However, there are some robberies with a stroke of the pen, whereby a highly placed official, especially amongst political office holders in government departments, and corporation executives appropriate millions (or even billions) of Dollars or other currencies. Unfortunately, many of such officials, when apprehended, often receive little or no sentence in comparison with armed robbers no matter how much is taken away by the armed robber. The major difference between the armed robber and a pen robber is that while the former is ready to kill or inflict physical bodily harm on his victim, the pen robber may not, notwithstanding that the results of the pen robber's act may be more far reaching in the long run.

Money from Scamming.

Another form of stealing is scamming – defrauding or swindling by trick or under false pretenses. In Nigeria it is more popularly known as "419" (four-one-nine), derived from the code number of the section of the Nigerian Criminal Code that deals with the fraud, the charges and penalties for offenders. It is also known as Advance Fee Fraud. Initially it was a local thing but gradually, with the growth or advancement in the Internet and globalization, 419 went international. This fraud style has earned Nigerians a very bad name to the extent that when a Nigerian abroad introduces himself as a Nigerian, people immediately begin to mistrust him or look at him as a criminal notwithstanding that it is only a few hundreds of people out of a population of about 200 million that perpetrate the evil.

Meanwhile it has been established that it is foreign nationals who are as greedy as the fraudsters that are successfully defrauded. And scams also happen in other nations in different magnitudes and different ways. The word, SCAM is not any Nigerian vernacular word. It is English! If it were not happening in the other English-speaking world, especially Great Britain and America, SCAM would not have been in their vocabulary or dictionary. Whatever happens, it is evil. Money acquired by this means is ill-gotten and does not last.

Money from (Hard) Drug Dealing.

Someone has said that drug dealing is all about money. Hard Drug Dealing, another means of making money involves trafficking and abuse of hard drugs. Hard drugs, also known as narcotics are highly addicting (chemical) substances that influence the user/abuser to the extent of losing self-control and becoming callous and shameless.

There are very many hard drugs, some of which are grouped by Center on Addiction [13] and listed as COMMONLY USED ILLEGAL DRUGS are as follows under the following subheadings:

CANNABINOIDS: Marijuana; Hashish.

OPIOIDS: Heroin; Opium

STIMULANTS: Cocaine; Amphetamine; Methamphetamine

CLUB DRUGS: MDMA (Methylenedioxymethamphetamine), Flunitrazepam, GHB (Gamma-hydroxybutyrate). The last two of these are said to have been used to perpetrate rape crimes.

DISSOCIATIVE DRUGS: Ketamine; PCP and Analogs (Phency clidine); Salvia Divinorum; Dextromethorphan (DXM).

HALLUCINOGENS: LSD (Lysergic acid diethylamide); Mescaline; Psilocybin.

OTHER COMPOUNDS: Anabolic Steroids; Inhalants.

You may observe that I did not include the manufacturers of the drugs in my description above of the term, Drug Dealing. It's because the substances are meant primarily for prescribed medical treatment of some ailments, especially severe pains, but because of their addictive effects and their ability to produce some other effects (side effects really), some people abuse them to heighten

---

[13] Center on Addiction:
https://www.centeronaddiction.org/addiction/commonly-used-illegal-drugs May 30, 2020

their psyches such that they have destroyed many lives including theirs. That's the more reason the dispensing and distribution of the drugs are controlled by 43 agencies.

Most of these hard drugs are very expensive. They make people rich! The barons or lords bask in millions of Dollars until they are arrested. Another set of drug dealers that make money, though not as much as the barons are the couriers, who move the drugs from source to their countries. Also the peddlers who do the local trafficking of the drugs become wealthy. Most of the abusers of hard drugs are rich people that can afford to pay for them.

Unfortunately, these days many nations of the world have risen up against the drug dealers. Many of the countries give life or capital sentences to the dealers when apprehended. Drug trafficking is a dangerous, evil way of making money, in view of the destructive effects on abusers.

Money from Prostitution

Webster's Dictionary defines prostitute as "one who engages in sexual activities for money."[14] Therefore, the act of engaging in sexual activities for money is prostitution. The principal synonym for prostitute is harlot, which the same dictionary defines as "a woman who engages in sexual activities esp. for money." Another synonym for prostitute is whore. Harlot and whore/whoredom and

---

[14] Webster's All-In-One Dictionary & Thesaurus, 2010.

related terms have more occurrences in the Bible than prostitute/prostitution.

Prostitution is said to be the oldest known business especially amongst women because of the saying, 'use what you have to get what you want' during tough times. As early in the Bible as in Genesis 34:31 the word, harlot appears: "But they said, "Should he treat our sister like a harlot?" A few harlots were named or described in the Bible apart from the use of the term by many of the Old Testament prophets to describe the wayward behavior of Israel towards God. Some of such names and descriptions are as follows:

- Tamar

And it was told Tamar, saying, "Look, your father-in-law is going up to Timnah to shear his sheep." [14] So she took off her widow's garments, covered herself with a veil and wrapped herself, and sat in an open place which was on the way to Timnah; for she saw that Shelah was grown, and she was not given to him as a wife. [15] When Judah saw her, he thought she was a harlot, because she had covered her face. [16] Then he turned to her by the way, and said, "Please let me come in to you"; for he did not know that she was his daughter-in-law. So she said, "What will you give me, that you may come in to me?" [17] And he said, "I will send a young goat from the flock." So she said, "Will you give me a pledge till you send it?" [18] Then he said, "What pledge shall I give you?" So she said, "Your signet and cord, and your staff that is in your hand." Then he gave them to her, and went in to her, and she conceived by him (Genesis 38:13-18 NKJV).

- Rahab

Now Joshua the son of Nun sent out two men from Acacia Grove to spy secretly, saying, "Go, view the land, especially Jericho." So they went and came to the house of a harlot named Rahab, and lodged there (Joshua 2:1 NKJV).

- Jephthah's mother (not named).

Now Jephthah the Gileadite was a mighty man of valor, but he was the son of a harlot; and Gilead begot Jephthah. (Judges 11:1 NKJV).

- Delilah

Now Samson went to Gaza and saw a harlot there, and went in to her.

Afterward it happened that he loved a woman in the Valley of Sorek, whose name was Delilah (Judges 16:1, 4 NKJV).

- Two Harlots (unnamed) Before King Solomon.

Now two women who were harlots came to the king, and stood before him. (1 Kings 3:16 NKJV).

It is worth mentioning that some religions have a kind of prostitution whereby sexual intercourse is carried out as part of religious worship. It has been termed temple prostitution, sacred prostitution or cult prostitution. Some scholars have suggested that instead of any form of prostitution, it should be termed sacred sex or sacred sexual rites because no monetary payment may be involved.[15]

In the United States of America, except in some counties in the state of Nevada, and many other nations of the world, prostitution is prohibited or legal with conditions, even though it is practiced in one way or the other. On the other hand, it is legal in many European countries. Some people and, even governments, make lots of money from prostitution by running brothels, [16] advertisements and direct employment by companies. Some governments also make lots of money by legalizing and taxing the industry.

A serious situation has arisen as a result of global unemployment – worse in many African countries – where young ladies are deceived and trafficked abroad, especially to Europe. Such ladies are promised lucrative jobs, only to get there and be assigned rooms in brothels, where they should "sell" and make financial returns to their sponsors. Some women practice their prostitution in their own homes where some rich customers patronize them.

Unfortunately, however, no matter how profitable prostitution may appear to be, it is morally debasing and socially

---

[15] "Sacred Prostitution."
https://en.wikipedia.org/wiki/Sacred_prostitution June 1, 2020.
[16] Webster's Dictionary defines brothel as "a house of prostitution."

unacceptable, especially as it has always served as a major means of transmitting some deadly sexually transmitted diseases (STDs). Spiritually, it is sinful behavior to present oneself (to sell sex), or patronize the prostitute, for it is fornication or adultery. The seventh of the Ten Commandments is "Thou shalt not commit adultery" (exodus 20:14). The apostle Paul wrote in 1 Corinthians 6:16-18

(ESV), "Or do you not know that he who is joined to a prostitute becomes one body with her? For, as it is written, "The two will become one flesh." [17] But he who is joined to the Lord becomes one spirit with him. [18] Flee from sexual immorality. Every other sin a person commits is outside the body, but the sexually immoral person sins against his own body."

Read what the Lord says to the angel of the church in Thyatira, "But I have this against you, that you tolerate that woman Jezebel, who calls herself a prophetess and is teaching and seducing my servants to practice sexual immorality and to eat food sacrificed to idols. [21] I gave her time to repent, but she refuses to repent of her sexual immorality. [22] Behold, I will throw her onto a sickbed, and those who commit adultery with her I will throw into great tribulation, unless they repent of her works. (Revelation 2:20-22 ESV, emphases added). Secondly, the final verdict is that "or the cowardly, the faithless, the detestable, as for murderers, the sexually immoral, sorcerers, idolaters, and all liars, their portion will be in the lake that burns with fire and sulfur, which is the second death." (Revelation 21:8 ESV, emphases added).

Money from Exploitation

Some entrepreneurs in capitalist economies like the USA would rather give donations that would boost their egos than promptly and properly or appropriately remunerate their employees. Some award contracts to smaller contractors and wouldn't pay them, resulting in the smaller contractors owing their workers. If you deliberately owe your workers when you have the ability to pay them, their money in your bank accounts or pockets is not a blessing to you. Some employers deliberately underpay their workers because such employers believe the workers have no easy choice but to stay with them – all in the name of maximizing profit. The Bible says, "You shall not muzzle an ox while it treads out the grain," and, "The laborer is worthy of his wages." (1 Timothy 5:18 NKJV).

Some governments do exploit the poor by offering them false hope in lotteries, which people hardly ever win. Unfortunately, gullible gamblers are caught in the web. Many of them get so addicted to gambling that they lose all they have in the hope and attempt to win some huge sums someday. Promoters of lotteries may claim that they do not coerce their patrons to participate, but they lead us into temptation by their kinds of enticing and deceitful advertisements. Although the word, gambling is not explicitly declared sinful in Scriptures, yet it exposes greed in the gamblers. Greed is one of the sins for which people will not inherit the kingdom of God.[17] Webster's Dictionary defines greed as "acquisitive or selfish desire beyond reason." πλεονέκται (pleonektai) translated greedy from the Greek is also translated as "a covetous person" or "an avaricious one." Gambling is also not a good investment.

Money from Ritual Killing and Killing for Body Parts

It is often in the news these days that people get missing – adult, children, boys and girls, whose bodies may be found a few days later, dumped somewhere and sometimes devoid of some parts. In the western world some of such murders are with the intention to sell parts harvested from the victims to patients needing transplant, if the murder is not intended to conceal a crime. But in some developing nations especially in some African countries, some people superstitiously believe that with human blood and body parts herbalists can give them power and means for making lots of money. Consequently, the numbers of cases of kidnapping for ritual murders increase close to general elections in some of

---

[17] "Or do you not know that the unrighteous will not inherit the kingdom of God? Do not be deceived: neither the sexually immoral, nor idolaters, nor adulterers, nor men who practice homosexuality, [10] nor thieves, nor the greedy, nor drunkards, nor revilers, nor swindlers will inherit the kingdom of God." (1 Corinthians 6:9-10 ESV).

such countries. Such people lured into human sacrificing are then ushered into cults of bloodthirsty fellows.

If truly money comes by such means, it's another example of acquiring wealth from the devil, which will eventually land the recipient in sorrow, pain and regrets. Anyone that can do anything possible to acquire wealth, irrespective of the consequences has too much love for money. The apostle Paul said, "For the love of money is the root of all evil: which while some coveted after, they have erred from the faith, and pierced themselves through with many sorrows." (1 Timothy 6:10).

3.3 Good Use or Application of Money.

Over time, the power of money has been put into various uses all over the world. Some of such uses were (and are) good, commendable, acceptable and progressive, especially when they were for the benefit of humanity. Similarly, money has been used despicably and in destructive manners, or for purposes that are anti-human, which are described in the next section as abuses of money power. Meanwhile, this section looks into good application of the power of money in the olden times as per the Old Testament and New Testament Bible, and in contemporary times.

Abraham.

In Genesis 13:2 (NKJV) we read that Abraham was very rich in livestock, in silver and in gold. This was further exposed by the words of Abraham's servant as follows: "The Lord has greatly blessed my master, and he has become great. He has given him flocks and herds, silver and gold, male servants and female servants, camels and donkeys." (Genesis 24:35-36 ESV).

Although there is no explicit project credited to Abraham's use of his wealth, yet God saw him as a faithful, rich man that He could use to bring to pass His plan for the world. God said, "For I have known him, in order that he may command his children and his household after him, that they keep the way of the LORD, to do righteousness and justice, that the LORD may bring to Abraham what He has spoken to him." (Genesis 18:19).

<u>Boaz</u>

This man was a wealthy relative (kinsman) of Elimelech, the late husband of Naomi, to whose late son a foreign woman, Ruth was originally married (Ruth 2:1). Boaz arrived at his farm from Bethlehem one day and saw a strange woman gleaning and gathering grains behind the official reapers. He asked his supervisor who she was, and Ruth was introduced to him as the young Moabite woman, who returned with Naomi from Moab. Rather than take advantage of her as a normal capitalist employer, Boaz gave her some incentives including a formal authority to glean regularly on his field, and when thirsty she should drink from the water vessels provided by the male workers. Also, Boaz invited Ruth to lunch along with the reapers. He let her glean close to the reapers till the end of the wheat and barley harvest.

At the mother-in-law's advice, Ruth indicated her wish for Boaz to redeem her being a kinsman to her erstwhile husband. Boaz did not jump at it because he was a wealthy man, but followed the laid-down procedure for such – allowing a closer kinsman to do it. It was only after the closer kinsman declined that Boaz married Ruth.

"Then [Boaz] said to the close relative, "Naomi, who has come back from the country of Moab, sold the piece of land which belonged to our brother Elimelech. [4] And I thought to inform you, saying, 'Buy it back in the presence of the inhabitants and the elders of my people. If you will redeem it, redeem it; but if you will not redeem it, then tell me, that I may know; for there is no one but you to redeem it, and I am next after you.' "And he said, "I will redeem it." (Ruth 4:3-4 NKJV)

"[8] Therefore the close relative said to Boaz, "Buy it for yourself." So he took off his sandal. [9] And Boaz said to the elders and all the people, "You are witnesses this day that I have bought all that was Elimelech's, and all that was Chilion's and Mahlon's, from the hand of Naomi. [10] Moreover, Ruth the Moabitess, the widow of Mahlon, I have acquired as my wife, to perpetuate the name of the dead through his inheritance, that the name of the dead may not be cut off from among his brethren and from his position at the gate. You are witnesses this day." (Ruth 4:8-10 NKJV).

Ruth became the mother of Obed, the grandfather of King David. In the New Testament some rich people were mentioned. Some of these include Joseph of Arimathaea, Cornelius, Dorcas, Aquilla and Priscilla, and Philemon. Below is a brief of the good use their God-given wealth by two of these persons.

Joseph of Arimathaea was a rich man (Matthew 27:57), a prominent member of the Jewish Council – likely the Sanhedrin who was looking forward for the kingdom of God (Mark 15:43; Luke 23:51), and a good and just man (Luke 23:50). Joseph did not give consent to the crucifixion of Jesus Christ. When Jesus died on the cross Joseph went to Governor Pontus Pilate to beg for permission to bury the body. With permission granted Joseph provided linen cloths for shrouding the body and with the assistance of Nicodemus, another Pharisee, he laid the body of Jesus in his Never-used tomb before the Sabbath began.

It is worthy of note that all four Gospels recorded the contribution of Joseph of Arimathaea because of the value placed on the actions of such a rich man in humility.

Cornelius (Acts 10:1-2) was "a centurion of what was called the Italian Regiment, a devout man and one who feared God with all his household." A centurion was an officer of the Roman Army commanding between eighty and one hundred soldiers, depending on the size of the legion[18] to which the century (or centuria) belonged. Cornelius was said to be devout and God-fearing – he and his household. And he gave much alms. Alms are not given to the rich but for the poor and needy. That Cornelius did alms giving always indicates that he was generous towards the poor that would not be able to pay him back. He used his money to help the poor and needy in line with the teaching of Jesus Christ, that, ". . . when you give a feast, invite the poor, the crippled, the lame, the blind, [14] and you will be blessed, because they cannot repay you. For you will be repaid at the resurrection of the just." (Luke 14:13-24 ESV).

Contemporarily there have been people who have used their money to advance the well-being of humanity. Many of them were or are Christians and many others unbelievers. Such people these days are described as philanthropists, which word stems from the Greek φιλανθρωπία (transliterated filanthropía) meaning philanthropy. Synonyms of Philanthropy include graciousness charity, charitableness, benevolence, humanity, etc. In an online article, "Past Philanthropists: How Giving was Evolved" by Shariaz Musaffer the vision of John D. Rockefeller and Andrew Carnegie were highlighted. The writer quoted Carnegie that it is

---

[18] *Legion* was a collection of between 4,600 and 6,000 men of the Roman Army.

the duty of the wealthy to allow other people the opportunity to be wealthy. He added that Bill Gates also made that clear.[19]

3.4 Misuse or Abuse of Money

Money is worthless until and unless it is spent or used. Money is used for good causes and good things. It is also used to do evil. Over the ages up till the present people have wielded the power of money for the benefit, or to the detriment, of mankind and the environment.

Although there does not seem to be specific names of individual wealthy men that abused their money in the Old Testament times, yet that does not imply that none did. At least, God would not have instituted laws against greed and covetousness if there would not be such issues. The ninth and tenth commandments say thus:

"Thou shalt not bear false witness against thy neighbour.

Thou shalt not covet thy neighbour's house, thou shalt not covet thy neighbour's wife, nor his manservant, nor his maidservant, nor his ox, nor his ass, nor any thing that is thy neighbour's." (Exodus 20:16-17).

Another proof that there were rich men who abused money is contained in the words of caution and rebuke of the LORD through His prophets. Some of such words are as follows:

---

[19] https://www.bbc.com/news/business-19272109 August 1, 2020.

"Is not this the fast that I have chosen? to loose the bands of wickedness, to undo the heavy burdens, and to let the oppressed go free, and that ye break every yoke?

[7] Is it not to deal thy bread to the hungry, and that thou bring the poor that are cast out to thy house? when thou seest the naked, that thou cover him; and that thou hide not thyself from thine own flesh?" (Isaiah 58:6-7)

"As a cage is full of birds, so are their houses full of deceit: therefore they are become great, and waxen rich. [28] They are waxen fat, they shine: yea, they overpass the deeds of the wicked: they judge not the cause, the cause of the fatherless, yet they prosper; and the right of the needy do they not judge." (Jeremiah 5:27-28).

"The people of the land have used oppression, and exercised robbery, and have vexed the poor and needy: yea, they have oppressed the stranger wrongfully. [30] And I sought for a man among them, that should make up the hedge, and stand in the gap before me for the land, that I should not destroy it: but I found none. [31] Therefore have I poured out mine indignation upon them; I have consumed them with the fire of my wrath: their own way have I recompensed upon their heads, saith the Lord God." (Ezekiel 22:29-31).

"Are there yet the treasures of wickedness in the house of the wicked, and the scant measure that is abominable? [11] Shall I count them pure with the wicked balances, and with the bag of deceitful weights? [12] For the rich men thereof are full of violence, and the inhabitants thereof have spoken lies, and their tongue is deceitful in their mouth. [13] Therefore also will I make thee sick in smiting thee, in making thee desolate because of thy sins." (Micah 6:10-13).

There were some rich fellows mentioned in the Bible, who applied their money to wicked or wrong acts that displeased God. One of such men was King Solomon, the third king of the nation of Israel. From 1 Kings 10:14-29 we excerpt the following as some of the resources of King Solomon: Notwithstanding that Solomon built a magnificent temple for the LORD in Jerusalem, he misused the wealth that GOD had endowed him with. Some of his resources were as follows:

- Yearly receipt of 666 talents of gold, excluding the revenues from merchants and traders and from all the Arabian kings and the governors of the territories.
- 200 large shields of hammered gold each of which consisted of 600 shekels of gold.
- 300 small shields of hammered gold, each with three minas of gold.
- A great throne covered with ivory and overlaid with fine gold, having six steps and its back with a round top.
- All his "goblets were gold, and all the household articles in the Palace of the Forest of Lebanon were pure gold."

- "A fleet of trading ships at sea along with the ships of Hiram. Once every three years it returned, carrying gold, silver and ivory, and apes and baboons." (1 Kings 10:22 NIV)
- "Year after year, everyone who came brought a gift—articles of silver and gold, robes, weapons and spices, and horses and mules." (1 Kings 10:25 NIV).
- 1400 chariots and 12,000 horses.

Solomon was excessively wealthy, living in a luxurious palace, the construction of which culminated in excessively tasking and taxing the people. NIV comment on 1 Kings 10:26-11:3 notes that "The more luxurious Solomon's court became, the more the people were taxed. Excessive taxation created unrest, and soon conditions became ripe for a revolution."[20]

Although God gave Solomon – and by extension the people of Israel – peace and commercial popularity internationally, it is not explicitly stated in Scriptures the good things he might have done for the people, if any, apart from building the Temple of God in Jerusalem. It appears he was self-centered. "But Solomon married seven hundred wives and had three hundred concubines, all of royal blood, and in defiance of God's command."[21] It was sinful

---

[20] Life Application Study Bible, 514.
[21] Daniel Ukadike Nwaelene, ThD. "Jesus Christ: Savior, Judge & King of the World" (Bloomington, IN: WestBow Press, 2017), 38.

enough that he was so polygamous in marriage with foreign women against God's commandment to Israel, Solomon encouraged idolatry by allowing each of the women to carry along the deities (gods and goddesses) of their nations of origin. He built altars for all the idols and gods as well as goddesses that his seven hundred wives took to Israel from their idolatrous nations (1Kings 11:1-10). So, Solomon was wicked in the sight of God, hence such a man of great wisdom and wealth fell and ended up a failure. God tore his kingdom in two, leaving only two-twelfths (1/6) of the twelve tribes to his son Rehoboam while the 10 tribes went with Jeroboam the son of Nabat.

Haman

When the Jews were in exile in Babylon, there came a time when Haman, one of the senior officials of the empire plotted to have all the Jews in the empire exterminated, promising to pay large sums of money into the treasury for the officials that would carry out the evil act. His reason for that resolve was that one Jew by the name Mordecai refused to kneel down to give him honor, and discovering that all of Mordecai's people had the same attitude (to bow or kneel before the almighty God alone), Haman decided to kill not only the one offender, but all the Jews in the empire. (Esther 3:1-5).

This plot exemplifies how someone would want to spend large sums of money to perform a project that would not be profitable to the people or bring glory to God. This story of Haman will be re-visited under the Power, as abuse of power is also in it.

Others

Rebuke by prophets of the Old Testament reveals that the Bible recognizes that some rich people gained their wealth by injustice. Such rebukes also tell that many of the rich people spent their money to oppress and marginalize the poor and needy as well as strangers. Some of the Bible passages that rebuke the rich are as follows:

"Hear this word, you cows of Bashan, who are in the mountain of Samar'ia, who oppress the poor, who crush the needy, who say to their husbands, 'Bring, that we may drink!' [2] The Lord God has sworn by his holiness that, behold, the days are coming upon you, when they shall take you away with hooks, even the last of you with fishhooks." (Amos 4:1-2 RSV).

"They hate him who reproves in the gate, and they abhor him who speaks the truth. [11] Therefore because you trample upon the poor and take from him exactions of wheat, you have built houses of hewn stone, but you shall not dwell in them; you have planted pleasant vineyards, but you shall not drink their wine. [12] For I know how many are your transgressions, and how great are your sins—you who afflict the righteous, who take a bribe, and turn aside the needy in the gate." (Amos 5:10-12 RSV).

"Your rich men are full of violence; your inhabitants speak lies, and their tongue is deceitful in their mouth." (Micah 6:12 RSV).

"Do you think you are a king because you compete in cedar? Did not your father eat and drink and do justice and righteousness? Then it was well with him. [16] He judged the cause of the poor and needy; then it was well. Is not this to know me? says the Lord. [17] But you have eyes and heart only for your dishonest gain, for shedding innocent blood, and for practicing oppression and violence." (Jeremiah 22:15-17 RSV).

Jewish Leaders.

Roman soldiers securely guarded Jesus Christ's burial place while Jesus remained in the tomb. But at God's appointed time, sequel to a violent earthquake an angel of the Lord rolled away the stone used to block the entrance to the tomb and sat on it. The appearance of the angel was like lightning, and his clothes were white like snow. The Roman guards were so afraid that they shook and became like dead men. This marked the resurrection of the Lord Jesus Christ (Matthew 28:1-4).

Some women that went to the tomb to anoint the body of Jesus but were told by the angel that Jesus was no longer there, and they should go to Galilee to meet Him. While they were on their way, some of the guards went into the city and narrated to the chief priests their experience capable of earning the guard's capital punishment. The chief priests met with some Jewish elders and agreed to bribe the soldiers with large sums of money to change the narrative – to say to people that while they slept (on guard) at night the disciples of Jesus went and stole His body. They also promised to defend the guards if the report got to the authorities. Bribery! (Matthew 28:11-15).

Contemporarily, in most of the developing nations, especially in Africa, many rich people abuse money. They oppress the poor with impunity because they can easily buy justice or acquittal with money. They use their wealth to acquire much more wealth from their nations at the expense of the generality of the people, so much that a few people put together become richer that their nations. Most of such rich people are so corrupt that they spend money to silence machineries of government that fight corruption. The rich in many African countries of today help by their exploitation and diversion of money to private pockets to destroy public institutions and infrastructure that should be accessible to all, and go abroad or send their families abroad to receive the benefits they should otherwise derive at home. Examples of such institutions are healthcare and education.

This is not to imply that the "developed nations" do not have rich people that abuse money and oppress the less privileged with their wealth. But theirs is done in style, with some sophistication and tact in such a way that it is not too glaring.

Pushing and Peddling Hard Drugs.

In recent years hard drugs such as cocaine, heroin, etc. have destroyed many lives. Most of these hard drugs were meant for solving some health issues, but because such medications are addicting, many people that have tasted them become addicted to their use to their personal destruction. It is mostly the rich and, unfortunately, their children that can afford to buy hard drugs for use.

Hard drugs are expensive all over the world and they are a great money-spinner. Rich men buy them and use poor people to courier them abroad – from one nation to another. Many nations have outlawed hard drug peddling/abuse, with severe penalties up to and including death for perpetrators of drug businesses. However, since in most cases, when caught the couriers do not accept to expose their sponsors, perhaps because of non-disclosure agreements (NDAs) they sign to that effect with their sponsors. In that case, the poor folk used to courier the drug suffers punishment that may arise, which may be death, while the rich owner or sponsor goes Scot-free without any remorse or regret.

Jesus Christ cast out very powerful demons from the Gadarene demoniac who called himself Legion. Jesus directed the demons into a swine at the request of the demons, and the swine numbering about 2000 pigs rushed into the sea and were destroyed. The owners of the swine asked Jesus to leave their neighborhood. They were not pleased that a human being was saved, though to the detriment of pigs – animals lower in value than man – because that healing affected the business incomes of the people (Matthew 8:28-34; Mark 5:1-20). Similarly in recent times in the United States groups of people have been fatally attacked with guns of various sorts including assault rifles meant for wars.

All efforts to control the acquisition and use of weapons of mass destruction have continued to be blocked by moneybags, whose wealth depends on the manufacture and sale of such weapons, in preference to preserving lives of fellow Americans including children. Abuse of money for sure! Rather than agree to the control of the weapons, the moneybags have been pressing for people to buy more for protecting themselves. And that would further enrich them, notwithstanding the inherent dangers on the people.

3.5 Contribution of Money to the Downfall of a Man.

To the astonishment of some people many great and rich men have fallen far into poverty, from grace to grass – sometimes into wretchedness. Some who had many houses, cars, fat bank accounts, ranches, mineral wealth such as gold, silver, diamond and so on lost all and could barely feed. Stories abound of some erstwhile chief executive officers that earned large sums of money as salaries but died penniless – some of them committing suicide. It is not that they desired it that way, but many things could account for such a fall. The Bible gives some possible causes of a rich man's fall as follows: -

1. Pride.

People that are proud hardly accept that they are. Several other words or collections of words describe, or are synonyms of pride thus:

- "Inordinate self-esteem; justifiable self-respect; elation over an act or possession; haughty behavior; ostentatious display;"[22]

- " Self-exaltation; conceit; arrogance; putting oneself above others; looking down upon others."[23]

"Pride goeth before destruction, and an haughty spirit before a fall." (Proverbs 16:18). "When pride comes, then comes shame; but with the humble is wisdom." (NKJV). "Before his downfall a man's heart is proud, but humility comes before honor." (Proverbs 18:12 BSB).

2. Greed.

This is intense desire to acquire (possessions); lust for more; covetousness.

---

[22] Webster's All-in-one Dictionary & Thesaurus.

[23] Practical Word Studies in the New Testament Vol. 2 L-Z, 1610.

"For from within, out of the heart of men, proceed evil thoughts, adulteries, fornications, murders, [22] Thefts, <u>covetousness</u>, wickedness, deceit, lasciviousness, an <u>evil eye</u>, blasphemy, pride, foolishness: [23] All these evil things come from within, and defile the man." (Mark 7:21-23 emphases added).

"He that is greedy of gain troubleth his own house; but he that hateth gifts shall live." (Proverbs 15:27).

The story of the healing of Naaman in 2Kings 5:1-19 ended on a bad note for Gehazi, Prophet Elisha's attendant. He would probably have become the greatest prophet in the Bible but for greed for money. Elisha was a very powerful prophet of God. He received a double portion of the anointing of Prophet Elijah. If Gehazi had patiently completed his apprenticeship and, may be, received a double portion of the anointing of Elisha, Gehazi would have had a record greater than Elisha's and Elijah's.

After Naaman was healed of leprosy by God at the word of Elisha, Naaman offered great financial and material gifts, which Elisha turned down. But Gehazi secretly ran after Naaman and lied to receive just a bit of all that Naaman had brought to give to Elisha. Elisha cursed Gehazi and inflicted him with leprosy, then Gehazi left Elisha's presence an incurable leper.

3. Selfishness or self-centeredness.

To be selfish or self-centered is the act of being concerned about oneself only; having or giving no consideration for others; or being mainly concerned about one's own personal pleasure or gain. The Scriptures counsel as follows regarding selfishness and the opposite thereof, generosity or liberality:

"The generous soul will be made rich, And he who waters will also be watered himself. [26] The people will curse him who withholds grain," (Proverbs 11:25-26 NKJV).

"Be devoted to one another in love. Honor one another above yourselves. [13] Share with the Lord's people who are in need. Practice hospitality." (Romans 12:10, 13 NIV).

"Bear one another's burdens, and so fulfill the law of Christ." (Galatians 6:2).

But do not forget to do good and to share, for with such sacrifices God is well pleased." (Hebrews 13:16).

4. Love of Money.

Loving money implies placing money (wealth) ahead of God and all things else in such a way that the one is ready and willing to do anything to acquire it. Money is not the root of all evil, as some people misquote the passage of the Bible below, rather it is the love of money that is. Money is necessary and good to have. But going after it by all means is dangerous and sinful. The apostle Paul counsels thus:

"But they that will be rich fall into temptation and a snare, and into many foolish and hurtful lusts, which drown men in destruction and perdition. [10] For the love of money is the root of all evil: which while some coveted after, they have erred from the faith, and pierced themselves through with many sorrows. [11] But thou, O man of God, flee these things; and follow after righteousness, godliness, faith, love, patience, meekness." (1 Timothy 6:9-11).

5. Lack of Appreciation of the Giver of Wealth.

"Then beware lest thou forget the Lord, which brought thee forth out of the land of Egypt, from the house of bondage." (Deuteronomy 6:12 NKJV).

"Beware that thou forget not the Lord thy God, in not keeping his commandments, and his judgments, and his statutes, which I command thee this day:

[12] Lest when thou hast eaten and art full, and hast built goodly houses, and dwelt therein; [13] And when thy herds and thy flocks multiply, and thy silver and thy gold is multiplied, and all that thou hast is multiplied; [14] Then thine heart be lifted up, and thou forget the Lord thy God, which brought thee forth out of the land of Egypt, from the house of bondage; [15] Who led thee through that great and terrible wilderness, wherein were fiery serpents, and scorpions, and drought, where there was no water; who brought thee forth water out of the rock of flint; [16] Who fed thee in the

wilderness with manna, which thy fathers knew not, that he might humble thee, and that he might prove thee, to do thee good at thy latter end; ¹⁷ And thou say in thine heart, My power and the might of mine hand hath gotten me this wealth.

"¹⁸ But thou shalt remember the Lord thy God: for it is he that giveth thee power to get wealth, that he may establish his covenant which he sware unto thy fathers, as it is this day. ¹⁹ And it shall be, if thou do at all forget the Lord thy God, and walk after other gods, and serve them, and worship them, I testify against you this day that ye shall surely perish. ²⁰ As the nations which the Lord destroyeth before your face, so shall ye perish; because ye would not be obedient unto the voice of the Lord your God." (Deuteronomy 8:11-20).

"Can a maid forget her ornaments, or a bride her attire? yet my people have forgotten me days without number." (Jeremiah 2:32).

6. Oppression of the Poor

"He that oppresseth the poor to increase his riches, and he that giveth to the rich, shall surely come to want." (Proverbs 22:16).

"Woe to them that devise iniquity, and work evil upon their beds! when the morning is light, they practise it, because it is in the power of their hand. ² And they covet fields, and take them by violence; and houses, and take them away: so they oppress a man and his house, even a man and his heritage.

³ Therefore thus saith the Lord; Behold, against this family do I devise an evil, from which ye shall not remove your necks; neither shall ye go haughtily: for this time is evil.

⁴ In that day shall one take up a parable against you, and lament with a doleful lamentation, and say, we be utterly spoiled: he hath changed the portion of my people: how hath he removed it from me! turning away he hath divided our fields.

⁵ Therefore thou shalt have none that shall cast a cord by lot in the congregation of the Lord.

⁶ Prophesy ye not, say they to them that prophesy: they shall not prophesy to them, that they shall not take shame.

⁷ O thou that art named the house of Jacob, is the spirit of the Lord straitened? are these his doings? do not my words do good to him that walketh uprightly?

⁸ Even of late my people is risen up as an enemy: ye pull off the robe with the garment from them that pass by securely as men averse from war.

⁹ The women of my people have ye cast out from their pleasant houses; from their children have ye taken away my glory for ever.

¹⁰ Arise ye, and depart; for this is not your rest: because it is polluted, it shall destroy you, even with a sore destruction.

¹¹ If a man walking in the spirit and falsehood do lie, saying, I will prophesy unto thee of wine and of strong drink; he shall even be the prophet of this people.

^{12} I will surely assemble, O Jacob, all of thee; I will surely gather the remnant of Israel; I will put them together as the sheep of Bozrah, as the flock in the midst of their fold: they shall make great noise by reason of the multitude of men.

^{13} The breaker is come up before them: they have broken up, and have passed through the gate, and are gone out by it: and their king shall pass before them, and the Lord on the head of them. (Micah 2:1-13).

And I will come near to you to judgment; and I will be a swift witness against the sorcerers, and against the adulterers, and against false swearers, and against those that oppress the hireling in his wages, the widow, and the fatherless, and that turn aside the stranger from his right, and fear not me, saith the Lord of hosts." (Malachi 3:5).

7. God's Punishment for Ill-gotten Wealth

In view of God's disapproval of acquisition of wealth by evil means, He has prescribed and reserved punishment for the wicked that enrich themselves by such means. Some of such punishments are stated below:

"Fret not thyself because of evildoers, neither be thou envious against the workers of iniquity. ^{2} For they shall soon be cut down like the grass, and wither as the green herb.

[9] For evildoers shall be cut off: but those that wait upon the Lord, they shall inherit the earth. [10] For yet a little while, and the wicked shall not be: yea, thou shalt diligently consider his place, and it shall not be. [11] But the meek shall inherit the earth; and shall delight themselves in the abundance of peace. [12] The wicked plotteth against the just, and gnasheth upon him with his teeth. [13] The Lord shall laugh at him: for he seeth that his day is coming. [14] The wicked have drawn out the sword, and have bent their bow, to cast down the poor and needy, and to slay such as be of upright conversation. [15] Their sword shall enter into their own heart, and their bows shall be broken. [16] A little that a righteous man hath is better than the riches of many wicked. [17] For the arms of the wicked shall be broken: but the Lord upholdeth the righteous.

[20] But the wicked shall perish, and the enemies of the Lord shall be as the fat of lambs: they shall consume; into smoke shall they consume away.

[38] But the transgressors shall be destroyed together: the end of the wicked shall be cut off." (Psalm 37:1- 2, 9-17, 20, 38).

"Wealth gotten by vanity shall be diminished: but he that gathereth by labour shall increase." (Proverbs 13:11).

"He that is greedy of gain troubleth his own house; but he that hateth gifts shall live." (Proverbs 15:27).

"Go to now, ye rich men, weep and howl for your miseries that shall come upon you.

² Your riches are corrupted, and your garments are moth eaten.
³ Your gold and silver is cankered; and the rust of them shall be a witness against you, and shall eat your flesh as it were fire. Ye have heaped treasure together for the last days." (James 5:1-3).

To fall, in the context of this work means "to become lower in degree or level" or "to become lowered. "²⁴ Pursuit of money, or focus on it has brought about the collapse of many Christian ministries, pastors and institutions. Many pastors who want to be like the (rich and flamboyant) Joneses have fallen. It has been noted that often times, two or more pastors, especially of the Pentecostal extraction, who start a church in partnership, remain together until their church's membership grows and a lot of money begins to be realized. Quickly they split and go their separate ways, each taking along some loyal members of the old partnership.

Some pastors make much ado about growth in membership or size of their congregations. It is a good thing to desire and work for growth in membership of a church, provided the motive is not mainly for growth in financial gains rather than to reduce the number of souls headed for hell. But unfortunately, some preachers have been reported to have gone to powers of darkness to seek power to grow their 'churches', principally for the purpose

---

²⁴ Merriam-Webster [online] Dictionary

of becoming rich. Goats, cows, human bodies have been exhumed from underneath some churches' pulpits, all being rituals for more money to flow in. Unfortunately, 'pastors' who committed such heinous atrocity had always lived to regret it. 1Timothy 6:9-11 (quoted above) is an important reminder here.

Some folks become too boastful, full of themselves so much that they feel they can do anything and cover it up with money. Such people are ready to and do spend lots of money to cover their evil tracks, and gradually their money takes up wings and they fall into penury. When most of such people fall, they never rise again.

3.6 Bible Passages Teaching About Money (Riches, Wealth).

The Word of God is rich in teachings, warnings and counsels concerning money, riches or wealth. Some of the Bible verses instruct and teach to guard against greed, which often opens doors to other forms of sin. People that were/are wise and smart have heeded many of the teachings and it augured well with them. The teachings are all quoted below:

Exodus 20:15, 17 (NKJV) "You shall not steal.

[17] "You shall not covet your neighbor's house; you shall not covet your neighbor's wife, nor his male servant, nor his female servant, nor his ox, nor his donkey, nor anything that is your neighbor's."

Deuteronomy 8:18 "But thou shalt remember the Lord thy God: for it is he that giveth thee power to get wealth, that he may establish his covenant which he sware unto thy fathers, as it is this day."

Deuteronomy 23:19 NKJV "You shall not charge interest to your brother — interest on money or food or anything that is lent out at interest."

Deuteronomy 15:7-8 "If there be among you a poor man of one of thy brethren within any of thy gates in thy land which the Lord thy God giveth thee, thou shalt not harden thine heart, nor shut thine hand from thy poor brother: [8] But thou shalt open thine hand wide unto him, and shalt surely lend him sufficient for his need, in that which he wanteth."

Deuteronomy 15:11 "For the poor shall never cease out of the land: therefore I command thee, saying, Thou shalt open thine hand wide unto thy brother, to thy poor, and to thy needy, in thy land."

Deuteronomy 19:14 (NKJV) "You shall not remove your neighbor's landmark, which the men of old have set, in your inheritance which you will inherit in the land that the Lord your God is giving you to possess.

Deuteronomy 21:16 (NKJV) "then it shall be, on the day he bequeaths his possessions to his sons, that he must not bestow firstborn status on the son of the loved wife in preference to the son of the unloved, the true firstborn."

Deuteronomy 23:19-20 (NKJV) "You shall not charge interest to your brother—interest on money or food or anything that is lent out at interest. [20] To a foreigner you may charge interest, but to your brother you shall not charge interest, that the Lord your God may bless you in all to which you set your hand in the land which you are entering to possess."

1 Chronicles 29:12a (NKJV) "Both riches and honor come from You, And You reign over all."

Psalm 15:5 (NKJV) "He who does not put out his money at usury, Nor does he take a bribe against the innocent. He who does these things shall never be moved.

Psalm 37:21 "The wicked borroweth, and payeth not again: but the righteous sheweth mercy, and giveth."

Psalm 39:6 (NKJV) "Surely every man walks about like a shadow; Surely they busy themselves in vain; He heaps up riches, And does not know who will gather them."

Psalm 49:6-7 (NKJV) "Those who trust in their wealth and boast in the multitude of their riches, [7] None of them can by any means redeem his brother, Nor give to God a ransom for him—"

Psalm 49:10 (NKJV) "For he sees wise men die; Likewise the fool and the senseless person perish, And leave their wealth to others."

Psalm 52:7 (NKJV) "Here is the man who did not make God his strength, But trusted in the abundance of his riches, And strengthened himself in his wickedness."

Psalm 62:10 (NKJV) "Do not trust in oppression, Nor vainly hope in robbery; If riches increase, Do not set your heart on them."

Psalm 112:5 (NKJV) "A good man deals graciously and lends; He will guide his affairs with discretion."

Psalm 112:9 (NKJV) "He has dispersed abroad, He has given to the poor; His righteousness endures forever; His horn will be exalted with honor."

Proverbs 3:9 (NKJV) "Honor the Lord with your possessions, And with the firstfruits of all your increase."

Proverbs 10:22 (NKJV) "The blessing of the Lord makes one rich, And He adds no sorrow with it."

Proverbs 10:4 (NKJV) "He who has a slack hand becomes poor, But the hand of the diligent makes rich."

Proverbs 11:4 (NKJV) "Riches do not profit in the day of wrath, But righteousness delivers from death."

Proverbs 11:28 (NKJV) "He who trusts in his riches will fall, But the righteous will flourish like foliage."

Proverbs 13:11 (NKJV) "Wealth gained by dishonesty will be diminished, But he who gathers by labor will increase."

Proverbs 13:22 (NKJV) "A good man leaves an inheritance to his children's children, But the wealth of the sinner is stored up for the righteous."

Proverbs 14:31 (NKJV) "He who oppresses the poor reproaches his Maker, But he who honors Him has mercy on the needy."

Proverbs 20:21 (NKJV) "An inheritance gained hastily at the beginning Will not be blessed at the end."

Proverbs 22:1 (NKJV) "A good name is to be chosen rather than great riches, Loving favor rather than silver and gold."

Proverbs 22:4 (NKJV) "By humility and the fear of the Lord Are riches and honor and life."

Proverbs 22:9 (NKJV) "He who has a generous eye will be blessed, For he gives of his bread to the poor."

Proverbs 28:22 (NKJV) "A man with an evil eye hastens after riches, And does not consider that poverty will come upon him."

Proverbs 27:24 (NKJV) "For riches are not forever, Nor does a crown endure to all generations."

Proverbs 29:3 (NKJV) "Whoever loves wisdom makes his father rejoice, But a companion of harlots wastes his wealth."

Ecclesiastes 5:19 (NKJV) "As for every man to whom God has given riches and wealth, and given him power to eat of it, to receive his heritage and rejoice in his labor—this is the gift of God."

Ecclesiastes 5:10 (NKJV) "He who loves silver will not be satisfied with silver; Nor he who loves abundance, with increase. This also is vanity."

Ecclesiastes 6:1-2 (NKJV) "There is an evil which I have seen under the sun, and it is common among men: [2] A man to whom God has given riches and wealth and honor, so that he lacks nothing for himself of all he desires; yet God does not give him power to eat of it, but a foreigner consumes it. This is vanity, and it is an evil affliction."

Jeremiah 9:23 (NKJV) "Thus says the Lord: "Let not the wise man glory in his wisdom, Let not the mighty man glory in his might, Nor let the rich man glory in his riches;"

Jeremiah 17:11 (NKJV) "As a partridge that broods but does not hatch, So is he who gets riches, but not by right; It will leave him in the midst of his days, And at his end he will be a fool."

Ezekiel 18:5, 7-9 (ESV) "If a man is righteous and does what is just and right— ···, [7] does not oppress anyone, but restores to the debtor his pledge, commits no robbery, gives his bread to the hungry and covers the naked with a garment, [8] does not lend at interest or take any profit, withholds his hand from injustice, executes true justice between man and man, [9] walks in my statutes, and keeps my rules by acting faithfully—he is righteous; he shall surely live, declares the Lord God."

Ezekiel 28:5-7 (ESV) "by your great wisdom in your trade you have increased your wealth, and your heart has become proud in your wealth— [6] therefore thus says the Lord God: Because you make your heart like the heart of a god, [7] therefore, behold, I will bring foreigners upon you, the most ruthless of the nations; and they shall draw their swords against the beauty of your wisdom and defile your splendor."

Micah 3:11-12 (ESV) "Its heads give judgment for a bribe; its priests teach for a price; its prophets practice divination for money; yet they lean on the Lord and say, "Is not the Lord in the midst of us? No disaster shall come upon us." [12] Therefore because of you Zion shall be plowed as a field; Jerusalem shall become a heap of ruins, and the mountain of the house a wooded height."

3.7 Conclusion About Money

Money in itself is good, not evil.

It is a good thing to have money.

It is as well necessary to possess money.

The need for money abounds always and

"Money answers all things" (Ecclesiastes 10:19).

But do not love money because

Love of money is root of all sorts of evil (1Timothy 6:10).

Do not allow money to control you, your thoughts or actions.

Do not desire it lustfully.

Do not want to acquire money by all means.

If you do not have money yet,

Do not envy them that do.

Be content with what you have, and be grateful to God

For you could have been worse off.

God gives power to get wealth (Deuteronomy 8:18 NKJV "And you shall remember the Lord your God, for it is He who gives you power to get wealth, that He may establish His covenant which He swore to your fathers, as it is this day.").

Pray Him to give you and He will (Matthew 7:7 NKJV: "Ask, and it will be given to you; seek, and you will find; knock, and it will be opened to you.")

When you have money –

Look not down on them that have not.

Put money where it belongs: your servant,

Never above, or equal to, God.

Use your money to worship and serve God.

Use it to bless fellow men.

Do not hoard money, else you may lose it.

The following are divine counsel of the Lord Jesus Christ: Matthew 6:19-21, 31-33 NIV:

"Do not store up for yourselves treasures on earth, where moths and vermin destroy, and where thieves break in and steal. [20] But store up for yourselves treasures in heaven, where moths and vermin do not destroy, and where thieves do not break in and steal. [21] For where your treasure is, there your heart will be also.

[31] So do not worry, saying, 'What shall we eat?' or 'What shall we drink?' or 'What shall we wear?' [32] For the pagans run after all these things, and your heavenly Father knows that you need them. [33] But seek first his kingdom and his righteousness, and all these things will be given to you as well."

CHAPTER FOUR

POWER

Power is a popular word that means different things to different people and is used in respect of different real-life issues. Examples of the noun form of power are as follows:

-   Power as "ability to act or produce an effect."
-   As legal or official authority, capacity or right.
-   Possession of control, authority, or influence over others e.g., sovereign state.
-   A controlling group: Establishment – often used in the phrase, "the powers that be;"
-   Physical might.
-   Political control or influence.
-   An order of angels.
-   A source or means of supplying energy such as electricity.
-   The mathematical number of times as indicated by an exponent that a number occurs as a factor in a product e.g., x^2; 2^{64}, etc.

Synonyms of Power.

The following are synonyms of power:

Arm	Control	Mastery
Authority	Death grip	Reign
Clutch	Dominion	Rein (s)
Command	Hold	Sway

For our subject, we are considering power as the ability to act and/or produce an effect, using legal, official, financial or other authority or influence at one's disposal.

Just like money, power has led, and often does lead, to the downfall of people and nations/empires, especially when used excessively or unnecessarily. When power is used excessively it is bound to cause a revolt. George Orwell in his book, Animal Farm that I read over 50 years ago, said that "Power corrupts, and absolute power corrupts absolutely." George Orwell's observation then is as true now in the 21st century as it was in the mid 19th century and earlier. It is not wrong to wield power within the ambits of the law or within the limits of one's authority. But when one begins to be power-drunk and act ultra vires (beyond his powers) with impunity the end result is a fall to destruction.

Below is a list of some symptoms of power-drunkenness, which must be watched in and by everyone in a position of authority:

- Oppression of the less powerful or helpless.
- Seeing oneself as the most knowledgeable person or repository of knowledge.
- Not listening to advice or hearing advice but refusing to weigh it against own ideas.
- Not taking criticism lightly.
- Trying to be the only voice heard – every opposing voice must be silenced or intimidated.

- Never wanting, planning or accepting to relinquish power – this is perpetuation of power.

- Using position to illegally amass wealth at the expense of others – persons or society.

- Being self-centered in everything, irrespective of how the people feel or the effect on them.

- Using power to acquire more power, changing existing laws in the statute books to accommodate personal excesses.

4.1 Greek Words Translated as Power in the English Bible.

About thirty-seven Hebrew words and twenty-one Greek words in the Bible (Old and New Testaments) have been translated as power and power's synonyms (as nouns, adverbs and adjectives) in the English Bible, according to Strong's Concordance with Hebrew & Greek Lexicon. However, for the purpose of this work only the noun form of a few of the Greek words are listed below:

1. **ἀρχή** (Gr. 746*)* *archē* pronounced ar-khay' translated as Authority (like Governor), principality. Examples are Luk. 20:20 ". . . so they might deliver him unto the <u>power</u> and <u>authority</u> of the governor."

Mark 10:6 "But from the beginning of the creation God made them male and female.."

2. **ἄρχων** (Gr. 758) *Archon* pronounced: ar'-khone translated Ruler, prince, chief, magistrate, chief ruler. Examples of usage are Matt. 9:18 ". . . behold, there came a certain ruler, and worshipped him,"

John 3:1 "There was a man of the Pharisees, named Nicodemus, a ruler of the Jews:"

3. **βασιλεύς** (Gr. 935) *basileus.* Pronounced: bas-il-yooce translated as King, King (of the Jews), King (God or Christ). Examples: Matt. 17:25 ". . . What thinkest thou, Simon? of whom do the kings of the earth take custom or tribute?

Luke 22:26 And he said unto them, The kings of the Gentiles exercise lordship over them; and they that exercise authority upon them are called benefactors.

4. **δύναμις** (Gr. 1411) *dynamis.* Pronounced: doo'-nam-is translated as <u>Power</u>, mighty work, miracle, might, strength. References are 2Cor. 4:7 "But we have this treasure in earthen vessels, that the excellency of the power may be of God, and not of us."

Acts 4:7 "And when they had set them in the midst, they asked,
By what <u>power,</u> or by what name, have ye done this?"

Rev. 17:13 "These have one mind, and shall give their <u>power</u> and strength unto the beast."

5. δυνατός (Gr. 1415) dynatos pronounced: doo-nat-os, translated as able, powerful, mighty, strong, possible. References are Matt. 19:26 "But Jesus beheld them, and said unto them, With men this is impossible; but with God all things are possible"

Rom. 4:21 "And being fully persuaded that, what he had promised, he was able also to perform."
Heb. 11:19"Accounting that God was able to raise him up, even from the dead; . . . "

Rom. 9:22 "What if God, willing to shew his wrath, and to make his power known, ..."

6. ἐξουσία (Gr. 1849) exousia pronounced: ex-oo-see'-ah, translated as Power, authority, right, liberty, jurisdiction, strength. Usage examples are Matt. 21:23 "And when he was come into the temple, the chief priests and the elders of the people came unto him as he was teaching, and said, By what authority doest thou these things? and who gave thee this authority?"

Rom. 9:21 "Hath not the potter power over the clay, of the same lump to make one vessel unto honour, and another unto dishonour?"

7. ἐπιτροπή (Gr. 2011) epitropē Pronounced: ep-ee-trop-ay,' translated as permission, power, commission. Example is Acts 26:12 "Whereupon as I went to Damascus with authority and commission from the chief priests,"

8. θρόνος (Gr.2362) thronos, translated as Throne seat, kingly power, royalty. Examples of Usage are Luke 1:32 "He shall be great, and shall be called the Son of the Highest: and the Lord God shall give unto him the throne of his father David:"

Heb. 12:2 "Looking unto Jesus the author and finisher of our faith; who for the joy that was set before him endured the cross, despising the shame, and is set down at the right hand of the throne of God."

Rev. 20:11a "And I saw a great white throne, and him that sat on it, from whose face the earth and the heaven fled away;"

9. ἰσχύς (Gr.2479) ischys pronounced: is-khoos, translated as Ability, force, strength, might. References are 2Thes 1:9

"Who shall be punished with everlasting destruction from the presence of the Lord, and from the glory of his power"

2Pet. 2:11 "Whereas angels, which are greater in power and might, bring not railing accusation against them before the Lord."

10. κράτος (Gr.2904) kratos. Translation: force, strength, power, might. Examples: Eph. 6:10 Finally, my brethren, be strong in the Lord, and in the power of his might."

Colossians 1:11 "Strengthened with all might, according to his glorious power, unto all patience and longsuffering with joyfulness;"

11. μεγαλειότης (Gr. 3168) megaleiotēs Pronounced: meg-al-i-ot'-ace. Translation: magnificence, majesty, mighty power (superbness i.e. splendor or glory).

Luke 9:43 "And they were all amazed at the mighty power of God. But while they wondered every one at all things which Jesus did, he said unto his disciples,

2Pet. 1:16 "For we have not followed cunningly devised fables, when we made known unto you the power and coming of our Lord Jesus Christ, but were eyewitnesses of his majesty"

4.2 Sources of Power and Methods of Acquisition of Power

Technically speaking, there are two main sources of power – God and the devil. But ultimately, all powers belong to God. The psalmist says, "God hath spoken once; twice have I heard this; that power belongeth unto God." (Psalm 62:11). He created all things and powers and He gives it to whom He chooses, for the purpose of doing service for/to Him. The Bible says in Romans 13:1-5:

"Let every soul be subject unto the higher powers. For there is no power but of God: the powers that be are ordained of God. [2] Whosoever therefore resisteth the power, resisteth the ordinance of God: and they that resist shall receive to themselves damnation. [3] For rulers are not a terror to good works, but to the evil. Wilt thou then not be afraid of the power? do that which is good, and thou shalt have praise of the same: [4] For he is the minister of God to thee for good. But if thou do that which is evil, be afraid; for he beareth not the sword in vain: for he is the minister of God, a revenger to execute wrath upon him that doeth evil. [5] Wherefore ye must needs be subject, not only for wrath, but also for conscience's sake."

It is expected, therefore, that all God-given powers are obtained legitimately and are meant for good deeds. There are several methods of acquiring this God-given power, including election or appointment, heredity, expert knowledge, imputation, etc.

Let's consider some examples in the Bible:

A. Acquisition of Power by Election/Appointment

(a) Abraham: God in His infinite wisdom and foreknowledge chose and elected Abraham for the purpose of establishing a nation from which to raise the Savior of mankind.

"Now the Lord had said unto Abram, Get thee out of thy country, and from thy kindred, and from thy father's house, unto a land that I will shew thee: [2] And I will make of thee a great nation, and I will bless thee, and make thy name great; and thou shalt be a blessing: [3] And I will bless them that bless thee, and curse him that curseth thee: and in thee shall all families of the earth be blessed." (Genesis 12:1-3).

"For I know him, that he will command his children and his household after him, and they shall keep the way of the LORD, to do justice and judgment; that the LORD may bring upon Abraham that which he hath spoken of him." (Genesis 18:19).

(b) Moses: Moses was a Hebrew that was brought up as the adopted son of an Egyptian princess in the palace of Pharaoh. While in self-exile and shepherding flock God called Moses out of the burning bush to go back to Egypt to deliver the people of Israel from the bondage and slavery of the Egyptians into a land flowing with milk and honey.

"And the Lord said, I have surely seen the affliction of my people which are in Egypt, and have heard their cry by reason of their taskmasters; for I know their sorrows; [8] And I am come down to deliver them out of the hand of the Egyptians, and to bring them up out of that land unto a good land and a large, unto a land flowing with milk and honey; unto the place of the Canaanites, and the Hittites, and the Amorites, and the Perizzites, and the Hivites, and the Jebusites.

[9] Now therefore, behold, the cry of the children of Israel is come unto me: and I have also seen the oppression wherewith the Egyptians oppress them. [10] Come now therefore, and I will send

thee unto Pharaoh, that thou mayest bring forth my people the children of Israel out of Egypt" (Exodus 3:7-10).

(c) <u>Joshua</u>: After Moses led the Israelites forty years from Egypt through the desert and died, God appointed Joshua, who was the servant of Moses, to lead the people into the Promised Land and conquer the original occupants of the land to occupy it. The Bible says:

"Now after the death of Moses the servant of the Lord it came to pass, that the Lord spake unto Joshua the son of Nun, Moses' minister, saying, [2] Moses my servant is dead; now therefore arise, go over this Jordan, thou, and all this people, unto the land which I do give to them, even to the children of Israel. [3] Every place that the sole of your foot shall tread upon, that have I given unto you, as I said unto Moses." (Joshua 1:1-3).

(d) <u>Israel's Judges</u>: Subsequent to the death of Joshua and for a period of about 305 years God appointed judges to lead Israel especially to war against their enemies. Samuel was the last of the judges.

(e) <u>King Saul</u>: Late in the days of Samuel as judge of Israel, the people demanded from God a human king so as to be like other nations. Although the demand displeased God as it was a rejection of His theocratic leadership, He appointed for them a king in the person of Saul who became the first king of Israel.

"And Samuel said unto all Israel, Behold, I have hearkened unto your voice in all that ye said unto me, and have made a king over you. [2] And now, behold, the king walketh before you:" (1 Samuel 12:1-2a).

(f) <u>King David</u>: Following God's rejection of Saul as king due to disobedience, God chose David and instructed Samuel to go and anoint him king of Israel.

"And the Lord said unto Samuel, How long wilt thou mourn for Saul, seeing I have rejected him from reigning over Israel? fill thine horn with oil, and go, I will send thee to Jesse the Bethlehemite: for I have provided me a king among his sons. [13] Then Samuel took the horn of oil, and anointed him in the midst of his brethren: and the Spirit of the Lord came upon David from that day forward." (1 Samuel 16:1, 13).

(g) <u>King Cyrus:</u> Cyrus was a Persian king that allowed/sponsored the Jews in exile in Babylon to return to Jerusalem to rebuild the temple. Scriptures say God anointed him.

"Thus saith the Lord to his anointed, to Cyrus, whose right hand I have holden, to subdue nations before him; [3] And I will give thee the treasures of darkness, and hidden riches of secret places, that thou mayest know that I, the Lord, which call thee by thy name, am the God of Israel. [4] For Jacob my servant's sake, and Israel mine elect, I have even called thee by thy name: I have surnamed thee, though thou hast not known me. [5] I am the Lord, and there is none else, there is no God beside me: I girded thee, though thou hast not known me:" (Isaiah 45:1a, 3-5).

"Thus saith Cyrus king of Persia, The Lord God of heaven hath given me all the kingdoms of the earth; and he hath charged me to build him an house at Jerusalem, which is in Judah." (Ezra 1:2)

(h) The Prophets of God: No one became a prophet because his father was one. God called them all at different times to different locations, and each with a peculiar and specific message.

B. Acquisition of Power by Heredity

This is the system of one ascending to the position of power by virtue of being the son (or occasionally daughter) of the incumbent occupant of the position. Some examples are as follows:

(i) Sons of Aaron – as priests of Israel. Levites, descendants of Levi, one of the twelve sons of Jacob, were selected by the LORD to serve in and around the Tabernacle that preceded the Holy Temple in Jerusalem temple.

(ii) King Solomon: Although Solomon was God's choice of successor to the throne of Israel after King David, he was anointed king because he was a son of the king.

(iii) Rehoboam: He succeeded his father as king over Israel being the son of King Solomon. He turned out to be the last king of United Kingdom of Israel as ten northern tribes seceded under the leadership if Jeroboam. So, Rehoboam continued to be king over the remaining two tribes, which took the name Judah.

(iv) <u>The Kings of Judah</u>: From Rehoboam to Zedekiah who was killed by the Babylonians, there were nineteen kings and one queen; and of all the rulers only the queen, Athaliah was not a descendant of David.[25] In effect every king succeeded his father or acquired power by heredity.

(v) <u>European and African Monarchies.</u>

A monarch (king, queen or emperor) is someone that holds preeminent position of power, reigning over the people of a kingdom, empire or city. The kind of government in such a constituency is a monarchy.

Merriam-Webster's online Dictionary states, "monarchy is a government having hereditary chief of state with life tenure and powers varying from nominal to absolute."

In Europe there are seven kingdoms, namely Belgium, Denmark, Netherlands, Norway, Spain, Sweden and the United Kingdom of Great Britain and Northern Ireland (the UK for short). Each of these kingdoms has a king or queen as the monarch, and succession to the throne of each is hereditary.

As at date the longest reigning of all the living monarchs in Europe is Queen Elizabeth II of the UK. She has been on the

---

[25] Daniel U. Nwaelene. Jesus Christ: Savior, Judge & King of the World. (Bloomington, IN: WestBow Press, 2017), 55.

throne since February 6, 1952 (now 70 years), succeeding her father, King George VI. Her heir apparent is her eldest 74 years old first son, Prince Charles, Prince of Wales.[26]

The other monarchies in Europe include the Principality of Andora (Urgel and France), Principality of Liechtenstein, Grand Duchy of Luxembourg, Principality of Monaco, and the Vatican City State.

In Africa there are currently only three national monarchies – Morocco, having hereditary succession; Eswatini (formerly Swaziland) having hereditary/elective succession, and Lesotho also having hereditary/elective succession. There are many other monarchies in Africa, which are all sub-national constituencies of some sovereign African states. Wikipedia states, "Traditional authority is vested in the monarchs of these constituencies by virtue of customary law as a general rule, although some of them also enjoy either a constitutional or a statutory recognition of their titles in the states that play host to them. Such figures as the Nigerian traditional rulers and the Zulu King of South

---

[26] Note that before the publishing of this book, "On 8 September 2022, at 15:10 BST, Elizabeth II, Queen of the United Kingdom and the other Commonwealth realms, and the longest-reigning British monarch, died at Balmoral Castle in Aberdeenshire, Scotland, at the age of 96. Her death was publicly announced at 18:30. She was succeeded by her eldest son, Charles III. Wikipedia"
https://en.wikipedia.org/wiki/Death_and_state_funeral_of_Elizabeth_II

Africa typify the class."[27] Succession to the throne in most of the kingdoms is hereditary.

C. Power Acquisition by Imputation

There are powers or forms of authority that are imputed unto people only by the LORD. These include power to be saved and become a member of God's Family; power to witness and exercise the gifts of the Holy Spirit; and power to make wealth.

(a) Power for Salvation

Jesus Christ alone gives power for salvation, which is not available from anywhere else. Several Bible verses support this e.g.

John 1:11-13 "He came unto his own, and his own received him not. [12] But as many as received him, to them gave he power to become the sons of God, even to them that believe on his name: [13] Which were born, not of blood, nor of the will of the flesh, nor of the will of man, but of God." (Emphasis added).

———————————————

"The coronation of Charles III and his wife, Camilla, as king and queen of the United Kingdom and the other Commonwealth realms, took place on Saturday, 6 May 2023 at Westminster Abbey. Charles acceded to the throne on 8 September 2022 upon the death of his mother, Elizabeth II. The ceremony was structured around an Anglican service of Holy Communion. Wikipedia"
https://en.wikipedia.org/wiki/Coronation_of_Charles_III_and_Camilla

[27] "Monarchies in Africa"
https://en.wikipedia.org/wiki/Monarchies_in_Africa March 1, 2022

John 3:16-18 "For God so loved the world, that he gave his only begotten Son, that whosoever believeth in him should not perish, but have everlasting life. [17] For God sent not his Son into the world to condemn the world; but that the world through him might be saved. [18] He that believeth on him is not condemned: but he that believeth not is condemned already, because he hath not believed in the name of the only begotten Son of God."

Acts 4:11-12 "This is the stone, which was set at nought of you builders, which is become the head of the corner. [12] Neither is there salvation in any other: for there is none other name under heaven given among men, whereby we must be saved."

Acts 16:29-31 "Then [the jailor] called for a light, and sprang in, and came trembling, and fell down before Paul and Silas, [30] And brought them out, and said, Sirs, what must I do to be saved? [31] And they said, <u>Believe on the Lord Jesus Christ, and thou shalt be saved</u>, and thy house." (Emphasis added).

(b) Power for Witnessing

Witnessing for Him is the primary assignment that Jesus Christ left to His disciples. Witnessing involves performing the activities Jesus performed during His earthly ministry, including evangelizing, preaching, teaching, healing, deliverance, helping, etc. He said, "Verily, verily I say unto you, he that believeth in

Me, the works that I do he shall do also; and greater works than these shall he do, because I go unto My Father." (John 14:12).

In order to be able to witness effectively, one needs the spiritual power or enablement for it, which only God gives. Before He ascended into heaven Jesus gave His disciples (then and in the future) the authority to witness but to begin only after the Holy Spirit – the Enabler – had come on them. Look at the references:

Matthew 28:18-20 "And Jesus came and spake unto them, saying, All power is given unto me in heaven and in earth. [19] Go ye therefore, and teach all nations, baptizing them in the name of the Father, and of the Son, and of the Holy Ghost: [20] Teaching them to observe all things whatsoever I have commanded you: and, lo, I am with you always, even unto the end of the world. Amen."

Mark 16:15-18 "And he said unto them, Go ye into all the world, and preach the gospel to every creature. [16] He that believeth and is baptized shall be saved; but he that believeth not shall be damned. [17] And these signs shall follow them that believe; In my name shall they cast out devils; they shall speak with new tongues; [18] They shall take up serpents; and if they drink any deadly thing, it shall not hurt them; they shall lay hands on the sick, and they shall recover."

Acts 1:8 "But ye shall receive power, after that the Holy Ghost is come upon you: and ye shall be witnesses unto me both in

Jerusalem, and in all Judaea, and in Samaria, and unto the uttermost part of the earth." (Emphasis added)

(c) Power to Make Wealth

Acquiring wealth that lasts and brings blessings is given people only by God. Wealth acquired by powers contrary to God's brings sorrows. The devil gives one with one hand and takes two with the other hand. See the two references below:

Deuteronomy 8:18 "But thou shalt remember the Lord thy God: for it is he that giveth thee power to get wealth, that he may establish his covenant which he sware unto thy fathers, as it is this day." (Emphasis added).

Proverbs 10:22 "The blessing of the Lord, it maketh rich, and he addeth no sorrow with it."

D. Power by Expert Knowledge.

Another source of power is expert knowledge of a needed discipline. When this knowledge is acquired, usually by education and training (of course, God gives all knowledge), the one becomes an authority in the field and may begin to wield the power occasioned by that knowledge. An example of this is when a professional in a particular field is required to lead and his/her knowledge comes into play.

E. Power by Delegation

Delegation is another important method of acquiring genuine power. When responsibility is assigned someone by another of higher authority, some power/authority is also given the delegate to enable him to discharge the responsibility. The delegator of the responsibility and authority does not relinquish totally the power and authority, since he still remains accountable.

The one delegated the responsibility, and commensurate authority is obligated to faithfully and appropriately discharge the responsibility and render account to the delegator. However, at times a delegate abuses the power given him in various ways, including acting ultra vires (beyond the powers given him).

During the cause of His ministry and before the (final) Great Commission, Jesus delegated power to the twelve apostles and seventy disciples at different times (Matthew 10:1-15; John 20:21-23). The power (Gk. exousia) was more spiritual than physical – "power against unclean spirits, to cast them out, and to heal all manner of sickness and all manner of disease."

Every Christian, beginning with the apostles, has from Jesus Christ the delegated responsibility to witness for Him, with the authority to heal the sick, cast out devils and win the world for Him (Matthew 28:18-20; Mark 16:15-17; Acts 1:8)[28]. Jesus did

---

[28] Matthew 28:18-20 "And Jesus came and spake unto them, saying, All power is given unto me in heaven and in earth. [19] Go ye therefore, and teach all nations, baptizing them in the name of the Father, and of the Son, and of the Holy Ghost: [20] Teaching them to observe all things

this delegating and commissioning after His resurrection from the dead but before ascending physically into heaven. He asserted that all power had been given to Him 'in heaven and in earth' (Matthew 28:18), and everyone that uses this power delegated by Jesus Christ to perform the responsibility He left is accountable to Him. Anyone that abuses the power will face Jesus in judgment. The ungodly source of power is the devil, and he gives these powers through various means via various agents. Examples of such means and agents include:

-   Secret cults and Lodges.
-   Witchcraft/wizardry/sorcery/principalities and rulers of darkness.
-   Usurpation and conquering; etc.

The principal characteristic of powers given by the evil one is that such powers are used to oppress, manipulate and harm other people and at times, themselves. Holders of such powers often

---

whatsoever I have commanded you: and, lo, I am with you always, even unto the end of the world. Amen."

Mark 16:15-17 "And he said unto them, Go ye into all the world, and preach the gospel to every creature. [16] He that believeth and is baptized shall be saved; but he that believeth not shall be damned. [17] And these signs shall follow them that believe; In my name shall they cast out devils; they shall speak with new tongues;"

Acts 1:8 "But ye shall receive power, after that the Holy Ghost is come upon you: and ye shall be witnesses unto me both in Jerusalem, and in all Judaea, and in Samaria, and unto the uttermost part of the earth."

counterfeit genuine divine powers but use theirs for evil. Three instances in the Acts of the Apostles are as follows:

Acts 8:9-11 "But there was a certain man, called Simon, which beforetime in the same city used sorcery, and bewitched the people of Samaria, giving out that himself was some great one: ¹⁰ To whom they all gave heed, from the least to the greatest, saying, This man is the great power of God. ¹¹ And to him they had regard, because that of long time he had bewitched them with sorceries."

Acts 16:16-20 (NKJV): Now it happened, as we went to prayer, that a certain slave girl possessed with a spirit of divination met us, who brought her masters much profit by fortune-telling. ¹⁷ This girl followed Paul and us, and cried out, saying, "These men are the servants of the Most High God, who proclaim to us the way of salvation." ¹⁸ And this she did for many days. But Paul, greatly annoyed, turned and said to the spirit, "I command you in the name of Jesus Christ to come out of her." And he came out that very hour. ¹⁹ But when her masters saw that their hope of profit was gone, they seized Paul and Silas and dragged them into the marketplace to the authorities. ²⁰ And they brought them to the magistrates, and said, "These men, being Jews, exceedingly trouble our city;"

Acts 13:6-12 (NKJV): "Now when they had gone through the island to Paphos, they found a certain sorcerer, a false prophet, a

Jew whose name was Bar-Jesus, [7] who was with the proconsul, Sergius Paulus, an intelligent man. This man called for Barnabas and Saul and sought to hear the word of God. [8] But Elymas the sorcerer (for so his name is translated) withstood them, seeking to turn the proconsul away from the faith. [9] Then Saul, who also is called Paul, filled with the Holy Spirit, looked intently at him [10] and said, "O full of all deceit and all fraud, you son of the devil, you enemy of all righteousness, will you not cease perverting the straight ways of the Lord? [11] And now, indeed, the hand of the Lord is upon you, and you shall be blind, not seeing the sun for a time."

And immediately a dark mist fell on him, and he went around seeking someone to lead him by the hand. [12] Then the proconsul believed, when he saw what had been done, being astonished at the teaching of the Lord."

It is noteworthy that one of the commands to Israel in the days of Moses was to allow no witch (a woman that practiced witchcraft or sorcery) to remain alive (Exodus 22:18). Through the mouth of Prophet Micah God proposed to wipe out witchcraft from among His people. He said, "I will destroy your witchcraft and you will no longer cast spells" (Micah 5:12 NIV).

In some cultures, herbalists are able to invoke evil powers and bring about "blessings" on their client/victims. Of course, because the devil is the source of such "blessings" the good benefits of the "blessings" are short-lived, and the real evil (or death) encapsulated in the "blessings" become manifest. The "blessing" could be children, money, and all sorts of material possessions that people long for. In the case of "preachers" or "men of God" who obtain powers from evil sources, their congregations grow rapidly because of the fake miracles they perform, and with time such men of God get exposed and they fall forever. The Bible says that the blessing of God makes one rich and adds no sorrow with it (Proverbs 10:22). The converse is also true: the blessing of the devil enriches but adds sorrows with it.

F. Power by Usurpation

People also do usurp power from the true holders thereof. They plot and execute coups-d'états to overthrow the incumbent. This could take any of several shapes. Coups to overthrow a government could be with arms (bloody) or without (bloodless); gossip and slander; intimidation with money power, taking advantage of a vulnerable leader (Esau and Jacob in Genesis for example).

Overrunning or conquering is another way of usurpation. It was rampant in ancient times when empires conquered other empires, and the conquering emperor dethroned or even killed the conquered one. Examples abound in the Holy Bible and in History, including Assyrian empire, Babylonian empire, Persian

Empire, Greek empire, Roman empire, etc. There were also many other empires[29] not mentioned in the Bible such as -

- Ottoman Empire (16th to 17th centuries).
- Spanish Empire (16th Century).
- Byzantine Empire or Eastern Roman Empire (the Roman Empire during the Middle Ages).
- British Empire (from late 15th Century to late 20th Century (precisely 1997));[30]
- The Holy Roman Empire (Middle Ages to early 19th Century).
- The Russian Empire (1721 to 1917).

4.3 Good Uses or Application of Power

The Holy Bible has records of people that exercised power to benefit humanity in one way or the other. Examples include the following:

Joshua, Son of Nun

Sequel to the death of Moses the servant of God, God chose and appointed Joshua and empowered him to lead the Israelites to

---

[29] "Top 10 Greatest Empires in History."
https://listverse.com/2010/06/22/top-10-greatest-empires-in-history/
03/31/22.
[30] "British Empire." https://en.wikipedia.org/wiki/British_Empire
03/31/2022.

conquer and occupy the Promised Land of Canaan according to Numbers 27:18-20 (NKJV):

"And the Lord said to Moses: "Take Joshua the son of Nun with you, a man in whom is the Spirit, and lay your hand on him; [19] set him before Eleazar the priest and before all the congregation, and inaugurate him in their sight. [20] And you shall give some of your authority to him, that all the congregation of the children of Israel may be obedient.""

It should be noted here, how Moses, who had led the people for forty years was to transfer power to his successor according to God's instruction. Other references for this are Deuteronomy 31:1-8, 14-15, 23.

Effectively, God was with Joshua as he led the people of Israel through the River Jordan into the Promised Land, engaged the original occupants of the land in wars and defeated them. According to God's instructions Joshua allocated the land to the tribes of Israel. He did not use the authority available to him to acquire parts of the land for himself. Although the book of Joshua is basically not about him, but about God, Joshua was very obedient to God and was a great instrument in the hand of God for taking the people of Israel into the Promised Land.

King David

God endowed David with power. He got Samuel the priest/prophet to anoint David king over Israel while a youth and the youngest of all the seven sons of Jesse (1Samuel 16:6-13)[31]. The Bible says, "Blessed is the man that trusteth in the Lord, and whose hope the Lord is." (Jeremiah 17:7).

There are indications that King David trusted in the Lord from his youth. And as he said in Psalm 125:1 a man that trusts in the Lord is like Mount Zion that cannot be moved. As a young man, David killed Goliath – a warrior-giant. In those days wars were fought with spears, javelins and such devices, in a face-to-face combat. While Goliath was armed with his spear, had on his protective wears, David was only armed with a sling and a few pieces of stone with the name of the Lord. David had had good intentions for that battle – to project the name of the Lord – to remove the

---

[31] 1 Samuel 16:6-13 NKJV So it was, when they came, that he looked at Eliab and said, "Surely the Lord's anointed *is* before Him!" [7] But the Lord said to Samuel, "Do not look at his appearance or at his physical stature, because I have refused him. For *the Lord does* not *see* as man sees; for man looks at the outward appearance, but the Lord looks at the heart." [8] So Jesse called Abinadab, and made him pass before Samuel. And he said, "Neither has the Lord chosen this one." [9] Then Jesse made Shammah pass by. And he said, "Neither has the Lord chosen this one." [10] Thus Jesse made seven of his sons pass before Samuel. And Samuel said to Jesse, "The Lord has not chosen these." [11] And Samuel said to Jesse, "Are all the young men here?" Then he said, "There remains yet the youngest, and there he is, keeping the sheep."
And Samuel said to Jesse, "Send and bring him. For we will not sit down till he comes here." [12] So he sent and brought him in. Now he *was* ruddy, with bright eyes, and good-looking. And the Lord said, "Arise, anoint him; for this *is* the one!" [13] Then Samuel took the horn of oil and anointed him in the midst of his brothers; and the Spirit of the Lord came upon David from that day forward. So Samuel arose and went to Ramah.

disgrace from the people of Israel by killing the "uncircumcised Philistine" that had defied the armies of the Lord. (1 Samuel 17:26 – "And David spake to the men that stood by him, saying, What shall be done to the man that killeth this Philistine, and taketh away the reproach from Israel? for who is this uncircumcised Philistine, that he should defy the armies of the living God?)

That David trusted in the Lord is fully evident in the story of how he went about the destruction of Goliath, thus:

"David said moreover, The Lord that delivered me out of the paw of the lion, and out of the paw of the bear, he will deliver me out of the hand of this Philistine. And Saul said unto David, Go, and the Lord be with thee.

"And Saul armed David with his armour, and he put an helmet of brass upon his head; also he armed him with a coat of mail. [39] And David girded his sword upon his armour, and he assayed to go; for he had not proved it. And David said unto Saul, I cannot go with these; for I have not proved them. And David put them off him. [40] And he took his staff in his hand, and chose him five smooth stones out of the brook, and put them in a shepherd's bag which he had, even in a scrip; and his sling was in his hand: and he drew near to the Philistine.

[41] And the Philistine came on and drew near unto David; and the man that bare the shield went before him. [42] And when the Philistine looked about, and saw David, he disdained him: for he

was but a youth, and ruddy, and of a fair countenance. [43] And the Philistine said unto David, Am I a dog that thou comest to me with staves? And the Philistine cursed David by his gods. [44] And the Philistine said to David, Come to me, and I will give thy flesh unto the fowls of the air, and to the beasts of the field.

[45] Then said David to the Philistine, Thou comest to me with a sword, and with a spear, and with a shield: but I come to thee in the name of the Lord of hosts, the God of the armies of Israel, whom thou hast defied. [46] This day will the Lord deliver thee into mine hand; and I will smite thee, and take thine head from thee; and I will give the carcases of the host of the Philistines this day unto the fowls of the air, and to the wild beasts of the earth; that all the earth may know that there is a God in Israel. [47] And all this assembly shall know that the Lord saveth not with sword and spear: for the battle is the Lord's, and he will give you into our hands.

[48] And it came to pass, when the Philistine arose, and came, and drew nigh to meet David, that David hastened, and ran toward the army to meet the Philistine. [49] And David put his hand in his bag, and took thence a stone, and slang it, and smote the Philistine in his forehead, that the stone sunk into his forehead; and he fell upon his face to the earth. [50] So David prevailed over the Philistine with a sling and with a stone, and smote the Philistine, and slew him; but there was no sword in the hand of David. [51] Therefore

David ran, and stood upon the Philistine, and took his sword, and drew it out of the sheath thereof, and slew him, and cut off his head therewith. And when the Philistines saw their champion was dead, they fled." (1 Samuel 17:37-51).

Samuel anointed David king on the instructions of God, to take the place of King Saul. This is found in 1 Samuel 16:10-13: "Again, Jesse made seven of his sons to pass before Samuel. And Samuel said unto Jesse, The Lord hath not chosen these. [11] And Samuel said unto Jesse, Are here all thy children? And he said, There remaineth yet the youngest, and, behold, he keepeth the sheep. And Samuel said unto Jesse, Send and fetch him: for we will not sit down till he come hither. [12] And he sent, and brought him in. Now he was ruddy, and withal of a beautiful countenance, and goodly to look to. And the Lord said, Arise, anoint him: for this is he. [13] Then Samuel took the horn of oil, and anointed him in the midst of his brethren: and the Spirit of the Lord came upon David from that day forward. So Samuel rose up, and went to Ramah."

When King Saul went after David to kill him out of jealousy, David had opportunities to kill Saul; but David restrained himself from killing 'the Lord's anointed one.' "And he said unto his men, The Lord forbid that I should do this thing unto my master, the Lord's anointed, to stretch forth mine hand against him, seeing he is the anointed of the Lord." (1 Samuel 24:6).

David conquered Jerusalem, a city of the Jebusites. He then made Jerusalem Israel's capital, making it the "darling city" of all nations and religions. Jerusalem will equally be the world's capital when Jesus Christ returns to establish the Millennial Reign.

David wrote over seventy psalms, and established a strong dynasty, which the Lord said shall be forever. (2 Samuel 7:16 "And thine house and thy kingdom shall be established for ever before thee: thy throne shall be established for ever.")

Queen Esther

Esther was one of the Hebrews taken into captivity in the Medo-Persian kingdom of King Ahasuerus. Esther was a pretty, young orphan lady, brought up by her cousin, who became her adoptive father. She was selected to be queen in place of Queen Vashti that was banished from ever appearing before the king. As first lady of the Medo-Persian kingdom, Esther became a "powerful" lady of some sort.

At a point in History, Haman the son of Hammedatha the Agagite, the number one prince (official) of the kingdom plotted to exterminate all the Jews in the kingdom, encompassing one hundred twenty-seven (127) provinces, extending from India to Ethiopia. Haman's reason for the plot was that one Jewish man, Modeccai refused to bow to reverence him.

Esther 3:2, 12-15 (KJV): "And all the king's servants, that were in the king's gate, bowed, and reverenced Haman: for the king had so commanded concerning him. But Mordecai bowed not, nor did him reverence."

"[12] Then were the king's scribes called on the thirteenth day of the first month, and there was written according to all that Haman had commanded unto the king's lieutenants, and to the governors that were over every province, and to the rulers of every people of every province according to the writing thereof, and to every people after their language; in the name of king Ahasuerus was it written, and sealed with the king's ring.

[13] And the letters were sent by posts into all the king's provinces, to destroy, to kill, and to cause to perish, all Jews, both young and old, little children and women, in one day, even upon the thirteenth day of the twelfth month, which is the month Adar, and to take the spoil of them for a prey.

[14] The copy of the writing for a commandment to be given in every province was published unto all people, that they should be ready against that day. [15] The posts went out, being hastened by the king's commandment, and the decree was given in Shushan the palace. And the king and Haman sat down to drink; but the city Shushan was perplexed." Instructions to all provinces were sent under the authority of the king, which made it mandatory and irreversible - according to the laws of the Medes and Persians. If

the plot had sailed through, it would have been similar to what Adolph Hitler did in 1945 in Germany, where over six million Jews were killed in gas chambers. But Esther used her authority/influence to reverse the irreversible! She took a serious risk of her life for the sake of her people: Nobody in the kingdom, no matter who, went into the presence of the king or inner court uninvited by the king. Offenders of the rule had only one punishment – death.

But Esther proposed to fast and pray with her maidens, and requested for all Jews in Shushan to pray for her. She proposed to go to the king on behalf of her people, the Jews. Esther 4:16 (KJV) "Go, gather together all the Jews that are present in Shushan, and fast ye for me, and neither eat nor drink three days, night or day: I also and my maidens will fast likewise; and so will I go in unto the king, which is not according to the law: and if I perish, I perish."

Note Esther's resolve as stated in Esther 8:6 (KJV): "For how can I endure to see the evil that shall come unto my people? or how can I endure to see the destruction of my kindred?"

It worked out well for Esther and the Jews: the plotter of the evil of extermination, Haman was hanged on the very gallows he built in his house on which to hang Modeccai. And the king gave Haman's house to Esther.

Record of the outcome of Esther's use of power at her disposal for good is found below:

Esther 8:11, 15-17 (KJV): "[11] Wherein the king granted the Jews which were in every city to gather themselves together, and to stand for their life, to destroy, to slay and to cause to perish, all the power of the people and province that would assault them, both little ones and women, and to take the spoil of them for a prey,"

"[15] And Mordecai went out from the presence of the king in royal apparel of blue and white, and with a great crown of gold, and with a garment of fine linen and purple: and the city of Shushan rejoiced and was glad. [16] The Jews had light, and gladness, and joy, and honour. [17] And in every province, and in every city, whithersoever the king's commandment and his decree came, the Jews had joy and gladness, a feast and a good day. And many of the people of the land became Jews; for the fear of the Jews fell upon them."

Till date the Jews still annually observe as "Purim" the victory God gave them via the submission of Queen Esther, notwithstanding that the event occurred around the 4th Century B.C.

Pharaoh of Egypt – "There arose up a new king over Egypt, which knew not Joseph," who enslaved and oppressed the people of Israel in Egypt. In spite of Pharaoh's treachery, wickedness and hardness of heart towards the people of Israel, it would fascinate to know that God raised him for the purpose of bringing glory to Him. Unknown to people everything King Pharaoh did or did not do in the process of the deliverance of the Israelites was in line with heaven's plans. "So then it is not of him who wills, nor of him who runs, but of God who shows mercy. [17] For the Scripture says to the Pharaoh, "For this very purpose I have raised you up, that I may show My power in you, and that My name may be declared in all the earth." (Romans 9:16-17 NKJV). Another reference for this is Exodus 9:14-17.

King Cyrus II of Persia (c. 600 – 530 BC) – also known as Cyrus the Great. He was a pagan king, popular among the Jews because it was during his reign that the Babylonian captivity of the Jews ended. He was the king of Persia, the empire that conquered Babylon. Babylon had held Judah in captivity from the days of King Nebuchadnezzar. Around 700 BC Prophet Isaiah prophesied of the anointed one that would act for God with regard to rebuilding the temple at Jerusalem. "Who says of Cyrus, 'He is My shepherd, And he shall perform all My pleasure, Saying to Jerusalem, "You shall be built," And to the temple, "Your foundation shall be laid." (Isaiah 44:28 NKJV).

The prophecy of Isaiah is also recorded in chapter 45:1-7, 13 as follows:

"Thus says the Lord to His anointed, To Cyrus, whose right hand I have held—

To subdue nations before him And loose the armor of kings,

To open before him the double doors, So that the gates will not be shut:

2 'I will go before you And make the crooked places straight;

I will break in pieces the gates of bronze And cut the bars of iron.

3 I will give you the treasures of darkness And hidden riches of secret places,

That you may know that I, the Lord, Who call you by your name, Am the God of Israel.

4 For Jacob My servant's sake, And Israel My elect, I have even called you by your name;

I have named you, though you have not known Me.

5 I am the Lord, and there is no other; There is no God besides Me.

I will gird you, though you have not known Me,

6 That they may know from the rising of the sun to its setting That there is none besides Me. I am the Lord, and there is no other;

7 I form the light and create darkness, I make peace and create calamity;

I, the Lord, do all these things.'

¹³ I have raised him up in righteousness, And I will direct all his ways;

He shall build My city And let My exiles go free, Not for price nor reward,"

Says the Lord of hosts." (Isaiah 45:1-7, 13 NKJV).

King Cyrus was believed to have gotten the information from the words of Prophet Jeremiah that God had chosen him as a deliverer for His people, the Jews, from the prophecy of Isaiah, which he read. He believed that since there was such a prophecy given many centuries before his birth, and the prophecy mentioned him by name, it was credible. And he opted to do as the Lord assigned. Ezra stated that God stirred up the spirit of Cyrus and he obeyed. Ezra 1:1-3 NKJV "Now in the first year of Cyrus king of Persia, that the word of the Lord by the mouth of Jeremiah might be fulfilled, the Lord stirred up the spirit of Cyrus king of Persia, so that he made a proclamation throughout all his kingdom, and also put it in writing, saying, ² Thus says Cyrus king of Persia:

All the kingdoms of the earth the Lord God of heaven has given me. And He has commanded me to build Him a house at Jerusalem which is in Judah. ³ Who is among you of all His people? May his God be with him, and let him go up to Jerusalem which is in Judah, and build the house of the Lord God of Israel (He is God), which is in Jerusalem.

So, with the authority that Cyrus had as king of the empire he took the following actions that changed for the better the cause of history of the Jews: -

(1) He ordered that the Temple at Jerusalem be rebuilt by the Jews (Ezra 1:2 quoted above);

(2) He decreed that financial and material support from the king's account be given anybody that was willing to go and do the work in Jerusalem (Ezra 1:4);

(3) Cyrus brought out, and caused to be returned to Jerusalem the articles/vessels of gold, silver and others, which Nebuchadnezzar had taken away from the temple and placed in the shrines of his gods in Babylon (Ezra 1:7-11). The gold and silver were carried in five thousand four hundred (5,400) basins.

(4) Cyrus released the Jews from captivity and the numbers of them that returned to Judah were Forty-two thousand three hundred and sixty (42, 360) in addition to Seven thousand three hundred and thirty-seven (7,337) maids and servants.

(5) He decreed that anyone who might attempt to reverse the decrees should be executed (Ezra 6:11). This was a confirmation of Cyrus' action by his successor, Darius.

Cyrus cooperated with God as God used him, a heathen nation's king, to deliver the people of Judah from captivity, and to rebuild the walls of Jerusalem and the temple at Jerusalem. This was to fulfill God's pronouncement through the prophet Jeremiah – to release the people after seventy years of captivity.

Alexander the Great (356 BC to 323 BC) led the Greeks to overthrow and conquer the Medo-Persian Empire.   Alexander was said to have employed a strategy of terror and kindness to carry out his conquests.

One of Alexander's main achievements was laying the foundation for the Hellenization of the world of the Greek Empire – making the whole empire imbibe the Greek culture including making Greek the official language of the empire. This singular action was advantageous to the spread of the gospel of Christ. Most of the then known world spoke Greek without losing their languages, hence the New Testament Scriptures were originally written in Greek.

Caesar Augustus was the first emperor of the Roman Empire (after Julius Caesar). Augustus was born September 23, 63 BC[32] and he died August 19, 44 AD.[33] He was a pagan emperor that believed in the many Roman gods. He himself was deified after his death.

There were indications or occasions of kindness in him, but he was seen as one of the cruel Caesars of Rome. For instance,

---

[32] Gaius Suetonius Tranquillus. Robert Graves (TR). THE TWELVE CAESARS (London: Penguin Books, 1957), 56.
[33] ibid, 110.

Tranquillus stated that he fought five civil wars, and "the underlying motive of every campaign was that [he] felt it as his duty, above all, to avenge Caesar and keep his decrees . . . he decided to surprise Brutus and Cassius by rapid and forceful actions; but they . . . escaped, so he had recourse to the law and prosecuted them for murder in their absence."[34]

About 700 years BC Prophet Micah announced that the Messiah, Jesus Christ would be born in Bethlehem of Judea. He said, "But thou, Bethlehem Ephratah, though thou be little among the thousands of Judah, yet out of thee shall he come forth unto me that is to be ruler in Israel; whose goings forth have been from of old, from everlasting." (Micah 5:2).

Around the time of the birth of Jesus, God used the Roman Emperor, Caesar Augustus to enact a decree that required the whole world to return to their places of origin to get registered for tax (Luke 2:1). That was why Joseph, to whom Mary the mother of Jesus was espoused, took her (already heavily pregnant) and had to return to Bethlehem, where Mary was delivered of the Baby, Jesus according to the prophecy of Micah. This is further confirmed by the event of the visit of the Magi from the East to the Child, Jesus, at which time they gave Him presents and worshipped Him as "King of the Jews." As the Magi were seeking direction from King Herod, Herod asked the Scribes and priests

---

[34] ibid, 58.

where the Messiah was to be born. And they confirmed that Bethlehem of Judaea was the prophesied place (Matthew 2:3-6 NKJV: "When Herod the king heard this, he was troubled, and all Jerusalem with him. [4] And when he had gathered all the chief priests and scribes of the people together, he inquired of them where the Christ was to be born.

[5] So they said to him, "In Bethlehem of Judea, for thus it is written by the prophet:

[6] 'But you, Bethlehem, in the land of Judah, Are not the least among the rulers of Judah; For out of you shall come a Ruler Who will shepherd My people Israel.'").

Pontius Pilate was procurator[35] (governor) of Judea during the days of the physical presence of Jesus Christ on earth. Pilate was the first procurator to bring the effigy of the Roman emperor Caesar to Jerusalem against the will and laws of the people. The people pleaded with him to remove them but he refused in order not to offend Caesar.[36]

In spite of the unfriendliness of Pilate with the Jews, God used him to bring to pass His plan of salvation – even though he "found no fault in [Jesus]" Pilate heeded the voice/will of the people to grant them authority to crucify Jesus on the cross for sins He did

---

[35] Procurator was an agent of the empire of Rome in countries that practiced Roman civil law.
[36] Flavius Josephus. William Whiston (TR). THE COMPLETE WORKS. (Nashville: Thomas Nelson, 1998), 575 – 576.

not commit, and release Barabbas, a criminal in prison. The references are as follows:

Luke 23:13-25 NKJV: Then Pilate, when he had called together the chief priests, the rulers, and the people, [14] said to them, "You have brought this Man to me, as one who misleads the people. And indeed, having examined Him in your presence, I have found no fault in this Man concerning those things of which you accuse Him; [15] no, neither did Herod, for I sent you back to him; and indeed nothing deserving of death has been done by Him. [16] I will therefore chastise Him and release Him" [17] (for it was necessary for him to release one to them at the feast).

[18] And they all cried out at once, saying, "Away with this Man, and release to us Barabbas"— [19] who had been thrown into prison for a certain rebellion made in the city, and for murder. [20] Pilate, therefore, wishing to release Jesus, again called out to them. [21] But they shouted, saying, "Crucify Him, crucify Him!" [22] Then he said to them the third time, "Why, what evil has He done? I have found no reason for death in Him. I will therefore chastise Him and let Him go."

[23] But they were insistent, demanding with loud voices that He be crucified. And the voices of these men and of the chief priests prevailed. [24] So Pilate gave sentence that it should be as they requested. [25] And he released to them the one they requested, who

for rebellion and murder had been thrown into prison; but he delivered Jesus to their will.

Matthew 27:16-26 NKJV: "And at that time they had a notorious prisoner called Barabbas. [17] Therefore, when they had gathered together, Pilate said to them, "Whom do you want me to release to you? Barabbas, or Jesus who is called Christ?" [18] For he knew that they had handed Him over because of envy. [19] While he was sitting on the judgment seat, his wife sent to him, saying, "Have nothing to do with that just Man, for I have suffered many things today in a dream because of Him.""

[20] But the chief priests and elders persuaded the multitudes that they should ask for Barabbas and destroy Jesus. [21] The governor answered and said to them, "Which of the two do you want me to release to you?" They said, "Barabbas!"

[22] Pilate said to them, "What then shall I do with Jesus who is called Christ?"

They all said to him, "Let Him be crucified!"

[23] Then the governor said, "Why, what evil has He done?"

But they cried out all the more, saying, "Let Him be crucified!"

[24] When Pilate saw that he could not prevail at all, but rather that a tumult was rising, he took water and washed his hands before the multitude, saying, "I am innocent of the blood of this just Person. You see to it."

²⁵ And all the people answered and said, "His blood be on us and on our children."

²⁶ Then he released Barabbas to them; and when he had scourged Jesus, he delivered Him to be crucified.

Mark 15:1-15 NKJV: "Immediately, in the morning, the chief priests held a consultation with the elders and scribes and the whole council; and they bound Jesus, led Him away, and delivered Him to Pilate. ² Then Pilate asked Him, "Are You the King of the Jews?"

He answered and said to him, "It is as you say."

³ And the chief priests accused Him of many things, but He answered nothing. ⁴ Then Pilate asked Him again, saying, "Do You answer nothing? See how many things they testify against You!" ⁵ But Jesus still answered nothing, so that Pilate marveled. ⁶ Now at the feast he was accustomed to releasing one prisoner to them, whomever they requested. ⁷ And there was one named Barabbas, who was chained with his fellow rebels; they had committed murder in the rebellion. ⁸ Then the multitude, crying aloud, began to ask him to do just as he had always done for them. ⁹ But Pilate answered them, saying, "Do you want me to release to you the King of the Jews?" ¹⁰ For he knew that the chief priests had handed Him over because of envy.

¹¹ But the chief priests stirred up the crowd, so that he should rather release Barabbas to them. ¹² Pilate answered and said to

them again, "What then do you want me to do with Him whom you call the King of the Jews?" [13] So they cried out again, "Crucify Him!"

[14] Then Pilate said to them, "Why, what evil has He done?" But they cried out all the more, "Crucify Him!" [15] So Pilate, wanting to gratify the crowd, released Barabbas to them; and he delivered Jesus, after he had scourged Him, to be crucified.

John 18:29-19:1 NKJV: Pilate then went out to them and said, "What accusation do you bring against this Man?" [30] They answered and said to him, "If He were not an evildoer, we would not have delivered Him up to you." [31] Then Pilate said to them, "You take Him and judge Him according to your law."

Therefore, the Jews said to him, "It is not lawful for us to put anyone to death," [32] that the saying of Jesus might be fulfilled which He spoke, signifying by what death He would die.

[33] Then Pilate entered the Praetorium again, called Jesus, and said to Him, "Are You the King of the Jews?"

[34] Jesus answered him, "Are you speaking for yourself about this, or did others tell you this concerning Me?" [35] Pilate answered, "Am I a Jew? Your own nation and the chief priests have delivered You to me. What have You done?" [36] Jesus answered, "My kingdom is not of this world. If My kingdom were of this world, My servants would fight, so that I should not be delivered to the Jews; but now My kingdom is not from here."

³⁷ Pilate therefore said to Him, "Are You a king then?" Jesus answered, "You say rightly that I am a king. For this cause I was born, and for this cause I have come into the world, that I should bear witness to the truth. Everyone who is of the truth hears My voice." ³⁸ Pilate said to Him, "What is truth?" And when he had said this, he went out again to the Jews, and said to them, "I find no fault in Him at all. ³⁹ "But you have a custom that I should release someone to you at the Passover. Do you therefore want me to release to you the King of the Jews?" ⁴⁰ Then they all cried again, saying, "Not this Man, but Barabbas!" Now Barabbas was a robber. 19 So then Pilate took Jesus and scourged Him.

One of the extra-Biblical writings that lays credence to the Bible record concerning Governor Pontius Pilate's action and/or inaction that culminated in the death of Jesus Christ is by Flavius Josephus. He wrote:

"Now there was about this time Jesus, a wise man, if it be lawful to call him a man, for he was a doer of wonderful works - a teacher of such men as receive the truth with pleasure. He drew over to him both many of the Jews, and many of the Gentiles. He was [the] Christ, and when Pilate, at the suggestion of the principal men amongst us, had condemned him to the cross, those that loved him at the first did not forsake him, for he appeared to them alive again the third day, on as the divine prophets had foretold these and ten thousand other wonderful things concerning him; and the tribe of Christians, so named from him, are not extinct at this day."[37]

Prophets Isaiah and Daniel, as well as the psalmists, especially King David, all prophesied that the Messiah would be executed (see the following prophecies:

Isaiah 52:13-14 (NET) "Look, my servant will succeed! He will be elevated, lifted high, and greatly exalted— [14] (just as many were horrified by the sight of you) he was so disfigured he no longer looked like a man; his form was so marred he no longer looked human;"

Isaiah 53:1-10 (NET) "Who would have believed what we just heard? When was the Lord's power revealed through him? [2] He sprouted up like a twig before God, like a root out of parched soil; he had no stately form or majesty that might catch our attention, no special appearance that we should want to follow him.

[3] He was despised and rejected by people, one who experienced pain and was acquainted with illness; people hid their faces from him; he was despised, and we considered him insignificant. [4] But he lifted up our illnesses, he carried our pain; even though we thought he was being punished, attacked by God, and afflicted for something he had done. [5] He was wounded because of our rebellious deeds, crushed because of our sins; he endured

---

[37] Flavius Josephus, 576

punishment that made us well; because of his wounds we have been healed. [6] All of us had wandered off like sheep; each of us had strayed off on his own path, but the Lord caused the sin of all of us to attack him. [7] He was treated harshly and afflicted, but he did not even open his mouth. Like a lamb led to the slaughtering block, like a sheep silent before her shearers, he did not even open his mouth. [8] He was led away after an unjust trial— but who even cared? Indeed, he was cut off from the land of the living; because of the rebellion of his own people he was wounded. [9] They intended to bury him with criminals, but he ended up in a rich man's tomb, because he had committed no violent deeds, nor had he spoken deceitfully. [10] Though the Lord desired to crush him and make him ill, once restitution is made, he will see descendants and enjoy long life, and the Lord's purpose will be accomplished through him.

Daniel 9:24-26a (NET) "Seventy weeks have been determined concerning your people and your holy city to put an end to rebellion, to bring sin to completion, to atone for iniquity, to bring in perpetual righteousness, to seal up the prophetic vision, and to anoint a Most Holy Place. [25] So know and understand: From the issuing of the command to restore and rebuild Jerusalem until an anointed one, a prince arrives, there will be a period of seven weeks and sixty-two weeks. It will again be built, with plaza and moat, but in distressful times. [26] Now after the sixty-two weeks, an anointed one will be cut off and have nothing."

If Pontius Pilate, the governor that tried Jesus had boldly insisted on releasing Jesus on the grounds of finding no fault in Him, he could have succeeded; but that would have derailed or stalled the salvation plan of God.

Former President Donald J. Trump was elected the 45th president of the United States in November 2016 on the ticket of the Republican Party. He was inaugurated in Washington DC on January 20, 2017, succeeding the 44th, first African-American president, President Barak H. Obama of the Democratic Party. The final contest that brought Trump to power was with a former Secretary of State, Mrs. Hilary R. Clinton (Democrat), wife of former President William (Bill) J. Clinton. While Hilary won the popular vote by a margin of about three million votes, Trump was declared winner by virtue of the Electoral College results. People asked whether Trump could have been God-sent to prevent the Democrats from continuing to perpetuate some practices that they supported but are offensive to Christianity and some Republicans: In 1973 the United States Supreme Court ruled in the case between Roe vs. Wade, 410 US113 (1973) that a pregnant woman was at liberty under the U.S. Constitution to have an abortion "without excessive government restriction." In other words, abortion of unborn babies was legalized by that decision in 1973.

For several years the Church in general has been kicking against the practice of fetal abortion as it was seen as murder of babies (life destruction or termination).

On June 26, 2015 during the administration of President Obama the Supreme Court of the U.S.A. legalized same-sex marriage in the fifty states. To the Church too, this is evil in view of the numerous scripture passages that condemn or forbid homosexuality such as the following:

Genesis 19:1-25 NKJV: Now the two angels came to Sodom in the evening, and Lot was sitting in the gate of Sodom. When Lot saw them, he rose to meet them, and he bowed himself with his face toward the ground. [2] And he said, "Here now, my lords, please turn in to your servant's house and spend the night, and wash your feet; then you may rise early and go on your way." And they said, "No, but we will spend the night in the open square."

[3] But he insisted strongly; so they turned in to him and entered his house. Then he made them a feast, and baked unleavened bread, and they ate.

[4] Now before they lay down, the men of the city, the men of Sodom, both old and young, all the people from every quarter, surrounded the house. [5] And they called to Lot and said to him, "Where are the men who came to you tonight? Bring them out to us that we may know them carnally."

⁶ So Lot went out to them through the doorway, shut the door behind him, ⁷ and said, "Please, my brethren, do not do so wickedly! ⁸ See now, I have two daughters who have not known a man; please, let me bring them out to you, and you may do to them as you wish; only do nothing to these men, since this is the reason they have come under the shadow of my roof."

⁹ And they said, "Stand back!" Then they said, "This one came in to stay here, and he keeps acting as a judge; now we will deal worse with you than with them." So they pressed hard against the man Lot, and came near to break down the door. ¹⁰ But the men reached out their hands and pulled Lot into the house with them, and shut the door. ¹¹ And they struck the men who were at the doorway of the house with blindness, both small and great, so that they became weary trying to find the door.

Sodom and Gomorrah Destroyed

¹² Then the men said to Lot, "Have you anyone else here? Son-in-law, your sons, your daughters, and whomever you have in the city—take them out of this place! ¹³ For we will destroy this place, because the outcry against them has grown great before the face of the Lord, and the Lord has sent us to destroy it."

¹⁴ So Lot went out and spoke to his sons-in-law, who had married his daughters, and said, "Get up, get out of this place; for the Lord will destroy this city!" But to his sons-in-law he seemed to be joking.

[15] When the morning dawned, the angels urged Lot to hurry, saying, "Arise, take your wife and your two daughters who are here, lest you be consumed in the punishment of the city." [16] And while he lingered, the men took hold of his hand, his wife's hand, and the hands of his two daughters, the Lord being merciful to him, and they brought him out and set him outside the city. [17] So it came to pass, when they had brought them outside, that he said, "Escape for your life! Do not look behind you nor stay anywhere in the plain. Escape to the mountains, lest you be destroyed."

[18] Then Lot said to them, "Please, no, my lords! [19] Indeed now, your servant has found favor in your sight, and you have increased your mercy which you have shown me by saving my life; but I cannot escape to the mountains, lest some evil overtake me and I die. [20] See now, this city is near enough to flee to, and it is a little one; please let me escape there (is it not a little one?) and my soul shall live."

[21] And he said to him, "See, I have favored you concerning this thing also, in that I will not overthrow this city for which you have spoken. [22] Hurry, escape there. For I cannot do anything until you arrive there." Therefore the name of the city was called Zoar.

[23] The sun had risen upon the earth when Lot entered Zoar. [24] Then the Lord rained brimstone and fire on Sodom and Gomorrah, from the Lord out of the heavens. [25] So He overthrew those cities,

all the plain, all the inhabitants of the cities, and what grew on the ground.

Leviticus 18:22 (NKJV): "You shall not lie with a male as with a woman. It is an abomination."

Leviticus 20:13 (NKJV): "If a man lies with a male as he lies with a woman, both of them have committed an abomination. They shall surely be put to death. Their blood shall be upon them."

Jude 6-7 (NKJV): "And the angels who did not keep their proper domain, but left their own abode, He has reserved in everlasting chains under darkness for the judgment of the great day; [7] as Sodom and Gomorrah, and the cities around them in a similar manner to these, having given themselves over to sexual immorality and gone after strange flesh, are set forth as an example, suffering the vengeance of eternal fire."

Romans 1:26-32 (NKJV): "For this reason God gave them up to vile passions. For even their women exchanged the natural use for what is against nature. [27] Likewise also the men, leaving the natural use of the woman, burned in their lust for one another, men with men committing what is shameful, and receiving in themselves the penalty of their error which was due.

[28] And even as they did not like to retain God in their know-ledge, God gave them over to a debased mind, to do those

things which are not fitting; [29] being filled with all un-

righteousness, sexual immorality,

wickedness, covetousness, maliciousness; full of envy, murder,

strife, deceit, evil mindedness; they are whisperers, [30] backbiters,

haters of God, violent, proud, boasters, inventors of evil things,

disobedient to parents, [31] undiscerning, untrustworthy, unloving,

unforgiving, unmerciful; [32] who, knowing the righteous judgment

of God, that those who practice such things are deserving of death,

not only do the same but also approve of those who practice

them."

1 Corinthians 6:9-10 (NKJV): "Do you not know that the

unrighteous will not inherit the kingdom of God? Do not be

deceived. Neither fornicators, nor idolaters, nor adulterers, nor

homosexuals, nor sodomites, [10] nor thieves, nor covetous, nor

drunkards, nor revilers, nor extortioners will inherit the kingdom

of God."

1 Timothy 1:8-11 (NKJV): "But we know that the law

is good if one uses it lawfully, [9] knowing this: that the law is

not made for a righteous person, but for the lawless and

insubordinate, for the ungodly and for sinners, for the

unholy and profane, for murderers of fathers and murderers of

mothers, for manslayers, [10] for fornicators, for sodomites, for

kidnappers, for liars, for perjurers, and if there is any other thing that is contrary to sound doctrine, [11] according to the glorious gospel of the blessed God which was committed to my trust."

Trump administration blocked flow of funds for Planned Parenthood Federation and other bodies over abortion referrals in 2019. "Facing a Trump administration rule that forbids referrals for abortion, the organization decided to reject federal funds for family planning for low-income women."[38]

The most intriguing action of former President Trump in his Foreign Policy was the official recognition of Jerusalem on December 6, 2017 as the official capital of Israel in place of Tel Aviv. Many other past presidents of the USA had thought of it but didn't implement it. "Presidents from both parties over the years have declared their support for making Jerusalem the capital of Israel, but have never taken the step to move the U.S. Embassy from Tel Aviv out of a belief that the future of Jerusalem should be decided through negotiations between Israelis and Palestinians."[39]

---

[38] "Planned Parenthood Refuses Federal Funds Over Abortion Restrictions" https://www.nytimes.com/2019/08/19/health/planned-parenthood-title-x.html?searchResultPosition=1 New York Times August 19, 2019

[39] "2012 ELECTION NEWS." https://www.reuters.com/article/us-usa-campaign-israel/democrats-backpedal-and-change-language-on-jerusalem-idUSBRE8841JC20120906 SEPTEMBER 5, 2012

From the days of King David, the second king of Israel, Jerusalem was the capital of Israel until Roman Emperor Titus invaded and destroyed the city with the Temple in the year A.D.70, an event that Jesus Christ predicted and wept for before His crucifixion, death and resurrection as per Luke 19:41-44 (ESV)

"And when he drew near and saw the city, he wept over it, [42] saying, "Would that you, even you, had known on this day the things that make for peace! But now they are hidden from your eyes. [43] For the days will come upon you, when your enemies will set up a barricade around you and surround you and hem you in on every side [44] and tear you down to the ground, you and your children within you. And they will not leave one stone upon another in you, because you did not know the time of your visitation."

Writing about the destruction of Jerusalem, Josephus described Jerusalem as "a city otherwise of great magnificence, and mighty fame among all mankind." [40]

But God had made pronouncements concerning the future of Jerusalem through His prophets as follows:

1Kings 11:13 (NKJV): "However I will not tear away the whole kingdom; I will give one tribe to your son for the sake of My servant David, and for the sake of Jerusalem which I have chosen."

---

[40] Flavius Josephus, 900.

2Kings 19:31 "For out of Jerusalem shall go forth a remnant, and they that escape out of mount Zion: the zeal of the Lord of hosts shall do this."

2Kings 21:4 (NKJV): "He also built altars in the house of the Lord, of which the Lord had said, "In Jerusalem I will put My name."

2 Chronicles 6:6 (NKJV): "Yet I have chosen Jerusalem, that My name may be there, and I have chosen David to be over My people Israel.'

2 Chronicles 33:4 (NKJV): "He also built altars in the house of the Lord, of which the Lord had said, "In Jerusalem shall My name be forever."

Psalm 147:2 (NKJV): "The Lord builds up Jerusalem; He gathers together the outcasts of Israel."

Isaiah 27:13 (NKJV): "So it shall be in that day: The great trumpet will be blown; They will come, who are about to perish in the land of Assyria, And they who are outcasts in the land of Egypt, And shall worship the Lord in the holy mount at Jerusalem."

Isaiah 30:19 (NKJV): "For the people shall dwell in Zion at Jerusalem; You shall weep no more. He will be very gracious to you at the sound of your cry; When He hears it, He will answer you."

Isaiah 33:20 (NKJV): "Look upon Zion, the city of our appointed feasts; Your eyes will see Jerusalem, a quiet home, A tabernacle that will not be taken down; Not one of its stakes will ever be removed, Nor will any of its cords be broken."

Isaiah 37:32 (NKJV): "For out of Jerusalem shall go a remnant, And those who escape from Mount Zion. The zeal of the Lord of hosts will do this."

Isaiah 40:9 (NKJV): "O Zion, You who bring good tidings, Get up into the high mountain; O Jerusalem, You who bring good tidings, Lift up your voice with strength, Lift it up, be not afraid; Say to the cities of Judah, "Behold your God!""

Isaiah 41:27 (NKJV): "The first time I said to Zion, 'Look, there they are!' And I will give to Jerusalem one who brings good tidings."

Isaiah 44:26 (NKJV): "Who confirms the word of His servant, And performs the counsel of His messengers; Who says to Jerusalem, 'You shall be inhabited,' To the cities of Judah, 'You shall be built,' And I will raise up her waste places;"

Isaiah 44:28 (NKJV): "Who says of Cyrus, 'He is My shepherd, And he shall perform all My pleasure, Saying to Jerusalem, "You shall be built," And to the temple, "Your foundation shall be laid."

'

Isaiah 52:9 (NKJV): "Break forth into joy, sing together, You waste places of Jerusalem! For the Lord has comforted His people, He has redeemed Jerusalem."

Isaiah 65:18-19 (NKJV): "But be glad and rejoice forever in what I create; For behold, I create Jerusalem as a rejoicing, And her people a joy. [19] I will rejoice in Jerusalem, And joy in My people; The voice of weeping shall no longer be heard in her, Nor the voice of crying."

Isaiah 66:10, 13, 20 (NKJV): "Rejoice with Jerusalem, And be glad with her, all you who love her; Rejoice for joy with her, all you who mourn for her;

[13] As one whom his mother comforts, So I will comfort you; And you shall be comforted in Jerusalem."

"[20] Then they shall bring all your brethren for an offering to the Lord out of all nations, on horses and in chariots and in litters, on mules and on camels, to My holy mountain Jerusalem," says the Lord, "as the children of Israel bring an offering in a clean vessel into the house of the Lord."

Jeremiah 3:17 (NKJV): "At that time Jerusalem shall be called The Throne of the Lord, and all the nations shall be gathered to it, to the name of the Lord, to Jerusalem. No more shall they follow the dictates of their evil hearts."

Daniel 9:25 (NKJV): "Know therefore and understand, That from the going forth of the command To restore and
 build Jerusalem Until Messiah the Prince, There shall be
seven weeks and sixty-two weeks; The street shall be built again, and the wall, Even in troublesome times."

Joel 2:32 (NKJV): "And it shall come to pass That whoever calls on the name of the Lord Shall be saved. For in Mount Zion and in Jerusalem there shall be deliverance, As the Lord has said, Among the remnant whom the Lord calls.

Zechariah 2:4 (NKJV): "who said to him, "Run, speak to this yo ung man, saying:

'Jerusalem shall be inhabited as towns without walls, because of the multitude of men and livestock in it."

Zechariah 8:3, 22 (NKJV): "Thus says the Lord: 'I will return to Zion, And dwell in the midst of Jerusalem. Jerusalem s hall be called the City of Truth, The Mountain of the Lord of hosts, The Holy Mountain.'

[22] Yes, many peoples and strong nations Shall come to seek the Lord of hosts in Jerusalem, And to pray before the Lord.'

Zechariah 12:2, 6 (NKJV): "Behold, I will make Jerusalem a cup of drunkenness to all the surrounding peoples, when they lay siege against Judah and Jerusalem.

[6] In that day I will make the governors of Judah like a firepan in the woodpile, and like a fiery torch in the sheaves; they shall devour all the surrounding peoples on the right hand and on the left, but Jerusalem shall be inhabited again in her own place— Jerusalem.

Zechariah 14:2, 11, 17 (NKJV): "For I will gather all the nations to battle against Jerusalem; The city shall be taken, The houses rifled, And the women ravished. Half of the city shall go into captivity, But the remnant of the people shall not be cut off from the city. [11] The people shall dwell in it; And no longer shall there be utter destruction, But Jerusalem shall be safely inhabited. [17] And it shall be that whichever of the families of the earth do not come up to Jerusalem to worship the King, the Lord of hosts, on them there will be no rain."

Malachi 3:4 (NKJV): "Then the offering of Judah and Jerusalem Will be pleasant to the Lord, As in the days of old, As in former years."

Galatians 4:26 (NKJV): "but the Jerusalem above is free, which is the mother of us all."

Hebrews 12:22 (NKJV): "But you have come to Mount Zion and to the city of the living God, the heavenly Jerusalem, to an innumerable company of angels,"

Revelation 3:12 (NKJV): "He who overcomes, I will make him a pillar in the temple of My God, and he shall go out no more. I will write on him the name of My God and the name of the city of My God, the New Jerusalem, which comes down out of heaven from My God. And I will write on him My new name."

Revelation 21:2, 10 (NKJV): "Then I, John, saw the holy city, New Jerusalem, coming down out of heaven from God, prepared as a bride adorned for her husband.

[10] And he carried me away in the Spirit to a great and high mountain, and showed me the great city, the holy Jerusalem, descending out of heaven from God,"

In view of the above prophecies about Jerusalem, could it be that God has used former President Trump to get fulfilled an aspect of the prophecies of His plans regarding the city? It may be safe, in view of Romans 13: 1-6 quoted above, to conclude that God sent Trump to America for a special purpose. Although the special commission that investigated Russia's involvement in the 2016 USA election, together with the various intelligence agencies, ruled that Russian government performed acts to help Trump to win that election, yet if God's hand had not been in it they would not have succeeded. Why? "Unless the Lord builds the house, They labor in vain who build it; Unless the Lord guards the city, The watchman stays awake in vain. (Psalm 127:1 (NKJV)).

JOSEPH OF ARIMATHAEA (Matthew 27:57-60; Mark 15:43-46; Luke 23:50-53; John 19:38-40).
This man was a Jew. He was so recognized that his name and what he did in relation to Jesus Christ appeared in all four gospels. He was a member of the ruling body – the Sanhedrin - in Israel, though was unable to wield enough influence to stop the Jewish leaders crucifying the Lord.

Matthew calls Joseph a rich man of Arimathaea (Matthew 27:57) and Jesus' disciple; Mark calls him an honorable counsellor (Mark 15: 43).

Joseph went to Pontius Pilate, the governor and begged for the body of Jesus, which he took down and wrapped in a clean linen cloth. He laid the body in his own new tomb in a rock in "wherein never man before was laid." (Luke 23:53); and he rolled a big stone on to the entrance of the tomb.

There were other rich people like Matthew and Zacchaeus amongst the disciples of Jesus and other people that had benefited from the ministry of Jesus. But it was Joseph of Arimathaea that went to Pilate to obtain the body of Christ for burial in a personal, brand-new tomb in which nobody had ever been buried. In other words, Joseph donated to Jesus his (Joseph's) personal, unused tomb. He also undertook the burial with the help of Nicodemus, a Pharisee that had visited Jesus privately by night to ask His questions.

REV. DR. S.W. MARTIN (1870 – 1976)

Rev. Dr. Samuel [N]Wadiei Martin was born and named Olisemeke Nwadiei at Issele-Uku, Nigeria about 1870. He disappeared from home in his teen years and was assumed to have died mysteriously after searches for him proved abortive. He later got to the USA in company of a missionary couple that he served somewhere in Nigeria. As the couple, Rev. & Mrs. A. E. Martin had no biological child they adopted Olisemeke and he adopted their last name, Martin.

The young Rev. Martin while in the USA received vocational education, served in the United States Army and received Theological education in Moody Bible Institute, Chicago.

In 1922 he returned to Issele-Uku, Nigeria, a town some 300 miles east of Lagos. Lagos was the only or most developed area of Nigeria that time. But when Rev. Martin arrived there from America he did not choose to remain in Lagos. Rather he chose to continue his journey to Issele-Uku, to live with his people, suffer for, and with them that needed the light. He established the Pilgrim Baptist Mission of Nigeria, INC.

Before he died in 1976, Rev. Dr. S. W. Martin had, with the aid of some American Christian Missions, established the following at Issele-Uku and other towns and villages around:

- Over fifty elementary (Primary) schools.
- One secondary modern school;[41]
- Two secondary grammar schools (high schools).
- One teacher training college;[42]
- Two vocational (post-primary) schools and
- One hospital.

---

[41] Secondary Modern School was a three-year post-primary institution that prepared people for subsequent two-part four years teacher training program. It was abolished in the late 1970s as the Nigerian educational system was evolving.

[42] Teacher training colleges were later phased out for colleges of education.

- A church was established in each of the villages where he planted primary schools.

Although Rev. Dr. Martin and his wife had no biological children, yet a lot of Nigerians (and even Cameroonians) became educated and/or Christians by his influence and philanthropy. He suffered a lot of hardships but made many lives better by his cooperation with God. Personally, I am a beneficiary of Dr. Martin's philanthropy as my father was a Pilgrim Baptist Mission teacher; my elementary and secondary education were in schools established by the mission, and to crown it all, I learnt of the love of God in Jesus Christ and became a Christian in Pilgrim Baptist Church.

4.4 Abuse of Power

In History and Contemporary Times

Abuse (synonym of 'misuse,' 'wrong application,' 'misemployment,''mishandling,' 'improper use,' 'mistreatment') of power is as old as power. Just as power has been beneficially used all over the world and throughout the ages, so power has been abused to the detriment of people, families and even nations. Oftentimes when some people acquire or receive power, they forget their past so much that they allow the power to get into their heads. Such people use this power to intimidate and oppress others; some destroy others outright, while some others use the power to corruptly enrich themselves to the detriment of the people.

Ten Ways To Identify Abuse Of Power

(1) Intimidation – while asserting power, the 'power-person' frightens or threatens subordinate or subjects to make them do his bidding.

(2) Distancing – He begins to distance himself from immediate associates.

(3) Frustration and removal of persons whom he perceives do not like him or his leadership style.

(4) He starts rejecting advice and suggestions.

(5) Distortion of information

(6) He harasses and bullies colleagues and subordinates.

(7) Causing or forcing people to break the law with disregard.

(8) He becomes secretive, ensuring that many things he does are kept from people, especially his critics.

(9) He begins to place self above the law, while making his power absolute.

(10)   He becomes double-faced – one person to a group and another person to other groups.

In my secondary (high) school days, students were taught and required to respect and obey their seniors. A senior was any student that was one or more years or classes ahead of you. Thus, as shown in the table below, a class-5 student was senior to all others in classes one to four. And a class-4 student was senior to all years one to three students, etc. Only the year-one students (freshmen) had no class persons to show seniority until the following school year when they are promoted to class 2.

CLASS	SENIORITY TO STUDENTS
Year 5	Year 4; Year 3; Year 2; and Year 1
Year 4	Year 3; Year 2; and Year 1
Year 3	Year 2 and Year 1
Year 2	Year 1
Year 1	None

Table 1: Students and levels of Authority

Although this arrangement was meant to infuse discipline and respect, some students abused the authority that the arrangement ascribed, to the extent that some very junior seniors such as Year 2 students, seized every opportunity to inflict punishment on their juniors for every act they deemed an offense. If a student felt unjustly punished, and reported to another senior, or to a member of the student-body administration (prefects), the reporting student was asked to obey before complaining.

The arrangement went on until the school authorities discovered the abuse inherent in the system and abolished it after I had graduated from the school.

I remember in my first year, a year 2 'senior' told one of my classmates who "trespassed" into the year 2 classroom, "Kneel down there, you fag! How can you be so bold to enter this class, you fresher? Because I am your senior today, I will punish you for this trespass, even though you may become my mate in future. "That was abuse of power par excellence! Unfortunately, that year-2 senior failed at the end of that year, and we became his classmates the following year. How pride goes before a fall!

Some Ways of Abuse of Power:

a) A medical doctor or related professional taking advantage of his female patient by turning her into a mistress or wife because she is at his mercy.

b) When a pastor turns a counseling session into a romance theatre is an abuse. A pastor was said to have chosen to test for virginity a girl that was getting ready for her wedding, by groping her.

c) A coach (soccer, football, athletics, etc.) that takes sexual advantage of his or her "coachees" or trainees is abusing power.

d) It is abuse for a class teacher to take advantage of his/her student either sexually or financially. Stories abound of professors and lecturers in some named universities, who insisted that their male students pay some minimum amounts of money to pass their courses – the higher the amount paid, the better the grade awardable. Such professors also offered ladies the option of releasing their bodies sexually; in this case the more frequent the lady yielded the better the grade awardable to her, irrespective of the quality of her paper or presentation.

e) An employer that insists on taking a lady (potential employee) to lunch and bed before offering her a job whether or not she is qualified for the job is abusive of his power, and is corrupt. Such employers are often found to do the same to their reports or subordinates in order to earn promotions at work, even when they merit such promotions by their work standards.

f) A governor accepted bribes to pardon prisoners including murderers.

g) An attorney general for a consumer protection agency shut down a restaurant due to a complaint by his daughter that she was not given a seat she wanted in the restaurant.

h) If the head of a nation's food and drug administration takes bribes from companies to register and approve their products that do not meet safety standards, it is abuse of power, and corruption.

i) When a police officer fires a gun at a fleeing, defenseless, unarmed man that has not committed an offence that's punishable by death, the officer abuses power.

j) A government official who diverts funds meant for some community project to personal use or to some preferred unauthorized project abuses power.

k) A female senator overseas recently alleged openly that the senate president in their country refused to allow her present to the floor her constituency's needs because she had resisted his sex advances. That is power abuse at the highest level.

Romans 13:1-6 "Let every soul be subject unto the higher powers. For there is no power but of God: the powers that be are ordained of God. [2] Whosoever therefore resisteth the power, resisteth the ordinance of God: and they that resist shall receive to themselves damnation. [3] For rulers are not a terror to good works, but to the evil. Wilt thou then not be afraid of the power? do that which is good, and thou shalt have praise of the same: [4] For he is the minister of God to thee for good. But if thou do that which is evil, be afraid; for he beareth not the sword in vain: for he is the minister of God, a revenger to execute wrath upon him that doeth evil. [5] Wherefore ye must needs be subject, not only for wrath, but also for conscience sake. [6] For for this cause pay ye tribute also: for they are God's ministers, attending continually upon this very thing."

The treacherous activities of tyrants sometimes make one doubt the veracity of this claim. {But All Scripture is inspired by God

(2Timothy 3:16-17) and must be believed} When a king or emperor goes to war, conquers another king/emperor, and annexes his kingdom or empire by force, there are elements of oppression from the conqueror. Also if a leader – king, president, emperor, or whatever title they bear – inflicts a lot of hardships on the subjects, one begins to wonder whether the loving God, who does not desire that anyone should perish could have appointed or anointed, or allowed to be enthroned such a leader over His people. Consider some instances below.

Below is a catalog of some persons that abused power in Bible times (Old and New Testament times), and in recent and contemporary times.

KING DAVID

David was the second, after King Saul, and the greatest king of Israel. His people or subjects loved him. God loved him too. God described him as the man after God's own heart (1 Samuel 13:14 NKJV "But now your kingdom shall not continue. The Lord has sought for Himself a man after His own heart, and the Lord has commanded him to be commander over His people, because you have not kept what the Lord commanded you."

Acts 13:22 NKJV "And when He had removed him, He raised up for them David as king, to whom also He gave testimony and said, 'I have found David the son of Jesse, a man after My own heart, who will do all My will.')

It is clear from 1Samuel 13:14 (quoted above) that the major reason God removed David's predecessor, Saul from kingship was disobedience, perhaps accompanied by pride. It can, therefore, be inferred that David was 'naturally' obedient and had a humble heart. Before embarking on most of his serious actions he enquired of the Lord. Three instances of such enquiries are as follows:

1 Samuel 30:8 NKJV "So David inquired of the Lord, saying, "Shall I pursue this troop? Shall I overtake them?" And He answered him, "Pursue, for you shall surely overtake them and without fail recover all."

1 Samuel 23:2-4 NKJV "Therefore David inquired of the Lord, saying, "Shall I go and attack these Philistines?" And the Lord said to David, "Go and attack the Philistines, and save Keilah." [3] But David's men said to him, "Look, we are afraid here in Judah. How much more then if we go to Keilah against the armies of the Philistines?" [4] Then David inquired of the Lord once again. And the Lord answered him and said, "Arise, go down to Keilah. For I will deliver the Philistines into your hand."

1 Samuel 23:10-12 NKJV "Then David said, "O Lord God of Israel, Your servant has certainly heard that Saul seeks to come to Keilah to destroy the city for my sake. [11] Will the men of Keilah deliver me into his hand? Will Saul come down, as Your servant has heard? O Lord God of Israel, I pray, tell Your servant." And

the Lord said, "He will come down." [12] Then David said, "Will the men of Keilah deliver me and my men into the hand of Saul?" And the Lord said, "They will deliver you."

David fought wars for Israel even from his youth. In spite of this his formidable record, however, he had his failures too as human. He abused power at a point in time. Though one cannot claim that he fell as a result of that abuse of power, yet the curse that followed it devastated his family. David's misuse of power is detailed in 2 Samuel 11:1-12:14.

In summary, David as king sent out his army commander, Joab and his servants to war with the Ammonites. He did not take the lead. While at home one evening as he walked on the roof of the king's house, he saw a very beautiful woman, Bathsheba bathing in her place. David sent messengers to bring her to him. Then he went to bed with the woman notwithstanding that he knew she was the wife of Uriah the Hittite, and the woman could not object the king's advances perhaps in order not to be a disobedient subject.

One sin begets another: It was bad enough that David used his authority as king to seduce the woman and put her in family way, he sought a way to cover his tracks of sin. He called back Uriah from the battlefront, got him drunk and suggested to him to go home and pass the night. But Uriah refused to go home and rather chose to pass the night with the king's servants.

David then exercised his authority again: he sent Uriah back to the battle with a letter to Joab, asking Joab to position him where he would be killed. Joab obeyed and Uriah was killed. Joab sent to inform the king that his order had been successfully executed. After Bathsheba mourned her husband, David took her in as wife. 2 Samuel 11:27b says, "But the thing that David had done displeased the Lord." 2 Samuel 12:7-12 is record of God's judgment through the prophet Nathan on David's abuse of power. David acknowledged his sin and repented, and God forgave him[43], for which reason the judgment of God did not adversely affect God's covenant with David. Notwithstanding, he suffered all the punishment that God pronounced apart from an early death. In effect, incest, murder, adultery/fornication, rebellion were occurrences in King David's household.

In summary, King David misused his power as king to seduce Bathsheba, put her in family way, killed her husband in an attempt to cover his sins of adultery, murder and covetousness, contrary to the following three of the Ten Commandments: -

Exodus 20:13, 14, 17 NKJV:

[13] "You shall not murder.

[14] "You shall not commit adultery.

---

[43] This gives credence to 1John 1:9 that " If we confess our sins, He is faithful and just to forgive us *our* sins and to cleanse us from all unrighteousness."

[17] "You shall not covet your neighbor's house; you shall not covet your neighbor's wife, nor his male servant, nor his female servant, nor his ox, nor his donkey, nor anything that is your neighbor's."

KING SOLOMON

Solomon was the third king of the United Kingdom of Israel, succeeding his father, David.

He was a son of David whose mother was Bathsheba. Solomon is often described as the wisest man that lived. However, some things he did in life could be seen as foolishness and abuse of power.

Very early in his life and reign, God appeared to him in a dream, asking him to ask for anything. Wisely, Solomon asked God to give him wisdom, which he needed for ruling God's people. God was pleased that he did not request for riches, long life, life of his enemies, or luxury, contrary to what other natural minds would have requested. So, God gave him wisdom and added wealth to it. Solomon, therefore, became the wisest man and the wealthiest king. Long life (longevity) for him was going to depend on if he walked in God's ways as David his father did (1Kings 3:10-14).

Solomon built a formidable palace for the king (himself), a beautiful temple for the Lord and moved in the Ark of God there. However, he also built a shrine for every idol (god or goddess) that each of his seven hundred wives brought to the kingdom, contrary to the commandment of God: You shall have no other gods before me (Exodus 20:3; Deuteronomy 5:7). Read how Solomon abused power by being disobedient to God due to his love for women:

"King Solomon, however, loved many foreign women besides Pharaoh's daughter—Moabites, Ammonites, Edomites, Sidonians and Hittites. [2] They were from nations about which the Lord had told the Israelites, "You must not intermarry with them, because they will surely turn your hearts after their gods." Nevertheless, Solomon held fast to them in love. [3] He had seven hundred wives of royal birth and three hundred concubines, and his wives led him astray. [4] As Solomon grew old, his wives turned his heart after other gods, and his heart was not fully devoted to the Lord his God, as the heart of David his father had been. [5] He followed Ashtoreth the goddess of the Sidonians, and Molek the detestable god of the Ammonites. [6] So Solomon did evil in the eyes of the Lord; he did not follow the Lord completely, as David his father had done." (1 Kings 11:1-6 NIV)

KING AHAB AND JEZEBEL

Ahab was a King in Israel and had a wife named Jezebel. He reigned over Israel for a period of twenty-two years and did evil in the sight of the Lord more than all the kings before him (1 Kings 16:29-30).

One of Ahab's sins that popularized his abuse of power was his oppression and murder of Naboth of Jezreel and one of his subjects (1 Kings 21:1-16). Ahab requested Naboth to release to him his vineyard for a garden, because it was behind his palace. Ahab offered to pay Naboth something for the vineyard if he would not accept an alternative location.

As Naboth turned down the king's request and offer because the vineyard was an inheritance the king felt displeased. When he explained the cause of his sadness to his wife, Jezebel, she consoled him with the following words of 1 Kings 21:7:

"And Jezebel his wife said unto him, Dost thou now govern the kingdom of Israel? arise, and eat bread, and let thine heart be merry: I will give thee the vineyard of Naboth the Jezreelite."

Jezebel wrote instructions on the king's letterhead to the leaders of Jezreel - Naboth's city - falsely accusing him of blaspheming God and the king. She raised two false witnesses to accuse Naboth. So Naboth was executed by stoning. When it was reported to Jezebel that the deed had been done she told her husband that Naboth was dead and he could go ahead to possess the vineyard which Naboth refused to give him for money. And Ahab did. The act displeased God as indicated by the punishment He pronounced quickly afterwards through the mouth of prophet Elijah thus:

And Ahab said to Elijah, Hast thou found me, O mine enemy? And he answered, I have found thee: because thou hast sold thyself to work evil in the sight of the Lord.

²¹ Behold, I will bring evil upon thee, and will take away thy posterity, and will cut off from Ahab him that pisseth against the wall, and him that is shut up and left in Israel,

²² And will make thine house like the house of Jeroboam the son of Nebat, and like the house of Baasha the son of Ahijah, for the provocation wherewith thou hast provoked me to anger, and made Israel to sin. ²³ And of Jezebel also spake the Lord, saying, The dogs shall eat Jezebel by the wall of Jezreel. (1 Kings 21:20-23).

THE ROMAN CAESARS.

Roman Empire was the empire that succeeded the Greek, which was championed by Alexander the Great. Roman Empire was ruled by emperors the first twelve of who were titled Caesars. Not much is said in the Bible about the Caesars except the little mention of Caesar Augustus in relation to the birth of Jesus Christ; and that the apostle Paul appealed to Caesar when he was about to be lynched by the Jews.

There were twelve Caesars beginning with Julius, who was a Roman dictator, but not an emperor. Although Julius Caesar was not an emperor, he was the leader of Rome until he was assassinated on the ides (15th) of March, 44 B.C. The first twelve emperors of Rome had "Caesar" as part of their titles, beginning from Octavian Augustus Caesar, born Sept 23, 31 B.C. He was the emperor at the time of the birth of Jesus Christ, and he died on August 19, 14 A.D.

Most of the Caesars were said to be ruthless. Ruthlessness is by no means a mark or good use of power. It actually portrays the characteristic of having no pity or compassion for others. Let's take a brief look at some of the most ruthless and the bloodiest Caesars of the ancient Rome. These include Tiberius, Gaius, Claudius, Nero and Domitian.

TIBERIUS CAESAR (B.C. 42 - A.D. 37)

Tiberius was born November 16, 42 BC in Rome. He became the second emperor after the death of Caesar Augustus, his stepfather. He ascended the imperial throne on September 18, 14 A.D. He was reluctant to be emperor for fear of danger that threatened him from several quarters, including a former slave's to avenge his former master's death, a noble man's secret plan for a revolt, and mutinies breaking out in Germany and Illyricum.[44]

But after he assumed office, he gradually began to show that he was the one in authority over the Roman Empire. He introduced/re-introduced some changes in the Roman culture such as promiscuous kissing and exchange of 'good-luck gifts' at New Year, abolishing foreign goods and cults from Rome, safe-guarding the nation against banditry and brigandage.

---

[44] Tranquillus, Gaius Suetonius. Tr. Robert Graves: The Twelve Caesars. (London: Penguin Books, 1957), 127.

But as Emperor Tiberius grew older he changed. He let state affairs slide. Suetonius said that "Some aspects of his criminal obscenity are almost too vile to discuss, much less believe"[45] He notoriously forced a wealthy man, Gnaeus Lentulus Augur to name him as his sole heir and then commit suicide. Tiberius Caesar was said to have starved to death two of his grandsons, who he had appointed to the Senate – Drusus and Nero. Nero was believed to have been forced to commit suicide when an executioner announced that he had the Senate's warrant, and displayed the noose with which to hang him.

Suetonius wrote that Tiberius had requested the Senate to select for him a council of twenty men, who along with some old friends would advise him on public affairs. Apart from two or three of the men that died a natural death, Tiberius killed all one way or another. Also, a professor of Literature, Seleucus was dismissed from his company and later forced to commit suicide for trying to find out from imperial servants the kinds of books the emperor read.[46]

The emperor was reported to have done many other wicked acts under the guise of reforming public morals, but in reality such acts were to gratify his lust for seeing people suffer. As his cruelty worsened, no day (no matter how holy the day was) passed

---

[45] ibid, 136.
[46] ibid, 141.

without an execution. Many of the men victims were punished with their children. Any word from and informant was believed and every offence, no matter how minor, was seen and treated as a crime punishable by death.

The time came finally when Tiberius began to be disgusted with himself. Eventually he collapsed and died sequel to suspected poisoning, and when the news of his death first broke, the news caused so much joy all over Rome that "people ran about yelling: 'To the Tiber with Tiberius!' and others offered prayers to Mother earth and other Infernal Gods to give him no home below except amongst the damned." Unfortunately, the people's hatred of Tiberius grew worse after his death due to the execution of persons that were earlier sentenced to death, but on whose cases the Senate had decreed a stay of execution of ten days, but the stay expired after the death of Tiberius and there was no one to appeal to, since Gaius had not been crowned. [47]

So Tiberius Caesar reigned over Roman Empire for twenty-three years five months and three days and died on March 16, 37 A.D. "Tiberius had brought a vast number of miseries on the best families of the Romans, since he was easily inflamed with passion in all cases, and was of such a temper as rendered his anger irrevocable, till he had executed the same, although he had taken a hatred against men without reason: for he was by nature fierce

---

[47] ibid, 151.

in all the sentences he gave and made death the penalty for the slightest offenses; . . . "[48]

CALIGULA GAIUS CAESAR (12 A.D. TO 41 A.D.).

Caligula was born August 31, 12 A.D. He was the adopted son of Tiberius Caesar, Caligula's paternal uncle. The Roman Senate unanimously conferred absolute power on Gaius, setting aside the will of Tiberius for Gaius to be joint-heir with Tiberius' other grandson that was still a child then.

Gaius made efforts to strengthen his popularity by every means possible. For instance, he recalled all exiles and dismissed all criminal charges that were pending before his enthronement. He also completed some projects, which the predecessor began but couldn't finish. "He established a shrine to himself as god, with priests, the costliest possible victims, and a life-sized golden image, which was dressed everyday in clothes identical with those that he happened to be wearing. All the richest citizens tried to gain priesthood here, either by influence or bribery." He habitually committed incest with his three sisters.

Some of the reasons Gaius was seen as brutal and blood-thirsty include the following: Nearness and services of some friends and relatives earned them cruel deaths.

---

[48] Josephus, Flavius. Tr. William Whiston, A.M. THE COMPLETE WORKS. (Nashville, TN: Thomas Nelson, 1998), 589.

He found it too expensive to feed animals he collected for one of his shows with butcher's meat, rather he fed them with criminals. Gaius ordered many men of decent families to be sawn in two, thrown to wild animals or some other inhuman punishments for offences as minor as criticizing his shows or failing to swear by his name. He made parents watch their sons executed and preferred that numerous injuries be inflicted on persons being executed – for them to die slowly.

When officially broke, Gaius raised money by false accusations, taxes and auctions. Suetonius wrote that Gaius committed many fearful crimes and contemplated even worse ones, such as killing the most prominent senators and knights, Two books were discovered amongst his papers – "The Dagger," and "The Sword, - each of them containing a list with addresses of persons he wanted to kill.

Eventually his reckless behavior provoked thoughts and plots for Gaius's assassination. He was stabbed to death at the age of 29 on January 24, 41 A.D., after a brief reign of three years and ten months.[49]

CLAUDIUS TIBERIUS CAESAR (10 B.C. – 54 A.D.)

Claudius Caesar was born August 1, 10 BC at Lugdunum. He had children by three wives. He did not initiate many public works but completed uncompleted, important projects of his predecessor.

---

[49] Suetonius, 153 - 183

Claudius was cruel and bloodthirsty, which appeared in great and small matters. He liked to watch proceedings of executions and gladiatorial shows, either staged by himself or others. He was the Roman Emperor that ejected all Jews from Rome recorded in the Bible - Acts 18:1-2: "After these things Paul departed from Athens and went to Corinth. 2 And he found a certain Jew named Acquilla, born in Pontus, who had recently come from Italy with his wife, Priscilla (because Claudius had commanded all the Jews to depart from Rome); and he came to them." (NKJV).

Claudius died, likely, by poisoning on October 13, 54 A.D., though it was not certain who did the poisoning. His death was not announced until all necessary arrangements for the succession had been made. He died at the age of 64 after being emperor for thirteen years.

NERO CLAUDIUS CAESAR (37 A.D. – 68 A.D.).

Emperor Nero was born to Domitius on December 15, 37 A.D. at Antium. He was said to have grown up in poor circumstances under the care of Domitia Lepida, his aunt, until his inheritance from his late father's will was restored to him when Claudius became emperor.[50]

Just like most, if not all, of the earlier emperors, Nero began his reign being nice, humane and generous. For instance, he promised to fashion his rule after the principles that Augustus Caesar laid

---

[50] ibid, 216

down. He seized every opportunity to show mercy or be generous. He lowered some heavy taxes and abolished some. He was reluctant to sign execution orders of felons.

But as time went on, Nero's true character began to manifest. In fact, Suetonius said, "Gradually, Nero's vices gained the upper hand, he no longer tried to laugh them off, or hide, or deny them, but openly broke into more serious crime."[51] He seduced free-born boys and married women, and raped the Vestal Virgin Rubria. Nero arranged for his mother, Agippina, with whom he was believed to have been committing incest, to be murdered for being too watchful and too critical of the things he said and did (his pronouncements and actions), which he felt he could no longer stand.

Nero ordered doctors to give his aunt, Domitia Lepida a laxative of fatal strength and killed her and seized her property. He criminally abused every family relationship. He had Antonia, daughter of Claudius executed on a purported charge of rebellion because she refused to take the place of Poppaea.

Nero was said to be as cruel to strangers as he was to members of his family. When he uncovered plot to kill him by Piso and Beneventum and condemned them, he banished all their children from Rome and starved or had them starved or poisoned to death. He gave no more than one hour grace to people he ordered to

---

[51] ibid, 227.

commit suicide, and anyone found still alive was required to be 'taken care' of by doctors.

Claiming to have become disgusted by what he called the drab old buildings and narrow and winding Roman streets, he sent his attendants to set the city of Rome ablaze. The fires lasted six days and seven nights. Properties raised included apartment blocks, mansions belonging to famous Roman generals, temples and even his own mansion.[52]

These and many more brought Nero down to the extent that all deserted him – his bodyguard, friends and the caretakers, who went with Nero's bed linen and box of poison. He equally could not find "Spiculus the gladiator or any other trained executioner to put an end to him." He indeed asked, "Have I then neither friends nor enemies left?"[53] Before he finally took his life he got to a point in his fear that he was heard muttering how ugly and vulgar his life had become. He stabbed himself in the throat and died at the age of thirty-one on June 9, 68 A.D., having been emperor for about twelve and one half (12½) years.

It would be interesting to note that when Nero died there was widespread rejoicing of the citizens of Rome, who ran through the streets wearing hats of freedom – just a confirmation of Scriptures that "When the righteous are in authority, the people rejoice: but

---

[52] ibid, 234 – 236.
[53] ibid, 242.

when the wicked beareth the rule, the people mourn" (Proverbs 29:2). It is equally noteworthy that Christianity suffered great persecution in the Roman Empire during the reign of Emperor Nero. Josephus describes Nero as the cruelest tyrant (page 1137) as he commented on Nero's publicly putting his mother to death, killed his wife Octavia, and many other illustrious people all under false accusation of plotting against him.[54]

EMPEROR DOMITIAN TITUS CAESAR (51 A.D. – 96 A.D.)

Domitian Titus, the last of the twelve Caesars was born in Rome on October 24, 51 A.D. He grew up in poverty and was said to have pretended to be extremely modest before he became emperor. Suetonius wrote that for a period of time Domitian governed in such a way that his vices were balanced by his virtues. Domitian made a couple of social changes including banning the castration of men; he paid great attention to the dispensation of justice. During his youthful years he disliked shedding of blood – not even of oxen for sacrifice. One great practice of his was that he checked informers and severely punished any that brought him false accusation for financial benefits. He said, according to Suetonius that "An Emperor who does not punish informers encourages them."

Soon afterwards Domitian's true treacherous character began to manifest. He executed many senators, some of who he accused of

---

[54] Josephus, 642.

conspiracy. He killed one Salvius Coccianus for continuing to celebrate the birthday of his uncle – Emperor Otho. Many minor and ordinary acts of people became offensive to Domitian. He was very cruel and cunning; confiscated properties; got his agents to collect taxes on Jews with some peculiar mercilessness. There's the saying that those whom the gods want to destroy they first make mad. Domitian became proud. Of his arrogance Suetonius wrote:

"Just as arrogantly he began a letter, which his agents were to circulate, with the words: 'Our Lord and God instructs you to do this!' and the Lord and God became his regular title both in writing and conversation."

In view of all these and more, Domitian's friends and favorite freedmen conspired to remove him. On September 14, 96 A.D. Domitian was stabbed to death in his bedroom. He had reigned over Rome fifteen years and he died at the age of forty-four years eleven months (one month short of forty-five years). His body was treated like a pauper's.[55]

Note that it is not only kings, queens, emperors and presidents that abuse power. Anyone who uses the power of his office to make life difficult for anyone else that is vulnerable is abusing power and with time such abuse will lead to a fall. Such people include

---

[55] Suetonius, 312. The life and times of Emperor Domitian Titus Caesar as per Suetonius is found on pages 300 to 314.

some professionals that have private/confidential relationships with people, police officers – especially of the "red states" of the USA and other law enforcement agents, some medical doctors (to their patients), teachers to students and pastor to his disciple.

There were many other tyrannical leaders all over the world found in history. Some of them, to mention but a few, include:

- Idi Amin Dada of Uganda.
- Adolf Hitler of Nazi Germany.
- Queen Mary of England (1516 to 1558).
- General Sani Abacha of Nigeria (1943 - 1998).
- Vladmir Lenin of USSR (1870 to 1924).
- Col. Moammar Ghaddafi of Libya (c.1942 to 2011).
- Vladmir Putin of Russia (1952 to date, being president since 2012).

Below are brief notes on some of these abusers of power.

Like the Roman Caesars most tyrants/dictators begin well – giving an impression that they are in to change anomalies in government. But as soon as they are "welcomed" by the people, and the dictators settle down, they consolidate power around themselves. In the process they destroy all oppositions in order to retain absolute power and use it absolutely as desired without opposition.

As 'no condition is permanent' and change is the one thing that is constant apart from God Almighty, there certainly comes a time when the tyrant falls. The people either succeed in removing him from office somehow, killing him or overpowering him in such a way that he "steps aside" shamefully. At this point the people rejoice like Nigerians celebrated everywhere in the week that the military head of state, General Sani Abacha died in 1998.

The difference between all tyrants and Jesus Christ is that tyrants start by pretending to love the people, but bring out their true color as time progresses. But Jesus Christ began His earthly ministry being kind, compassionate, showing and exercising 'agape'[56] and preaching the gospel of the kingdom of God. He continued in that – healing the sick, feeding the hungry crowds, delivering the demon-possessed or demon-oppressed, raising the dead, and so on – until the end. Even while He was facing judgment for offenses He did not commit, He healed Malchus, the chief priest's servant's ear which Peter had cut off. While Jesus was executed, out of His compassion He prayed His Father to forgive the people for they did not know what they were doing.

The apostle Paul instructs to imitate him as he did Jesus Christ (1Corinthians 11:1), who humbled Himself (Philippians 2:8).[57]

---

[56] Agape is the Greek word for God-kind of love - love that knows no bounds, is unconditional and not discriminatory as to its beneficiary and does not expect reciprocation. Agape is different from other forms of love in the Greek language, since it is extended to the unlovable.

[57] Philippians 2:6-8 reads, "Who, being in the form of God, thought it not robbery to be equal with God: 7 But made himself of no reputation, and took upon him the form of a servant, and was made in the likeness of

Leaders must humble themselves so that their people may always rejoice during the reign of such leaders and for them to not fall due to pride.

IDI AMIN DADA (c. 1925 to 2003).[58]

Idi Amin Dada was born in Koboko, Uganda about 1925. He became military president of Uganda from 1971 to 1979. "Popularly known as the butcher of Uganda, he was considered one of the cruelest despots in the world." He joined the British Colonial Army's "King's African Rifles" as a cook and rose to the rank of Lieutenant. He remained in the Ugandan Army when Uganda gained independence from Great Britain in 1962, and rose to the rank of Major, and was appointed commander of the Ugandan Army in 1965. He overthrew the government of Milton Obote in a coup d'état in 1971 when he knew that Obote was planning to arrest him for misappropriating army finances.

Idi Amin persecuted some ethnic groups and political dissidents. The Tanzanian Armed Forces ousted Idi Amin from power in April 1979, and he went into exile and died in August 2003 in Saudi Arabia.

---

men: [8] And being found in fashion as a man, he humbled himself, and became obedient unto death, even the death of the cross."

[58] Idi Amin. https://en.wikipedia.org/wiki/Idi_Amin September 18,2022.

"Amin's rule was characterized by rampant abuses of human rights, political repression, ethnic persecution, extra-judicial killings, nepotism, corruption, and gross economic mis-management." To support the nickname given him, international observers and human rights groups estimate the numbers of people killed in Idi Amin's reign at between 100,000 and 500,000.

GENERAL SANI ABACHA (1943 TO 1998).

General Sani Abacha was born September 20, 1943 in Kano City, in the then Northern Region of Nigeria. He enlisted in the Nigerian Army, received military training in Nigerian and British military institutions and was commissioned 2nd Lieutenant in 1963 at age 20. In 1993 Abacha had risen to a full four-star general in the Nigerian Army. He was Nigeria's military head of state from November 17, 1993 until his death on June 8, 1998. After the first coup d'état of January 1966 that terminated the first post-colonial democratic government, there were eight successive coups d'états in Nigeria as follows:

Table 2: Military Coups in Nigeria Between July 1996 and August 1993 (inclusive)[59]

---

[59] "Military coups in Nigeria."
https://en.wikipedia.org/wiki/Military_coups_in_Nigeria September 22, 2022.

S/N	DATE	COUP LEADER	REMARKS
1.	Jul. 29, 1966	Col. Yakubu Gowon	Bloody coup. Maj.-Gen. J. T. U. Aguiyi-Ironsi (interim head of state) was killed.
2.	Jul. 29, 1975	Brig.-Gen. Murtala Mohammed	Bloodless coup. Gowon was overthrown.
3.	Feb. 13, 1976	Col. Buka S. Dimka	Bloody coup was aborted. Gen. Olusegun Obasanjo took over. Plotters were executed.
4.	Dec. 31, 1983	Maj.-Gen. Muhammadu Buhari	Bloodless coup removed 2nd democratic government led by Shehu Shagari.
5.	Aug. 27, 1985	Maj.-Gen. Ibrahim B. Babangida	Bloodless coup; Buhari was removed
6.	Dec. 1985	Maj.-Gen. Mamman Vatsa	Alleged, failed bloodless coup. Alleged plotters were executed by firing squad.

7.	Apr. 22 1990	Maj. Gideon Okar	Failed, bloodless coup. Plotters were executed.
8.	Nov. 17, 1993	Gen. Sani Abacha	Bloodless palace coup, overthrowing the Interim civilian government led by Chief Ernest Shonekan.

Table 2: Coups d'états in Nigeria (1966 to 1993)

General Sani Abacha was said to have participated actively in all the successful military coups from, or after, the one that brought Yakubu Gowon to power, and he participated in all resultant governments in Nigeria from Gowon's, either as a senior military officer or a political office holder, which afforded him the opportunity to be a member of every ruling (executive) body.[60]

When General Ibrahim Badamasi Babangida (a.k.a. IBB), military president of Nigeria from 1985 "stepped aside" in August 1993, he set up an interim civilian government headed by Chief Ernest Shonekan, GCFR, and appointed Gen. Sani Abacha as Chief of Defense Staff and minister of defense.[61] Gen. Abacha

---

[60] "Sani Abacha." https://en.wikipedia.org/wiki/Sani_Abacha September 22, 2022.

[61] "Ernest Shonekan." https://en.wikipedia.org/wiki/Ernest_Shonekan September 22, 2022

overthrew Chief Shonekan's three months old interim government in a bloodless palace coup d'etat as Shonekan offered no resistance. Then Abacha assumed the office of head of state, and Commander-in-chief of the armed forces.

Personal Characteristics of Sani Abacha.

This man had a couple of qualities, which help in characterizing him as a tyrant as follows: -

(1) He had no forgiving spirit but was rather vindictive. He was said to have no recognition for generosity, and pursued his enemies unremittingly.[62] An instance of this was that he promised vengeance to Sultan Dasuki of Sokoto for asking him to swear to an oath before getting back his money which was previously kept for Abacha by the late son of the Sultan. At an opportune time shortly afterward, Abacha deposed Sultan Dasuki.[63]

(2) He was said to be indifferent to suffering of people, and intolerant and callous.[64]

(3) The General was said to be ruthless and neither entertained opposition, advice, nor disobedience. As a supreme leader whose opinions and decisions were infallible or

---

[62] Fagbemi Olorunfemi. "THE PERPLEXING AND BRUTAL RULE OF GENERAL SAMORI BALCHA – A TYRANT." (Middletown, DE, 2018), 45.
[63] ibid, 2.
[64] ibid, 46

unquestionable, any real or imagined opposition was summarily dealt with. In Fagbemi's opinion this attitude emanated from the fear of the unknown, in view of the way he rose to power.[65] An example of this was the phantom coup d'état which the general and his CSO (Chief Security Officer) "set up" to test the loyalty of the members of his team in order to keep others on their toes.[66]

(4) He was a professional coup plotter, said to be "the most successful coup plotter of his age in world history." He participated actively in nearly all the successful coups d'états from or after the one that brought General Yakubu Gowon to power in July 1966. Consequently, he was rewarded with juicy posts in the government that the coup culminated in.[67]

Abacha suffered some inferiority complex, which caused him to dislike for any subordinate to give an impression of being more knowledgeable in governance by making him suggestions.

His Administrative Style

General Abacha's government was authoritarian; he was described as a maximum dictator. Of course, he had an

---

[65] ibid, 47.

[66] ibid, 195

[67] ibid, 50.

administrative structure in place, yet his wish was law. Meetings of the governing council members were only meant for him to inform them of the decisions he had taken and none must oppose.[68] The Provisional Ruling Council was, therefore, a rubber stamp body.

He constantly intimidated and dismissed his ministers and concentrated power in himself – dictating what happened in every ministry.[69] For the flimsiest reason he fired and replaced his ministers.

"In September 1994 General Abacha promulgated a decree that placed his government above the jurisdiction of any court of law in the land, effectively thereby giving him absolute power." He also promulgated another decree which empowered him to arrest and detain anyone for up to three months without trial.[70]

During Abacha's reign his men (mostly in uniform – police and army) detained, raped, maimed, killed, and generally terrorized people – with or without orders, and for no offenses that posed a threat to national security.[71] Many citizens were jailed without trial, and a couple of places were bombed by his agents under the guise of N.A.D.E.C.O. (National Democratic Coalition – a group

---

[68] Ibid, 100.
[69] ibid, 101.
[70] www.en.wikipedia.org/wiki/sani_Abacha.
[71] Fagbemi, 93.

of nine democrats formed in May 1994 for the purpose of pressuring the military to quit government for democracy).

In view of alleged and reported human rights abuses, judging and executing political opponents, Abacha's government was sanctioned by the international community.

One of the characteristics of Abacha's government was looting the treasury. He was said to have treated the nation's treasury like a personal household safe. For that, he gave orders to the Governor of the Central Bank to deliver outrageous amounts of money (in local and foreign currencies) to his home and office.[72]

A great deal of the looted funds amounting to as much as USD3.624 Bn (3.624 billion US Dollars) has been recovered from America and Europe by succeeding governments of Nigeria under various heads of state up to May 2020.[73]

On June 8, 1998, General Sani Abacha died in Aso Rock (the presidential villa) at Abuja. No one has accounted for the actual cause of his death after a previous night engagement with one of his favorite generals and some foreign women.[74] Meanwhile, there was great jubilation all over the nation, Nigeria that Abacha had died. Beer parlors were teeming with people rejoicing and celebrating freedom from bondage and tyranny. The truth is that,

---

[72] ibid, 111.
[73] ibid, 254 – 272.
[74] ibid, 217.

according to Proverbs 29:2, "When the righteous are in authority, the people rejoice: but when the wicked beareth rule, the people mourn."

It is noteworthy that all of Nigeria's nine military heads-of-state (Maj.-Gen. J.T.U. Aguiyi-Ironsi, Gen. Yakubu Gowon, Brig.-Gen. Murtala Mohammed, Lt.-Gen. Olusegun Obasanjo, Maj.-Gen. Muhammadu Buhari, Gen. Ibrahim Badamasi Babangida, Gen. Abdusalami Abubakar and Gen. Sani Abacha) were dictators of whom Abacha was one of the two (the second being Buhari in his first coming) whose end of reign caused jubilation all over the nation.

ADOLF HITLER (20 April 1889 – 30 April 1945)

His Birth and Early Years

Adolf Hitler was born on April 20, 1889, in Braunau, Austria. His parents were Alois Hitler and Klara. Klara was Alois's third wife (sequel to the death of his first two wives) and Adolf was the third child of that third marriage. Adolf was a confirmed Roman Catholic.

In the opinion of one of Adolf's high (secondary) school teachers, Dr. Eduard Humer, he was talented in a narrow field, but "lacked self-discipline, being notoriously cantankerous, willful, arrogant, and bad-tempered. . . He reacted with ill-concealed hostility to advice or reproof: at the same time, he demanded from his fellow pupils their unqualified subservience, fancying himself in the role of leader. . . ."[75]

Adolf was said to live in a world of his own, satisfied with making his widowed mother provide for his needs, while "scornfully refusing to concern himself with such petty mundane affairs as money or a job."[76] This corroborates the testimony of his teacher, Dr. Humer quoted above, that Adolf was lazy. He had only one friend, Kubizek, with whom he shared an apartment in Vienna after his mother's demise; apart from Kubizek Adolf lived a solitary life. He showed indifference to ladies that were attracted to him.[77] No wonder he did not marry until about April 29, 1945 – one day before he jointly committed suicide with his wife, Eva Anna Paula Hitler (nee Braun, February 6, 1912 – April 30, 1945), who was Adolf's long-time mistress.[78]

Hitler's Anti-Semitism

Adolf Hitler was grossly antisemitic. It is said that everything he ever said about the Jews was certainly "a reflection of the antisemitic peripherals and pamphlets he read in Vienna before 1914." Like the Viennese antisemitism Hitler believed that "the

---

[75] Bullock, Alan. HITLER. A STDY OF TYRANNY. (New York: Konecky & Konecky, 1962), 27.

[76] ibid, 30.

[77] ibid, 31.

[78] **Eva Braun.** https://en.wikipedia.org/wiki/Eva_Braun November 20, 2022.

Jews were responsible for bringing negroes into the Rhineland with the ultimate idea of bastardizing the white race, which they hate, and thus lowering its cultural and political level so that the Jew might dominate."[79] All his beliefs and assertions about the Jews were not based on any facts.

Hitler believed that equality of individuals and races were unnatural - the opposite was a law of nature. He did not believe in such democratic institutions as parliament, free press or free speech. Discussion irritated him.[80]

In concluding 'The Formative Years' of Hitler as a party leader, Bullock said as follows:

"Those years between 1908 and the end of 1918 had hardened him, taught him to be self-reliant, confirmed his belief in himself, toughened the power of his will. From them he emerged with a stock of fixed ideas and prejudices, which were to alter a little in the rest of his life: hatred of the Jews; contempt for the ideals of democracy, internationalism, equality, and peace; a preference for authoritarian forms of government; an intolerant nationalism; a rooted belief in inequality of races and individuals; and faith in the heroic virtues of war."[81]

---

[79] Bullock, 39.
[80] ibid, 41.
[81] ibid, 56.

Bullock (page 95) also noted that Hitler's hatred was not for the French but the republic, "which he depicted as a corrupt racket run by the Jews at the expense of national interests. No accusation against the Jews was too wild for him, but his most bitter scorn was reserved for the 'respectable' parties of the Right who hesitated to act." The Jew embodied all that Hitler hated. Antisemitism was one of the most consistent themes in his career and thought. He believed and preached that the Jew was the author of all that Hitler hated including democracy, capitalism, parliamentarianism, freedom of speech and the press, and internationalism.

In the words of Bullock, "Hitler's purpose was plain and unwavering. He meant to carry out the extermination of the Jewish race in Europe, using the word, 'extermination' not in a metaphorical but in a precise and literal sense as the deliberate policy of the German State – and he very largely succeeded. On a conservative estimate between 4 and 4.2 million Jews perished in Europe under Hitler's rule – apart from the number driven from their homes who succeeded in finding refuge abroad. History records few, if any, crimes of such magnitude and of so cold-blooded a purpose."[82]

The Nazi Party

---

[82] Bullock, 407 - 408

The story of Adolf Hitler cannot be complete without mentioning the Nazi Party, "officially the National Socialist German Workers' Party, and a far-right political party in Germany. The party, (Nationalsozialistische-Deutsche-Arbeiterpartei) was founded by Anton Drexler at Munich, Germany on February 24, 1920. Nazi Party supported the ideology known as Nazism – a form of fascism, with disdain for liberal democracy and parliamentary system. It incorporated fervent antisemitism, anti-communism, scientific racism, and use of eugenics into its creed.[83] The Nazi Party died on October 10, 1945.

Adolf Hitler's Rise to Power

He did not seize power from anybody. He succeeded in coming to power in 1933 due to "a shoddy political deal with the "Old Gang" whom he had attacked for many months past. His success, according to Bullock, was attributable more to bad judgment of his political opponents and rivals, and luck.[84] However, I believe that rather than luck, Hitler's rise to power was a divine arrangement that was to culminate in the part-fulfillment of the Holy Scriptures with regard to the Jews. Deuteronomy 28:1-14 is a record of the blessings that would be their portion if fully obedient to the commands of the Lord, but 28:15-66 are curses

---

[83] NAZISM. https://en.wikipedia.org/wiki/Nazism November 24, 2022.
[84] Bullock, 253.

that would overtake them if disobedient. Unfortunately, Israel became idolatrous, worshipping idols in place of the true God. Some of the relevant curses in the passage above and other passages are stated below.

Deuteronomy 28:64-65 NKJV "Then the Lord will scatter you among all peoples, from one end of the earth to the other, and there you shall serve other gods, which neither you nor your fathers have known—wood and stone. [65] And among those nations you shall find no rest, nor shall the sole of your foot have a resting place; but there the Lord will give you a trembling heart, failing eyes, and anguish of soul."

Deuteronomy 29:24-28 NKJV "All nations would say, 'Why has the Lord done so to this land? What does the heat of this great anger mean?' [25] Then people would say: 'Because they have forsaken the covenant of the Lord God of their fathers, which He made with them when He brought them out of the land of Egypt; [26] for they went and served other gods and worshiped them, gods that they did not know and that He had not given to them. [27] Then the anger of the Lord was aroused against this land, to bring on it every curse that is written in this book. [28] And the Lord uprooted them from their land in anger, in wrath, and in great indignation, and cast them into another land, as it is this day.'"

Ezekiel 5:7-12 NKJV "Therefore thus says the Lord God: 'Because you have multiplied disobedience more than the nations that are all around you, have not walked in My statutes nor kept My judgments, nor even done according to the judgments of the nations that are all around you'— [8] therefore thus says the Lord God: 'Indeed I, even I, am against you and will execute judgments in your midst in the sight of the nations. [9] And I will do among you what I have never done, and the like of which I will never do again, because of all your abominations. [10] Therefore fathers shall eat their sons in your midst, and sons shall eat their fathers; and I will execute judgments among you, and all of you who remain I will scatter to all the winds.

[11] 'Therefore, as I live,' says the Lord God, 'surely, because you have defiled My sanctuary with all your detestable things and with all your abominations, therefore I will also diminish you; My eye will not spare, nor will I have any pity. [12] One-third of you shall die of the pestilence, and be consumed with famine in your midst; and one-third shall fall by the sword all around you; and I will scatter another third to all the winds, and I will draw out a sword after them.

This punishment in Germany, and the prevalent antisemitism all over the world, may be viewed as an extension of the captivities in Assyria and Babylon of Samaria and Judah, notwithstanding that God made some Jews return to rebuild and inhabit Jerusalem after seventy years in Babylon. Bear in mind that Jerusalem was destroyed again by the Roman government in the year A.D. 70 and the people scattered all over the world, the reason being that the people went back to idolatry and disobedience of the law not long after they returned from captivity. The following passages in the book of Malachi (the last prophet in Israel before the coming of the New Testament events) give a little of the prevalent life of the people of Israel before the Advent of Jesus Christ and up to the final destruction of Jerusalem in A.D. 70:

Malachi 2:1-9 NIV "And now, you priests, this warning is for you. [2] If you do not listen, and if you do not resolve to honor my name," says the Lord Almighty, "I will send a curse on you, and I will curse your blessings. Yes, I have already cursed them, because you have not resolved to honor me.

[3] "Because of you I will rebuke your descendants; I will smear on your faces the dung from your festival sacrifices, and you will be carried off with it. [4] And you will know that I have sent you this warning so that my covenant with Levi may continue," says the Lord Almighty. [5] "My covenant was with him, a covenant of life and peace, and I gave them to him; this called for reverence and he revered me and stood in awe of my name. [6] True instruction was in his mouth and nothing false was found on his lips. He walked with me in peace and uprightness, and turned many from sin.

[7] "For the lips of a priest ought to preserve knowledge, because he is the messenger of the Lord Almighty and people seek instruct-tion from his mouth. [8] But you have turned from the way and by your teaching have caused many to stumble; you have violated the covenant with Levi," says the Lord Almighty. [9] "So I have caused you to be despised and humiliated before all the people, because you have not followed my ways but have shown partiality in matters of the law." (Emphasis added).

Malachi 3:5-7 NIV "So I will come to put you on trial. I will be quick to testify against sorcerers, adulterers and perjurers, against those who defraud laborers of their wages, who oppress the widows and the fatherless, and deprive the foreigners among you of justice, but do not fear me," says the Lord Almighty.

[6] "I the Lord do not change. So you, the descendants of Jacob, are not destroyed. [7] Ever since the time of your ancestors you have turned away from my decrees and have not kept them. Return to me, and I will return to you," says the Lord Almighty.

"But you ask, 'How are we to return?'"

Malachi 3:13-15 NIV "You have spoken arrogantly against me," says the Lord.

"Yet you ask, 'What have we said against you?' [14] "You have said, 'It is futile to serve God. What do we gain by carrying out his requirements and going about like mourners before the Lord Almighty? [15] But now we call the arrogant blessed.

Certainly, evildoers prosper, and even when they put God to the test, they get away with it.'"

Adolf Hitler, a Dictator

One of Hitler's usual habits was being on the defensive and to accuse of malice and aggression people that opposed him. He claimed innocence and always the fault in the other side – he was never wrong. He always criticized the Jews, the Republican government, Communists, Czechs, Bolsheviks or the Poles for exhibiting intolerable behaviors that caused him to take far-reaching actions in defense of himself.[85]

Hitler had a rare background that facilitated his actions carelessly:

- He had no roots – neither a home nor family.
- He accepted no loyalties from anyone.
- He was not bound by any traditions.
- He had respect for neither God nor man.
- To take advantage of any situation, it did not matter to him how – whether by lying, being cunning, treacherous or unscrupulous.
- To him it was needful for millions of Germans to die for Germany; but towards his end, he would rather destroy Germany than surrender his power or accept defeat.[86]

---

[85] ibid, 376.
[86] ibid, 380.

Hitler was highly ambitious and lustful for power, which consumed him. He over-estimated his genius, which brought him defeat. Bullock wrote, "The sin which Hitler committed was that which the ancient Greeks called hybris, the sin overweening pride, of believing himself to be more than a man. No man was ever more surely destroyed by the image he had created than Adolf Hitler."[87]

It's said that Hitler believed that democracy was breeding ground for irresponsibility by abandoning decisions to an anonymous majority. In 1937 he campaigned that all traditional privileges in all of life's spheres especially in the political, and vest leadership of the nation on handpicked or appointed men based on their talents irrespective of their social and religious inclination, birth or descent.

DEATH OF ADOLF HITLER

On April 30, 1945, Adolf Hitler died by suicide along with Eva Braun, his wife, in Berlin. His death was preceded by a series of events including the Second World War (WWII), which Hitler initiated in Europe when, as the German dictator he invaded Poland on September 1, 1939, for which Britain and France declared war on Germany. Hitler invaded the Soviet Union in June 1941.

---

[87] ibid, 385

When in 1945 Hitler realized that he had lost the war as the Soviet forces were advancing in Berlin to the Chancellery, he decided to take his life rather than be captured by the Soviet Red Army. Shortly before dying, precisely on April 29 between 1:00 AM and 3:00 AM Hitler formally married Eva Braun, who agreed to die with him.

He appointed Admiral Donitz his successor as head of state and Joseph Goebbels as chancellor. He willed and instructed that his body and Eva's be burnt in order not to suffer the fate of Mussolini and his mistress, who were murdered in Italy and their bodies hung in the public and later dumped in the gutters.

It is believed that Eva poisoned herself with cyanide while Hitler, sitting beside her, shot himself on April 30, 1945 – ten days after his 56th birthday. And with many gallons of petrol their bodies were burnt to ashes.

Various historians have different views of Hitler, depending on the angles from which they viewed:

David Irving, author of Hitler's Wars, writing from the standpoint of Nazi Germany's reader, is quoted by Wikipedia as suggesting that Hitler was slandered by historians, while in actual sense he was a "rational, intelligent politician, whose only goal was to increase Germany's prosperity and influence in the continent, and who was constantly let down by incompetent and/or treasonous subordinates."[88]

The author was further quoted as of the opinion that Hitler's invasion of the Soviet Union was a "preventive war" forced on him. Hitler, to him had no knowledge of the holocaust, how much more being the author. Rather, Hitler was against the killing of the Jews.

On the other hand, another historian, Kershaw is quoted also by Wikipedia as opining that Hitler was "the embodiment of modern political evil." He said,

"Never in history has such ruination – physical and moral – been associated with the name of one man. That the ruination had far deeper roots and far more profound causes than the aims and actions of one man has been evident in the preceding chapters. That the previously unprobed depths of inhumanity plumbed by the Nazi regime could draw upon wide-ranging complicity at all levels of society has been equally apparent. But Hitler's name justifiably stands for all time as that of the chief instigator of the most profound collapse of civilization in modern times. The extreme form of personal rule which an ill-educated beerhall demagogue and racist bigot, a narcissistic, megalomaniac, self-styled national saviour was allowed to acquire and exercise in a

---

[88] *Hitler's War.* https://en.wikipedia.org/wiki/Hitler%27s_War
November 26, 2022

modern, economically advanced, and cultured land known for its philosophers and poets, was absolutely decisive in the terrible unfolding of events in those fateful twelve years."[89]

In his Epilogue, Bullock wrote of Hitler:

"The fact that his career ended in a failure, and that his defeat was pre-eminently due to his mistakes, does not by itself detract from Hitler's claim to greatness. The flaw lies deeper. For these remarkable powers were combined with an ugly and strident egotism, a moral and intellectual cretinism. The passions which ruled Hitler's mind were ignoble: hatred, resentment, the lust to dominate, and, where he could not dominate, to destroy. His career did not exalt but debased the human condition, and his twelve years' dictatorship was barren of all ideas save one – the further extension of his own power and that of the nation with which he had identified himself."[90]

Hitler was a cruel dictator par excellence, whose hunger for power, heartlessness and hatred for certain people not his favorites, especially the Jews dragged the world into wars that destroyed millions of people – military and civilian, in addition to intentionally attempting to totally exterminate such hated peoples.

---

[89] Ian Kershaw. *Hitler 1936 – 1945: Nemesis (2000)*. https://en.wikiquote.org/wiki/Ian_Kershaw   November 26, 2022
[90] Bullock, 806.

"Hitler's policies resulted in the killing of nearly two million non-Jewish Polish civilians, over three million Soviet prisoners of war, communists and other political opponents, homosexuals, the physically and mentally disabled, Jehovah's Witnesses, Adventists, and trade unionists. Hitler did not speak publicly about the killings, and seems to never have visited the concentration camps."[91]

Unfortunately, many other (recent) dictators tried to practice domination and suppression. What some of them have not done is succeeding to wipe out persons of certain ethnic groups or races. Dictators are doomed to fail, especially as they often lose value for human life not theirs.

4.5 Instrumentality of Power to a Leader's Downfall

It is said that most of the Caesars (Roman Emperors) were either assassinated by their enemies or killed at war. This is because they were ruthless and abusive of power. Abuse of power is an indication of pride and lack of the fear of God. Having the fear of God should make one respect fellow human beings created by God. The Bible says that "Pride goes before destruction And a haughty spirit before a fall." (Proverbs 16:18 NKJV). We also

---

[91] ADOLF HITLER. *The Holocaust.*
https://en.wikipedia.org/wiki/Adolf Hitler November 27, 2022

read in Proverbs 29:23 that "A man's pride will bring him low, But the humble in spirit will retain honor."

According to Proverbs 1:7, The fear of the Lord is the beginning of wisdom. But "The fool says in his heart that there is no God (Psalms 14:1). So, a fool cannot fear God. Meanwhile, the Scriptures also tell to "Fear God, and keep His commandments" (Ecclesiastes 12:13).

Fear here refers to reverence or respect for God – revering Him because He is God, greater than everybody and all things; because He created and sustains all things that exist, according to Genesis chapters one and two. A person that does not fear God cannot keep His commands. For instance, the Caesars of Rome, the communist leaders of ancient China and Russia/Soviet Union that claimed to be gods for their people, would not fear God. Pharaoh of Egypt thought he was a god and had no regard for the almighty God, the I AM that sent Moses, until the final plagues and miracles – Pharaoh and his army perished in the Red Sea, where the Israelites crossed on dry land.

Israel's King David was described as a man after God's own heart. This does not imply that David was a perfect man. He had his faults, and as observed earlier he abused power during his reign. But he repented when confronted with his sin. At most other times David, though a king, recognized that he was one subject to a greater King – God. He sought the consent of God before embarking on any project. God honored David and kept His covenant with him.

There is a popular saying, "The handwriting is on the wall." The writing was, "MENE, MENE, TEKEL, URPHASIN" on the wall of the palace of the king of Babylon, Belshazzar who succeeded his father, Nebuchadnezzar. Daniel interpreted the message to the king thus: "This is the interpretation of each word. MENE: God has numbered your kingdom, and finished it; [27] TEKEL: You have been weighed in the balances, and found wanting; [28] PERES: Your kingdom has been divided, and given to the Medes and Persians." (Daniel 5:26-28 NKJV). And in Daniel 5:30-31 we read, "That very night Belshazzar, king of the Chaldeans, was slain. [31] And Darius the Mede received the kingdom, being about sixty-two years old."

Exercising unchecked and uncontrolled power leads to authoritarianism. A great deal of such is found amongst kings and queens, emperors and the like. But occasionally, some democratically elected leaders enjoy power so much that it gets into their heads and they abuse it and refuse to leave office. There are men that God mightily used to achieve great exploits in Christendom but ended up dying miserably. Some were used of God to heal many mysterious and terrible sicknesses but died of minor ailments because they began to ascribe to themselves the glory due God alone. God said His glory cannot be shared with anybody.

Your ministry will continue to prosper for as long as you recognize that God is the Author and Giver of the success of the ministry. The Bible says that promotions come not from the east or the west, neither from the north nor from the south, but from the Lord (Psalm 75:6-7). But the moment you begin to see yourself as the achiever by your ingenuity, your ministry surely will nose-dive. If in doubt, ask King Nebuchadnezzar of Babylon. This king had a dream which he claimed to have forgotten but wanted his astrologers and magicians and sorcerers to interpret to him. When, as human beings, they confessed their inability to know the king's dream without him narrating it to them he threatened to kill all of them (Daniel 2:5). This is high-handedness and abuse of power.

King Nebuchadnezzar also had a vision that Daniel also interpreted to him: (Daniel 5:25 - They shall drive you from men, your dwelling shall be with the beasts of the field, and they shall make you eat grass like oxen. They shall wet you with the dew of heaven, and seven times shall pass over you, till you know that the Most High rules in the kingdom of men, and gives it to whomever He chooses.)

Subsequently, Daniel counseled the king: Daniel 4:27 (NKJV) "Therefore, O king, let my advice be acceptable to you; break off your sins by being righteous, and your iniquities by showing mercy to the poor. Perhaps there may be a lengthening of your prosperity."

But due to pride twelve months later the king spoke out a thought he had: ""The king spake, and said, Is not this great Babylon, that I have built for the house of the kingdom by the might of my power, and for the honour of my majesty?" (Daniel 4:30).

And the consequence of that is as follows:

Daniel 4:31-33 (KJV) "While the word was in the king's mouth, there fell a voice from heaven, saying, O king Nebuchadnezzar, to thee it is spoken; The kingdom is departed from thee. [32] And they shall drive thee from men, and thy dwelling shall be with the beasts of the field: they shall make thee to eat grass as oxen, and seven times shall pass over thee, until thou know that the Most High ruleth in the kingdom of men, and giveth it to whomsoever he will. [33] The same hour was the thing fulfilled upon Nebuchadnezzar: and he was driven from men, and did eat grass as oxen, and his body was wet with the dew of heaven, till his hairs were grown like eagles' feathers, and his nails like birds' claws."

When the king was restored to his senses and his throne after 'seven times' (seven years), he confessed that he lifted his eyes to heaven, his reasoning was restored to him and he "blessed the Most High and praised and honored Him who lives forever:

For His dominion is an everlasting dominion, And His kingdom is from generation to generation." (Daniel 4:34).

Then Nebuchadnezzar declared, "Now I, Nebuchadnezzar, praise and extol and honor the King of heaven, all of whose works are truth, and His ways justice. And those who walk in pride He is able to put down." (Daniel 4:37).

That conclusion of the king is in line with the teaching of Jesus Christ that "whoever exalts himself will be humbled, and he who humbles himself will be exalted" (Matthew 23:12).

Similarly, king Belshazzar held a great feast and served wine to his guests using the gold and silver vessels which the erstwhile king, Nebuchadnezzar had carted from the temple at Jerusalem when he took Judah into captivity, and the people drank and praised idols (Daniel 5:1-4). It is risky to transfer items dedicated to God to serve idols.

Then appeared a handwriting on the wall, MENE, MENE, TEKEL, UPHARSIN (Daniel 5:4-25). In the process of interpreting the writing on the wall, Daniel told the king of the pride of his grandfather, Nebuchadnezzar, with the consequences, which the young king knew about, yet he had not humbled himself. Rather he had lifted himself against the Lord of heaven by using vessels meant for the Lord's temple in worshipping and praising idols. For that reason:

- MENE – God had numbered his kingdom and finished it;

- TEKEL – He was weighed in the balance and was found wanting;
- PERES – His kingdom had been divided and given to the Medes and Persians (Daniel 5:17-28).

The same night Belshazzar was killed, and Darius of Mede took over the throne.

No matter how powerful a man or woman may think he or she is, he/she must avoid using for self or other purposes things dedicated to God or ascribe to self the glory that is due God. The Lord said, "I am the Lord: that is my name: and my glory will I not give to another, neither my praise to graven images." (Isaiah 42:8).

It is observed that most of the Roman Caesars (emperors) died young after reigning for brief periods. Initially they were nice and did a few nice and commendable things to help their people. But shortly afterwards, as they began to get used to power, they began to display their cruelty. They used their powers to oppress the people. Of course, people disliked them, and they fell too soon.

Modern day despots usually employ various instruments of office, such as the military (armed forces) and law enforcement agencies, to intimidate their subjects in order to perpetuate their reign. We have observed in the USA, a president that appointed into office only loyalists and relations that did not question or refuse his instructions, using such loyalists to bend and abuse the laws of the land. He tried to place himself above the law, and his appointees assisted him.

This is a clear indication that the type of people that surround a leader contributes immensely to the continuity of a leadership. Also such people, being sycophants, encourage the leader in his despotic acts because they benefit from the evils of that leader.

In addition, when a leader's friends or admired persons are tyrants in other nations, if not checked, the leader is in most cases doomed to want to behave like those despots. The adage is true that says, 'tell me with whom you go, and I'll tell you who you are.'

4.6 Bible Lessons on Power/Authority

The Word of God teaches a lot of lessons on power. But unfortunately, the teachings are never read or are not understood, read and understood but not applied due to ignorance, nonchalance or carelessness, or just disobedience.

Some of the relevant passages are reproduced as follows:

Psalms 37:34-35 NKJV "Wait on the Lord, And keep His way, And He shall exalt you to inherit the land; When the wicked are cut off, you shall see it. [35] I have seen the wicked in great power, And spreading himself like a native green tree."

Psalms 12:3-4 NKJV "May the Lord cut off all flattering lips, And the tongue that speaks proud things, [4] Who have said, "With

our tongue we will prevail; Our lips are our own; Who is lord
over us?"

Psalm 101:5 NKJV "Whoever secretly slanders his neighbor,
Him I will destroy;

The one who has a haughty look and a proud heart, Him I will
not endure."

Psalm 138:6 NKJV "Though the Lord is on high, Yet He regards
the lowly; But the proud He knows from afar."

Psalm 62:11 NKJV "God has spoken once, Twice I have heard
this: That power belongs to God."

Proverbs 8:13 NKJV "The fear of the Lord is to hate evil; Pride
and arrogance and the evil way. And the perverse mouth I hate."

Proverbs 11:2 NKJV "When pride comes, then comes shame;
But with the humble is wisdom."

Proverbs 16:18 NKJV "Pride goes before destruction, And a
haughty spirit before a fall."

Proverbs 29:23 NKJV "A man's pride will bring him low, But
the humble in spirit will retain honor."

Proverbs 29:2 NKJV "When the righteous are in authority,
the people rejoice;

But when a wicked man rules, the people groan."

Proverbs 6:16-19 NKJV "These six things the Lord hates, Yes,
seven are an abomination to Him: [17] A proud look, A lying
tongue, Hands that shed innocent blood, [18] A heart that devises

wicked plans, Feet that are swift in running to evil, [19] A false witness who speaks lies, And one who sows discord among brethren."

Proverbs 15:25 NKJV "The Lord will destroy the house of the proud,

But He will establish the boundary of the widow."

Proverbs 16:5 NKJV "Everyone proud in heart is an abomination to the Lord;

Though they join forces, none will go unpunished."

Proverbs 28:25 NKJV "He who is of a proud heart stirs up strife,

But he who trusts in the Lord will be prospered."

Ecclesiastes 4:1 NKJV "Then I returned and considered all

the oppression that is done under the sun: And look! The tears of the oppressed, But they have no comforter—

On the side of their oppressors there is power, But they have no comforter."

Ecclesiastes 8:4 NKJV "Where the word of a king is, there is power;

And who may say to him, "What are you doing?"

Ecclesiastes 8:8 NKJV "No one has power over the spirit to retain the spirit, And no one has power in the day of death. There is no release from that war, And wickedness will not deliver those who are given to it."

Isaiah 2:11 NKJV "The lofty looks of man shall be humbled,

The haughtiness of men shall be bowed down, And
the Lord alone shall be exalted in that day."

Jeremiah 50:31-32 NKJV "Behold, I am against you, O most
haughty one!" says the Lord God of hosts; "For your day has
come, The time that I will punish you. [32] The most proud shall
stumble and fall, And no one will raise him up; I will kindle a
fire in his cities, And it will devour all around him."

Zephaniah 2:10 NKJV "This they shall have for their pride,
Because they have reproached and made arrogant threats Against
the people of the Lord of hosts."

Zechariah 4:6 NKJV "So he answered and said to me:
"This is the word of the Lord to Zerubbabel: 'Not by might nor
by power, but by My Spirit,' Says the Lord of hosts."

Matthew 20:25 NKJV "But Jesus called them to Himself and
said, "You know that the rulers of the Gentiles lord it over them,
and those who are great exercise authority over them."

Matthew 23:12 NKJV "And whoever exalts himself will
be humbled, and he who humbles himself will be exalted."

Luke 18:14 NKJV [14] I tell you, this man went down to his house
justified rather than the other; for everyone who exalts himself
will be humbled, and he who humbles himself will be exalted."

1 Peter 5:5-6 NKJV "Likewise you younger people, submit
yourselves to your elders. Yes, all of you be submissive to one
another, and be clothed with humility, for "God resists the

proud, But gives grace to the humble." [6] Therefore humble yourselves under the mighty hand of God, that He may exalt you in due time,"

4.7 Conclusions and Recommendations

Power grabbing, lust for power, power tussles, and abuse of power are problems that will continue to plague humanity until Jesus Christ returns to reign in His kingdom on earth. This implies that man's inhumanity to man, which has been since the Garden of Eden days will continue to be on the rise, and people that perpetrate such atrocities will end up in hell fire – the destiny and final destination of the devil and all his agents and their followers (Matthew 25:41 – "Then shall he say also unto them on the left hand, Depart from me, ye cursed, into everlasting fire, prepared for the devil and his angels:")

Michelle Gibbings opined in her article[92] that in order to resist the temptation of power grabbing, and by extension, power-drunkenness, leaders should create the right culture by the following:

- They should not surround themselves with sycophants.

---

[92] Gibbings, Michelle. "MANAGERS & LEADERS : WARNING SIGNS YOUR LEADER MIGHT BE DRUNK ON POWER." https://www.michellegibbings.com/warning-signs-your-leader-might-be-drunk-on-power/ January 12, 2023

- They should be open to challenge and constructive debate [or criticism].

- They should create open and transparent process for decision making, "which enable people to be involved;"

- They should own their mistakes, seeking feedback and following with making amends where necessary. The buck must be seen to stop at their desks – for persons that delegate responsibility and authority.

A few antidotes to lust for power based on the Holy Bible teachings are briefly discussed below: -

(1) Love of Jesus Christ vs. Love of Power

Jesus taught that everyone that loves Him must keep His commands; and His command to us is to love our neighbors as ourselves and as He had loved us (John 13:34). When you love people, you cannot oppress them.

Jesus asked Apostle Peter (and by extension, Christians in leadership positions in the 21st Century) whether he loved Him more than "these" (John 21:15). It is not clear in Scriptures what "these" stands for, whether the other disciples or fishes. Since Peter answered in the affirmative, Jesus instructed him to feed His lambs.

Jesus asked Peter again whether he loved Him. Peter, again, answered that he did, and Jesus instructed him to <u>Tend His sheep</u> (John 21:16).

Jesus Christ emphatically asked Peter a third time whether he loved Him. Peter answered as usual in the affirmative, and Jesus asked him <u>to feed His sheep</u> (John 21:17).

Jesus referred to His followers as sheep and it must be borne in mind that a lamb is a baby-sheep. In effect, asking Peter to feed the lambs, tend the sheep and feed the sheep, Jesus was assigning Peter the responsibility of shepherding or caring for young and old followers of His – in fact, all followers.

A leader must love the Lord more than the led and more than power and all the world gives. He should then shepherd (lead, provide for, protect and guide) all the people just as Jesus would do them.

(2) <u>Repentance And Restitution</u>

As no man is infallible whether they are kings/monarchs, presidents, pastors, church leaders, public office holders or supervisors. Everyone in an exalted position must be able to repent when wrong. The story of King David, Israel's second human king is worth citing here. When the prophet Nathan confronted him with his sin which encompassed adultery, murder, lying, covering up, covetousness, all in taking Bathsheba to bed and getting her husband killed, David repented, and God forgave him. That repentance did not diminish him or his power. Read the story below:"Why have you despised the commandment of the Lord, to do evil in His sight? You have killed Uriah the Hittite with the sword; you have taken his wife to be your wife, and have killed him with the sword of the people of Ammon. [10] Now therefore, the sword shall never depart from your house, because you have despised Me, and have taken the wife of Uriah the Hittite to be your wife.' [11] Thus says the Lord: 'Behold, I will raise up adversity against you from your own house; and I will take your wives before your eyes and give them to your neighbor, and he shall lie with your wives in the sight of this sun. [12] For you did it secretly, but I will do this thing before all Israel, before the sun.'" [13] So David said to Nathan, "I have sinned against the Lord." And Nathan said to David, "The Lord also has put away your sin; you shall not die." (2 Samuel 12:9-13 NKJV).

Similarly, when King Nebuchadnezzar of Babylon learnt his lesson and repented, God forgave him and restored him both to humanity and his throne:

"That very hour the word was fulfilled concerning Nebuchadnezzar; he was driven from men and ate grass like oxen; his body was wet with the dew of heaven till his hair had grown like eagles' feathers and his nails like birds' claws. [34] And at the end of the time I, Nebuchadnezzar, lifted my eyes to heaven, and my understanding returned to me; and I blessed the Most High and praised and honored Him who lives forever: And His kingdom is from generation to generation." (Daniel 4:33-34 NKJV)

Repentance is the act of realizing that one has been wrong and turning one hundred eighty degrees to the behavior in question. In Luke 19:8 we read of a rich Publican of Jesus' day by the name Zacchaeus, who repented when he met Jesus Christ. He also offered a restitution for all he had forcefully acquired from people.

(3) <u>Self-Control And Prayer</u>

One of the characteristics of life controlled by the Holy Spirit of God is self-control, which in my own words is the ability to exercise restraint in times of tension and pressure. This and other virtues come not just by training or heredity, but by prayer and dependence on the Holy Spirit of God. Self-control is actually one of the "fruit of the Holy Spirit" described in Galatians 5:22-23 NKJV thus: "But the fruit of the Spirit is love, joy, peace, longsuffering,   kindness, goodness, faithfulness, [23] gentleness, self-control. Against such there is no law."

Exercising self-control will help you as a leader each time you are tempted to abuse power.

(4) <u>Humility</u>

Jesus Christ taught His disciples that anyone that wants to be a leader must see and place himself as a servant of all. Mark 9:35 –

(ESV) "And he sat down and called the twelve. And he said to them, "If anyone would be first, he must be last of all and servant of all.""

The leader must see himself as "primus inter pares" (first amongst equals), bearing in mind that leadership position could change at any moment and any of the followers can become the leader.

Learn from the humility of Jesus Christ. The Bible says in John 13:12-15, "When he had washed their feet and put on his outer garments and resumed his place, he said to them, "Do you understand what I have done to you? [13] You call me Teacher and Lord, and you are right, for so I am. [14] If I then, your Lord and Teacher, have washed your feet, you also ought to wash one another's feet. [15] For I have given you an example, that you also should do just as I have done to you.""

Read the apostle Paul's admonition on humility as follows:

Philippians 2:5-11 "Let this mind be in you, which was also in Christ Jesus: [6] Who, being in the form of God, thought it not robbery to be equal with God: [7] But made himself of no reputation, and took upon him the form of a servant, and was made in the likeness of men: [8] And being found in fashion as a man, he humbled himself, and became obedient unto death, even the death of the cross. [9] Wherefore God also hath highly exalted him, and given him a name which is above every name: [10] That at the name of Jesus every knee should bow, of things in heaven, and things in earth, and things under the earth; [11] And that every tongue should confess that Jesus Christ is Lord, to the glory of God the Father."

Humility should make you remember that any exalted position you hold is given you by God for a purpose and can be taken away ignominiously if abused. Jesus taught that "whosoever exalteth himself shall be abased; and he that humbleth himself shall be exalted" (Luke 14:11; 18:14; Matthew 23:12).

(5) <u>Power Belongs to God</u>

Acknowledge that power belongs to God. In Psalm 62:11 we read, "God hath spoken once; twice have I heard this; that power belongeth unto God." When you remember or bear in mind that ultimately all power belongs to God, you will remember that you will give an account to God of the way you have employed the power He lent you. Every account attracts a reward or punishment.

(6) <u>Time And Chance</u>

The Preacher says, "I returned, and saw under the sun, that the race is not to the swift, nor the battle to the strong, neither yet bread to the wise, nor yet riches to men of understanding, nor yet favour to men of skill; but time and chance happeneth to them all." (Ecclesiastes 9:11).

You are not in the position of leadership because you are the richest or most powerful person. The opportunity you are given to occupy the position of leadership could have been give to someone else and could still change hands away from you.

Pulpit Commentary explains this verse as follows: "Work as we may and must and ought, the results are uncertain and beyond our control."[93]

Interestingly, the current president of the United States of America Joseph Biden proposed to nominate an African American woman to the Supreme Court of the USA (SCOTUS), who would become the first black woman Justice in the SCOTUS. There were several women who were fingered as front runners - at least three of them were equally qualified and well qualified and well deserving to be in that position. They were seen to be not inferior to the present Justices already in the SCOTUS. But only one of the three equally qualified women was needed, and whoever was nominated should never boast of being the best and therefore allow the power to get into her head. It would be God's doing. It is heartwarming that Judge (now Justice) Ketanji Brown Jackson who was eventually nominated acknowledged this in one of her speeches at the White House after her Supreme Court confirmation when she said, "First, as always, I have to give

[93] https://biblehub.com/ecclesiastes/9-11.htm January 15, 2023.

thanks to God for delivering me as promised – (applause) – and for sustaining me throughout this nomination and confirmation process. As I said at the outset, I have come this far by faith, and I know that I am truly blessed. To the many people who have lifted me up in prayer since the nomination, thank you. I am very grateful.

Thank you, as well, Mr. President, for believing in me and for honoring me with this extraordinary chance to serve our country."[94]

WARNINGS IN SCRIPTURES AGAINST ABUSE OF POWER

"You shall neither mistreat a stranger nor oppress him, for you were strangers in the land of Egypt. [22] "You shall not afflict any widow or fatherless child. [23] If you afflict them in any way, and they cry at all to Me, I will surely hear their cry;" (Exodus 22:21-23 NKJV).

"You shall not oppress a hired servant who is poor and needy, whether one of your brethren or one of the aliens who is in your land within your gates." (Deuteronomy 24:14 NKJV).

"Do not rob the poor because he is poor, Nor oppress the afflicted at the gate; [23] For the Lord will plead their cause, And

---

[94] https://www.cnn.com/2022/04/08/politics/ketanji-brown-jackson-confirmation-speech/index.html January 15, 2023.

plunder the soul of those who plunder them." (Proverbs 22:22-23 NKJV)

"Do not oppress the widow or the fatherless, The alien or the poor.

Let none of you plan evil in his heart Against his brother.'" (Zechariah 7:10 NKJV).

"But Jesus called them to Himself and said, "You know that the rulers of the Gentiles lord it over them, and those who are great exercise authority over them. 26 Yet it shall not be so among you; but whoever desires to become great among you, let him be your servant. 27 And whoever desires to be first among you, let him be your slave—" (Matthew 20:25-27 NKJV also Mark 10:42-44). And He said to them, "The kings of the Gentiles exercise lordship over them, and those who exercise authority over them are called 'benefactors.' 26 But not so among you; on the contrary, he who is greatest among you, let him be as the younger, and he who governs as he who serves." (Luke 22:25-26 NKJV).

"Shepherd the flock of God which is among you, serving as overseers, not by compulsion but willingly, not for dishonest gain but eagerly; 3 nor as being lords over those entrusted to you, but being examples to the flock;" (1Peter 5:2-3 NKJV).

CHAPTER FIVE

SEX

Sex is the third in the series of three powerful traits that play major roles in the downfall of many people. The other two are money and power. Here, in our context sex, which in everyday conversations refers to sexual intercourse, stands for that and sexuality, which "encompasses an individual's thoughts, feelings, desires, and behaviors related to sex [as of gender], intimacy, and attraction."[95] In other words, in this book sex encompasses sexual relationships that involve or lead to sexual intercourse such as fornication, adultery, homosexuality/lesbianism, (all forms of sexual immorality). It should be noted that in the King James Version Bible the word, sex and words that take root form sex are not found. Rather other terms like 'know', and combination of words like 'lie with' are used. But some sex forms of words are found in some modern English versions of the Bible.

5.1 DEFINITIONS

<u>Sexual Intercourse</u> is an act during which a man inserts his genital into that of a woman. This is the original, and only used-to-be-

---

95

https://www.google.com/search?q=what+is+sexuality%3F&oq=what+is+sexuality%3F&gs_lcrp=EgZjaHJvbWUyBggAEEUYOTIKCAEQABixAxiABDIHCAIQABiABDIHCAMQABiABDIHCAQQABiABDIHCAUQABiABDIHCAYQABiABDIHCAcQABiABDIHCAgQABiABDIHCAkQABiABNIBCjExNDgwajBqMTWoAgywAgHxBSWtnAS49qs1&sourceid=chrome&ie=UTF-8

known way to do sex.[96] In some cultures it was (and still is in some cases) considered too vulgar of anyone to describe this act as has just been done. Rather they said such things as:

- He knew her – e.g., Genesis 4:1 "And Adam knew Eve his wife; and she conceived, and bare Cain, and said, I have gotten a man from the Lord."

  Genesis 4:17a reads, "And Cain knew his wife; and she conceived, and bare Enoch:"

- He lay with her – e.g., Leviticus 18:22 "Thou shalt not lie with mankind, as with womankind: it is abomination."

- He had an affair with her.

- He put her in family way.

- He did something with her.

- He used her.

- He went out with her; etc.

A mother giving her young daughter sex education in those days would say to her at her first menstrual flow, now that you are beginning to be like your mother, ensure that no man has anything to do with you – not even to touch you, because you'd get pregnant to your shame and the shame of your parents and

---

[96] Things like 'anal sex' where a man inserts his genital in the anus of a woman or another man; 'oral sex' – in which case a woman (or another man) with her mouth sucks the genitals of a man, or a man (or another woman) with the mouth sucks the clitoris of a woman; and 'masturbation' have all been deviantly introduced to humanity.

community. In sex education now, it is advisable to be explicit or blunt (not really sounding vulgar), mentioning the parts of the body involved in order to avoid confusion or misinterpretation that could arise in the child when she/he becomes a teenager – an explorer!

Sexual intercourse is the natural way to procreate. It is enjoyable, advisable and necessary between married couples. God created it and everything God created "was good," according to the Genesis creation account.

ADULTERY (SEXUAL)

An adulterer is a married man (such a woman is an adulteress) who engages in voluntary or consensual sexual intercourse with a woman that is not his or her married spouse. In effect, adultery is consensual sexual intercourse between a married man or woman and another person that is not his or her married spouse. This is also described as engagement in extra-marital affair or sex.

The seventh of the Ten Commandments of God in the Holy Bible is, "You shall not commit adultery." (Exodus 20:14; Deuteronomy 5:18 NKJV). This is an indication that God abhors adultery; therefore, it is a sin. In fact, Jesus Christ said adultery is the only grounds for divorce to be allowed (Matthew 19:9). However, for a child of God it is forgivable[97] because 1John 1:8-

---

[97] Nwaelene, Daniel U. JESUS CHRIST: SAVIOR, JUDGE AND KING OF THE WORLD. (Bloomington, IN: WestBow Press, 2017), 220-221.

9 reads, "If we say that we have no sin, we deceive ourselves, and the truth is not in us. [9] If we confess our sins, he is faithful and just to forgive us our sins, and to cleanse us from all unrighteousness." Meanwhile, a woman caught in adultery was brought without her male partner-in-the-act to Jesus Christ for His opinion. Jesus forgave her and warned her to go and sin no more. This is an interesting story recorded in John 8:1-11.

Adultery goes beyond sexual intercourse, according to Jesus Christ in His Sermon on the Mount: lustfully looking at someone of the opposite sex is also adultery (Matthew 5:27-28 – "Ye have heard that it was said by them of old time, Thou shalt not commit adultery: [28] But I say unto you, That whosoever looketh on a woman to lust after her hath committed adultery with her already in his heart.") People, including professionals, have suggested reasons for adultery. For example, A. Pawlowski listed eight reasons as follows:[98]

- Feeling of lack of love by the spouse - leading to boredom.
- Feeling of dissatisfaction with the sex life – leading to desire for more.

---

[98] Pawlowski, A. TODAY: 8 Reasons Why People Cheat. https://www.today.com/health/infidelity-8-reasons-why-people-cheat-become-unfaithful-t121512 February 5, 2023.

- Feeling of insufficient attention from the spouse. Feeling unappreciated.

- Finding yourself in a different setting, drunk or under stress or control.

- Desire for variety – to try many sexual experiences with different persons.

- Low commitment – unanticipated commitment to exclusive relationship.

- Seeking to improve sense of self-worth.

- Seeking to revenge the partner's cheating act.

I'd like to add, however, greed, lust, lack of contentment and self-control as additional reasons for adultery. These are all signs of a life that is not Holy Spirit-filled or controlled (Galatians 5:19-21).

FORNICATION (Greek: πορνεία – porneia)

The first occurrence of the Hebrew equivalent of this Greek word in the Old Testament Bible is found in Genesis 34:31 – "But they said, "Should he treat our sister like a <u>harlot?</u>" The Strong's Hebrew (2181) word here translated to "a whoring" or "harlot" is (זָנָה i.e., zanah) which means to commit fornication or be a harlot. Apart from this, it occurs about eighty-nine (89) other times, mostly to mean illicit or immoral relationship with other gods (idols). In other words, it means spiritual backsliding.

Fornication (πορνεία – porneia) generally or broadly means illicit sexual intercourse. It encompasses all pre-marital and extra-marital sexual intercourse, including adultery (described above), and others to be mentioned later. The word is found in several New Testament passages such as the following:

Matthew 5:32 ASV: "but I say unto you, that every one that putteth away his wife, saving for the cause of fornication, maketh her an adulteress: and whosoever shall marry her when she is put away committeth adultery."

Matthew 19:9 ASV: "And I say unto you, Whosoever shall put away his wife, except for fornication, and shall marry another, committeth adultery: and he that marrieth her when she is put away committeth adultery."

John 8:41 NKJV: "You do the deeds of your father." Then they said to Him, "We were not born of fornication; we have one Father—God."

Acts 15:20, 29 KJV: "But that we write unto them, that they abstain from pollutions of idols, and from fornication, and from things strangled, and from blood."

"[29] That ye abstain from meats offered to idols, and from blood, and from things strangled, and from fornication: from which if ye keep yourselves, ye shall do well. Fare ye well."

Acts 21:25 KJV: "As touching the Gentiles which believe, we have written and concluded that they observe no such thing, save only that they keep themselves from things offered to idols, and from blood, and from strangled, and from fornication."

1 Corinthians 5:1 KJV: "It is reported commonly that there is fornication among you, and such fornication as is not so much as named among the Gentiles, that one should have his father's wife."

1 Corinthians 6:13, 18 KJV: "Meats for the belly, and the belly for meats: but God shall destroy both it and them. Now the body is not for fornication, but for the Lord; and the Lord for the body." "[18] Flee fornication. Every sin that a man doeth is without the body; but he that committeth fornication sinneth against his own body."

2 Corinthians 12:21 KJV: "And lest, when I come again, my God will humble me among you, and that I shall bewail many which have sinned already, and have not repented of the uncleanness and fornication and lasciviousness which they have committed."

Galatians 5:19 ASV: "Now the works of the flesh are manifest, which are these: fornication, uncleanness, lasciviousness,"

Ephesians 5:3 KJV: "But fornication, and all uncleanness, or covetousness, let it not be once named among you, as becometh saints;"

Colossians 3:5 KJV: "Mortify therefore your members which are upon the earth; fornication, uncleanness, inordinate affection, evil concupiscence, and covetousness, which is idolatry:"

1 Thessalonians 4:3 KJV: "For this is the will of God, even your sanctification, that ye should abstain from fornication:"

Revelation 2:20-21 KJV: "Notwithstanding I have a few things against thee, because thou sufferest that woman Jezebel, which calleth herself a prophetess, to teach and to seduce my servants to commit fornication, and to eat things sacrificed unto idols. [21] And I gave her space to repent of her fornication; and she repented not."

Revelation 9:20-21 ASV: "And the rest of mankind, who were not killed with these plagues, repented not of the works of their hands, that they should not worship demons, and the idols of gold, and of silver, and of brass, and of stone, and of wood; which can neither see, nor hear, nor walk: [21] and they repented not of their murders, nor of their sorceries, nor of their fornication, nor of their thefts."

This is why some modern Bible translations have preferred 'immorality' to fornication (see NIV, ESV, NLT, AMP, etc.). But in everyday usage of the word amongst Christians, fornication implies sexual intercourse involving an unmarried person (single) – male or female – with anyone else (married or unmarried). An unmarried co-habiting couple is said to be living in fornication for as long as they live like married couples, doing things married couples do sexually.

Before God, fornication is sin and will send perpetrators to hell fire, unless they repent. References for this include the following 2 Bible passages:

Revelation 21:8 ASV: "But for the fearful, and unbelieving, and abominable, and murderers, and fornicators, and sorcerers, and idolaters, and all liars, their part shall be in the lake that burneth with fire and brimstone; which is the second death." (Emphasis added).

Galatians 5:19-21 ASV: "Now the works of the flesh are manifest, which are these: fornication, uncleanness, lasciviousness, [20] idolatry, sorcery, enmities, strife, jealousies, wraths, factions, divisions, parties, [21] envyings, drunkenness, revellings, and such like; of which I forewarn you, even as I did forewarn you, that they who practise such things shall not inherit the kingdom of God." (Emphases added).

INCEST

Webster's Dictionary defines incest as sexual intercourse between two persons that are too close to marry. Such close relationships are described in the following Bible passages in Leviticus 18:6-18 NLT: "You must never have sexual relations with a close relative, for I am the Lord.

[7] "Do not violate your father by having sexual relations with your mother. She is your mother; you must not have sexual relations with her.

[8] "Do not have sexual relations with any of your father's wives, for this would violate your father.

[9] "Do not have sexual relations with <u>your sister or half-sister,</u> whether she is your father's daughter or your mother's daughter, whether she was born into your household or someone else's.

[10] "Do not have sexual relations with <u>your granddaughter,</u> whether she is your son's daughter or your daughter's daughter, for this would violate yourself.

[11] "Do not have sexual relations with <u>your stepsister,</u> the daughter of any of your father's wives, for she is your sister.

[12] "Do not have sexual relations with <u>your father's sister,</u> for she is your father's close relative.

[13] "Do not have sexual relations with <u>your mother's sister,</u> for she is your mother's close relative.

[14] "Do not violate <u>your uncle,</u> your father's brother, by having sexual relations with <u>his wife, for she is your aunt</u>.

[15] "Do not have sexual relations with <u>your daughter-in-law;</u> she is your son's wife, so you must not have sexual relations with her.

[16] "Do not have sexual relations with <u>your brother's wife,</u> for this would violate your brother.

[17] "Do not have sexual relations with <u>both a woman and her daughter</u>. And do not take <u>her granddaughter,</u> whether her son's daughter or her daughter's daughter, and have sexual relations with her. They are close relatives, and this would be a wicked act.

[18] "While your wife is living, do not marry her sister and have sexual relations with her, for they would be rivals." (Leviticus 18:6-18 NLT, emphases added throughout).

The word, incest does not appear in the English Bible but is described in Leviticus 18:6 quoted above - "[to] approach anyone who is near of kin to him, to uncover his nakedness" or "to approach any close relative to have sexual relations" as stated in the NIV Bible. Incest is a form of fornication and is a sin in the sight of God. That is why Exodus 18:6 ends in "I Am the LORD."

HARLOT (PROSTITUTE OR WHORE).

"There shall be no ritual harlot of the daughters of Israel, or a perverted one of the sons of Israel." (Deuteronomy 23:17 NKJV).

Prostitution is the practice of offering oneself indiscriminately for sexual activities for money or some religious rites. So, a harlot (whore or prostitute) is someone (usually a woman) that engages in the above described practices. These days people try to beautify the terminologies by calling such a person a call girl or sex worker. While whore and harlot are used in the KJV Bible, prostitute is the word in most modern translations including NIV, ESV, NLT, etc.

HOMOSEXUAL (GAY)

Webster's Dictionary defines homosexual as relating to, or involving sexual intercourse between members of the same sex. This word has been variously translated in the Word of God as effeminate, pervert, sodomite/sodomy, which Webster's Dictionary also defines as anal or oral sexual intercourse with a member of the same sex. Related to these also is lesbianism, which means female homosexuality. Look into the following two passages:

1 Corinthians 6:9-10 KJV: "Know ye not that the unrighteous shall not inherit the kingdom of God? Be not deceived: neither fornicators, nor idolaters, nor adulterers, nor effeminate, nor abusers of themselves with mankind, [10] Nor thieves, nor covetous, nor drunkards, nor revilers, nor extortioners, shall inherit the kingdom of God."

Deuteronomy 23:17 KJV: "There shall be no whore of the daughters of Israel, nor a sodomite of the sons of Israel."

HETEROSEXUAL

This word is the opposite of homosexual, and means, according to Webster's Dictionary, "of, relating to, or marked by, sexual intercourse between members of opposite sex."

LUST/TO LUST

Lust as a noun means strong desire for someone or something. As an infinitive, the Greek word ἐπιθυμῆσαι (epithymēsai) – Strong's 1937 – is translated as "to long for," "to covet," "to lust after," or "to set the heart upon." With regard to sex, Webster's defines lust as "intense or unbridled sexual desire" or "intense longing for [sex]." Although lust appears for a good desire in Luke 22:15, Philippians 1:23 and 1Thessalonians 2:17, wherever else it appears in the Bible, it is in a bad sense. Let's consider some Bible passages bearing lust:

Psalm 81:11-12 KJV: "But my people would not hearken to my voice; and Israel would none of me. [12] So I gave them up unto their own hearts' lust: and they walked in their own counsels."

Proverbs 6:24-25 KJV: "To keep thee from the evil woman, from the flattery of the tongue of a strange woman. [25] Lust not after her beauty in thine heart; neither let her take thee with her eyelids."

Matthew 5:27-28 KJV: "Ye have heard that it was said by them of old time, Thou shalt not commit adultery: [28] But I say unto you, That whosoever looketh on a woman to lust after her hath committed adultery with her already in his heart.

Romans 1:27-28 NKJV: "Likewise also the men, leaving the natural use of the woman, burned in their lust for one another, men with men committing what is shameful, and receiving in themselves the penalty of their error which was due. [28] And even as they did not like to retain God in their knowledge, God gave them over to a debased mind, to do those things which are not fitting;"

1 Corinthians 10:5-6 NKJV: "But with most of them God was not well pleased, for their bodies were scattered in the wilderness. [6] Now these things became our examples, to the intent that we should not lust after evil things as they also lusted.

James 1:14-15 NKJV: "But every man is tempted, when he is drawn away of his own lust, and enticed. [15] Then when lust hath conceived, it bringeth forth sin: and sin, when it is finished, bringeth forth death."

James 4:1-2 NKJV: "Where do wars and fights come from among you? Do they not come from your desires for pleasure that war in your members? [2] You lust and do not have. You murder and covet and cannot obtain. You fight and war. "

2 Peter 1:2-4 NKJV: "Grace and peace be multiplied to you in the knowledge of God and of Jesus our Lord, [3] as His divine power has given to us all things that pertain to life and godliness, through the knowledge of Him who called us by glory and virtue, [4] by which have been given to us exceedingly great and precious promises, that through these you may be partakers of the divine nature, having escaped the corruption that is in the world through lust."

1 John 2:16-17 NKJV: "For all that is in the world—the lust of the flesh, the lust of the eyes, and the pride of life—is not of the Father but is of the world. ¹⁷ And the world is passing away, and the lust of it; but he who does the will of God abides forever."

1 Peter 4:1-2 NKJV: "Therefore, since Christ suffered for us in the flesh, arm yourselves also with the same mind, for he who has suffered in the flesh has ceased from sin, ² that he no longer should live the rest of his time in the flesh for the lusts of men, but for the will of God."

RAPE.

In our context, an on-line dictionary defines rape as "unlawful sexual intercourse or any other sexual penetration of the vagina, anus, or mouth of another person, with or without force, by a sex organ, other body part, or foreign object, without the consent of the person subjected to such penetration."[99]

The perpetrator of this crime usually has some power or weapon with which to intimidate the victim such as a gun, knife/dagger, office superiority or position.

Before the almighty God rape is a sin punishable by death if the woman is engaged for marriage as we see in Deuteronomy 22:25 NIV: "But if out in the country a man happens to meet a young woman pledged to be married and rapes her, only the man who has done this shall die."

---

[99] Rape. https://www.dictionary.com/browse/rape February 18, 2023

But the law was a bit lenient to one who raped a virgin:

Deuteronomy 22:28-29 NIV: "If a man happens to meet a virgin who is not pledged to be married and rapes her and they are discovered, [29] he shall pay her father fifty shekels of silver. He must marry the young woman, for he has violated her. He can never divorce her as long as he lives."

5.2 MODES OF ACCESS TO SEX

- Genuine
- Crooked

An adage says that it takes two to tangle. Every sexual act involves two people - a man and a woman, or a boy and a girl. However, there are abnormal instances whereby two persons of the same sex are involved - specifically two ladies (lesbianism), or more commonly two men, i.e., sodomy or homosexuality. Lesbianism is also a form of homosexuality.

The important thing here is that any of the sexual acts can only occur in either of two ways: Genuinely or crookedly.

Genuine access to sex implies the situation whereby the two persons involved give mutual consent to the act. Of course, one party may resist participating for a while and afterwards give in due to pressure of some sort from the other party. Because sexual intercourse is meant for married persons, there is, therefore, genuine access to lawful sex and genuine access to illicit or unlawful sex.

Genuine access to lawful sex implies the consenting of husband and wife at any time. Any man and woman accepting to go into marriage have automatically consented to involve themselves in sexual intercourse until death parts them. It is natural, godly and scriptural. There have been a couple of unhealthy and unnecessary debates regarding sex in marriage, which are not subject of this book. But rape should not be found in the dictionary of a married couple; else 'cheating' may get dangerously introduced into that marriage.

On the other hand, genuine access to illicit sex applies to the consenting two persons that are not husband and wife. That is sexual immorality, adultery, fornication or any other name by which such an act is known.

Crooked access to sex is the total exclusion of consent. When a man takes to bed a girl that is young enough to be his daughter or granddaughter, except they are married, it is a crooked access to sex. There abound lots of cases of men drugging ladies with the intention of having sexual intercourse with them as the ladies passed out or slept and were unable to resist or protest. This is rape!

Some ladies are forced into sexual intercourse at gun point or "knife point." It is not as if only men commit this crime of rape.

Some women have been reported to have solicited sex from boys young enough to be their sons or grandsons, especially where, like their type of men, they (the women) are in a position to determine or influence the victim's future – for example, a teacher and his/her student or pupil; a manager and his/her employee or potential employee that must yield to be promoted or offered a certain job. These are all crooked means of acquiring sexual intercourse, and are condemnable.

5.3 GOOD APPLICATION OF SEX.

When God created man, He made them male and female, giving them the ability to procreate and the responsibility of replenishing the earth. To perform this function, God blessed them to "be fruitful and multiply" (Genesis 1:28). The responsibility requires the meeting at sex of the man and his female counterpart called woman. In fact, the Bible says that Adam knew Eve his wife; and she conceived and bore Cain (Genesis 4:1). Subsequently, the teaming population of the world that is now in billions of people has been achieved by men and women having sexual intercourse. With only one exception[100] - Jesus Christ – everyone that has

---

[100] Luke 1:30-35 New King James Version: "Then the angel said to her, "Do not be afraid, Mary, for you have found favor with God. [31] And behold, you will conceive in your womb and bring forth a Son, and shall call His name Jesus. [32] He will be great, and will be called the Son of the Highest; and the Lord God will give Him the throne of His father David. [33] And He

passed through, or lives on, this earth resulted from the sexual act of one man and one woman. So, sex has been useful in carrying out God's assignment to mankind to procreate to fill and replenish the earth.

Sex helps to strengthen the love of a man and his wife. Note Apostle Paul on a man and his wife: "So husbands ought to love their own wives as their own bodies; he who loves his wife loves himself. [29] For no one ever hated his own flesh, but nourishes and cherishes it, just as the Lord does the church." (Ephesians 5:28-29 NKJV). The process of nourishing and cherishing includes sex in love. Ellicott's Commentary for English Readers on Ephesians 5:29 says, "There are two parts of the natural care for our own bodies; first, "to nourish" . . . and then "to cherish" (literally, to keep them warm), to provide all they need for health, and comfort, and life. In all that corresponds to both, the husband is to show love to the wife, not only as a self, but as a weaker self, for whom he is bound to think and to act."[101]

---

will reign over the house of Jacob forever, and of His kingdom there will be no end."

[34] Then Mary said to the angel, "How can this be, since I do not know a man?"

[35] And the angel answered and said to her, "*The* Holy Spirit will come upon you, and the power of the Highest will overshadow you; therefore, also, that Holy One who is to be born will be called the Son of God."

[101]   https://biblehub.com/commentaries/ellicott/ephesians/5.htm
February 19, 2023.

The role of sex in marriage cannot be over-emphasized. That's why the apostle Paul cautions that husband and wife do not stay apart for a long time, so that they do not fall into temptation (1Corinthians 7:5). [102] However, a long time is relative - not definite, and may vary from one couple to another.

Medical Science also tends to have proven that there are several health benefits in sexual intercourse and sexual relations. Some of such health and psychological benefits are listed below. But first, let's consider the description of healthy sex life:

- It should be within the ambits of the law – precisely marriage: husband and wife.

- The couple should both consent to the act.

- In the absence of any known sexually transmitted disease (STD) in either.

- It must not be during the woman's monthly period. In Leviticus 18:19 we read: "'Do not approach a woman to have sexual relations during the uncleanness of her monthly period." (NIV).

- In an atmosphere devoid of anxiety and fear.

---

[102] When a person has had a sexual intercourse experience, especially if it is not by rape, the urge for it comes back often. That's why when a married couple stay apart for a 'long time' the tendency or temptation arises to give in, with little persuasion or pressure, to a stranger to the marriage. And one good sex experience attracts another, to the extent that the new pair may become regular sex partners.

- Also, in an atmosphere devoid of abuse, which, of course, should not be mentioned in a marriage – more so a Christian one.

BENEFITS OF HEALTHY SEX LIFE[103]

Most often, considerations of sexual intercourse and sexual relations are mainly for procreation and pleasure without thoughts of possible health benefits thereof. It is

heartwarming to note that healthy sex life – including penile-vaginal-insertion (PVI) in marriage – offers such health benefits as follows: -

1. Helping to improve the woman's bladder control and urinary incontinence as sex impacts pelvic muscles.
2. It helps to keep and boost the immunity system especially for them that engage in it at least one or two times a week.
3. It helps with heart health in the woman – lowering risk of heart attack. It helps to lower blood pressure.
4. It can act or count as exercise at which some calories can be burnt.

---

[103] Cleveland Clinic. 5 Benefits of a Healthy Sex Life. https://health.clevelandclinic.org/benefits-of-sex/ February 25, 2023.

Sexual Health. "What are the Potential Benefits of Having Sex Every Day." https://www.healthline.com/health/healthy-sex/sex-daily February 25, 2023.

5. It lessens pains. It is said that research shows that sex does help to reduce pains in people who have migraine or headaches.

6. Sex relieves stress and anxiety, and helps to improve quality of sleep.

7. It helps to reduce the risk of prostate cancer.

8. It can put you in a good mood.

9. Lowers the risk of pre-eclampsia (a serious pregnancy complication that is capable of causing swollen legs and arms, headaches, nausea and seizures).

10. It helps to keep husband and wife closer and preserve marriage.

11. It boosts libido, and improves sexual function.

5.4 ABUSES OF SEX

Like was done in earlier subjects, in this we shall consider instances of sex abuse in Old Testament Bible times, New Testament times and contemporary times. Just as all other things in life, including money and power, have good uses or applications and abuses, sex has great benefits and uses, and people who have abused it. Of course, it is still abused these days. Sex abuse may be of a spouse (domestic violence-related), a child, a person with developmental disabilities, an unprotected elderly person, a person in dire financial need (poverty-stricken) or in need of employment, or a person whose progress depends on the abuser. As a reminder, abuse is wrong use, bad application, illegal use, misuse, improper use, of something or someone – in this case, of sex. Sex abuse, including rape and all other forms of sexual sin, is a problem that has plagued the world for ages.

The story of the end of Adonijah, the second son of King David of Israel, is a very good example of a man having to die because of lust for power as a remote cause, and a woman as immediate cause. The stories are found in 1Kings 1:5-8; 49-53 and 2:13-27. In summary, when King David had grown old Adonijah declared himself king in place of his father thereby exalting himself because he lusted for power. When it was reported to King David, the king instructed that Solomon be crowned and enthroned, and all Israel that had wrongly supported Adonijah dispersed. Then Adonijah sought refuge in the tabernacle. It was told to Solomon and Solomon forgave him, and asked him to go home and be of good behavior.

Shortly afterwards, trying to claim a right, Adonijah sent a request through Bathsheba (Solomon's mother) to the young King Solomon to release to him the virgin Shunamite woman who took care of King David their father, to become his (Adonijah's) wife (1Kings 2:15-17). This request angered Solomon. He then swore that Adonijah would pay with his life for such a demand, and had Adonijah executed (1 Kings 2:22-25). Perhaps Solomon might have left Adonijah alive after forgiving him for taking power that was not given him. But he added insult to injury by lusting after their father's woman, forgetting or ignoring that the one that became king inherited the late king.

In 1Corinthians 5:1 (NKJV) we read, "It is actually reported that there is sexual immorality among you, and such sexual immorality as is not even named among the Gentiles—that a man has his father's wife!" Apart from this revelation to the apostle Paul there doesn't appear to be any direct incident of sexual abuse in the New Testament Bible.

Sometime in the 1990s, a Computer Technology undergraduate girl, about twenty years of age made a confession: she said that she grew up in the army barracks with her father, who was an army officer. A neighbor who was a soldier sexually abused her from when she was thirteen years old, such that she had sex with him every day. That resulted in the problem that even when she was no longer close to the soldier, she desired to make love every day, and it did not matter to her with whom – not for money or anything else, but to satisfy the urge. Incessant urge for sex had become some kind of sickness for her!

Rape or sexual violence has become a common crime all over the world. Women and girls are mostly the vulnerable victims. Many rapists succeeded in times past in getting away with their nefarious crimes especially because it was impossible for the victim to produce witnesses to support her to prove her case. In recent times most rape incidents go with murder – most of the raped victims are subsequently murdered in order to cover the footprints of the criminal. Rape is a wicked and wrong way to obtain sexual satisfaction.

Going by RAINN[104] Statistics, it is on record that "As of 1998, an estimated 17.7 million American women had been victims of attempted or completed rape." Also as of the same year, "2.78 million men in the U.S. had been victims of attempted or completed rape."[105]

Apart from rape, some other ways sex becomes abusive or abused are[106]: -

1. Always asking to be told everything about previous sexual partners, and using the information to call the respondent

---

[104] RAINN is America's largest anti-sexual violence organization.

[105]"VICTIMS OF SEXUAL VIOLENCE: STATISTICS."
https://www.rainn.org/statistics/victims-sexual-violence February 28,2023. Source: 5. National Institute of Justice & Centers for Disease Control & Prevention, Prevalence, Incidence and Consequences of Violence Against Women Survey (1998). *(Statistic presents information on the total number of male and female victims in the United States, using a study from 1998.*

[106] PsychCentral. "7 WAYS A PERSON CAN BE ABUSED."
https://psychcentral.com/pro/exhausted-woman/2015/08/7-ways-a-person-can-be-abused#1 February 28, 2023

names. Frequently accusing that partner of being attracted to others, flirting, flaunting her body, and cheating.

2. Coercing the target (or partner) into having sex by using harassment, guilt, shame, blame, or rage, nagging and insulting the target until she/he concedes.

3. Bullying into doing uncomfortable sexual acts by threatening infidelity by dangling the possibility of another person in the relationship.

4. Completely withdrawing all sex from the relation ship; any request for sex is met with ridicule, rants about performance, and excessive excuses for abstinence.

5. Mild sadistic sex performance which may include immobilizing the target through drugs or alcohol, administering pain (whipping) during sex, confining target to a cage, typing up, blindfolding, or clamping sexual organs.

6. Severe sadistic sex performance which could lead to death, including "physical beatings, choking, psycho-logical torture, burning, cutting, stabbing, vampirism, and murder before, during or after sex."

7. Uncontrollable sex drive – turning oneself into a sex maniac.

8. Making sex a condition for love.

9. Sex as an obligation, thereby becoming just

mechanical.

10. In an exploitative manner rather than respectful and mutually satisfying.

11. Insisting on having sex even when it is unsafe, especially for the victim.

5.5 THE ROLE OF SEX IN THE FALL OF PEOPLE

Sex destroys careers, relationships and lives. It brings down kings and leaders, and causes people to lose respect. It is necessary to look back in History to note that there were highly placed persons that fell from (grace) their lofty positions (to grass) due to sex and/or sex-related actions. In the Old Testament Bible, we shall consider Samson, David and Solomon.

SAMSON

Samson was the last of Israel's thirteen judges recorded in the Book of Judges. After him was Eli before Samuel, the last judge before the establishment of the monarchy in Israel. While the stories of Eli and Samuel are in the first book of Samuel, Samson's story is in Judges chapters 13 to 16. During those days the Angel of the LORD appeared physically to Samson's mother – barren wife of Manoa of Zorah, and promised her a nazarite son, to be dedicated to God and would "begin the deliverance of Israel from the Philistines." Samson was to be a great man, separated to God (Judges 13:1-3). He was born and endowed with power as the Spirit of the LORD was on him. He killed a lion with his bare hands. With the jawbone of a donkey, he killed a thousand Philistine men (Judges 15:15). Before his birth, God had for forty years delivered Israel into the hands of the Philistines, Israel's greatest enemy, as punishment for Israel's sin.

Samson fell in love with a Philistine harlot named Delilah. The lords of the Philistines promised Delilah large sums of money to entice Samson to reveal his source of strength so that they could kill him (Judges 16:1-4 NKJV). Delilah pestered and pressured Samson every day for a long time, "so that his soul was vexed to death, [17] that he told her all his heart, and said to her, "No razor has ever come upon my head, for I have been a Nazirite to God from my mother's womb. If I am shaven, then my strength will leave me, and I shall become weak, and be like any other man." (Judges 16:15-17 NKJV).

Delilah arranged to have Samson shaven, rendering him powerless. The Philistines gouged out his eyes, but did not kill him. The people rejoiced, saying, "Our god has delivered into our hands our enemy, The destroyer of our land, And the one who multiplied our dead." (Judges 16: 24 NKJV).

His hair began to grow again and his strength began to be restored. About 3,000 Philistines were gathered to praise their god and they got Samson from   prison   to entertain them. He prayed, "O Lord God, remember me, I pray! Strengthen me, I pray, just this once, O God, that I may with one blow take vengeance on the Philistines for my two eyes!" (Judges 16:28). Samson held the two main pillars of the temple and pulled them down, killing all the over 3,000 Philistines present, thereby destroying more people in his death than in his lifetime.

Although we naturally condemn Samson for letting out his secret to a woman prostitute which caused his life to be cut short, our condemnation should be with some caution because, while his parents were not pleased that he was going down to uncircumcised Philistines for a wife, they "did not know that it was of the Lord—that He was seeking an occasion to move against the Philistines. For at that time the Philistines had dominion over Israel." (Judges 14:4 NKJV). No wonder Samson appeared in the roll call of the heroes of faith in Hebrews 11:23-33.

KING DAVID

King David was the second king of Israel. At the time that kings went to war, King David sent his soldiers to fight but stayed back at home in Jerusalem. One evening he was walking around on the roof of his palace, he saw a naked woman bathing at her house. She looked to him very beautiful. ". . . and David sent someone to find out about her. The man said, "She is Bathsheba, the daughter of Eliam and the wife of Uriah the Hittite." [4] Then David sent messengers to get her. She came to him, and he slept with her.

(Now she was purifying herself from her monthly uncleanness.)
Then she went back home. [5] The woman conceived and sent word
to David, saying, "I am pregnant." (2Samuel 11:3-5 NIV). Before
continuing the story, note the following points so far: -

i) When he saw a naked woman at her home and got attracted to
her, he made enquiries and was told who she was – Bathsheba,
Uriah's wife;

ii) That did not stop him. He summoned her with the power of his
office as king. There was no indication that she was more
beautiful than his wives.

iii) The woman was "purifying herself from her monthly
period" when no man should go into her; but it did not deter the
king.

Seeing that Bathsheba had become pregnant, in an attempt to
cover his tracks, he plotted and got Uriah killed, and took over the
woman as his wife, for which God disciplined David. This was an
abuse of power and of sex!

David was the greatest king Israel had, and he is always said to be
a man after God's own heart, yet his fame and good deeds may
hardly be told without any mention of this collapse of his
reputation caused by sexual immorality and its consequences for
him.

ABNER

Abner was King Saul's army commander. It was not hidden that Saul was seeking for a long time to kill David. After the death of Saul in a war with the Philistines, Abner became a powerful leader of the house of Saul and continued in the war against the house of David.

One day, the surviving son of Saul by the name Ishbosheth accused Abner of sleeping with his father's concubine, Rizpah. Abner was highly infuriated and asked whether, after all he had done for his father, Saul, and his family, finding fault in his having that woman was his reward. And Abner boasted, "May God strike me and even kill me if I don't do everything I can to help David get what the Lord has promised him! [10] I'm going to take Saul's kingdom and give it to David. I will establish the throne of David over Israel as well as Judah, all the way from Dan in the north to Beersheba in the south." (2Samuel 3:9-11 NLT). Abner made good his threat, persuaded the elders of the rest of Israel and went to Hebron to inform David that all the people of Israel and Benjamin had agreed to support him. Abner thereby helped to get all Israel under the kingship of David. But shortly afterwards, Joab, David's army commander killed Abner.

Though it was the will and plan of God for David to rule over Israel, it probably would not have come that easy if not for

Abner's sexual relationship with Saul's concubine, which Saul's son protested.

ADONIJAH

Adonijah was the second son of King David – after Absalom, who died in the process of usurping his father's throne. He became David's eldest surviving son. As King David became very old, Adonijah boasted to make himself king (1Kings 1:5) and worked towards it. He got some of his father's officials to assist him including Joab (the army commander) and Abiathar, the priest; Adonijah invited all his brothers—the other sons of King David except Solomon —and all the royal officials of Judah to make sacrifices.

When David realized what went on by information from Bathsheba (Solomon's mother), King David ordered Zadok the priest, Nathan the prophet, and Benaiah son of Jehoiada to take Solomon and anoint him king over Israel. They were to blow the ram's horn and shout, 'Long live King Solomon!' This brought an end to Adonijah's shot at the throne as all his guests jumped up in panic from the banquet table and quickly scattered. King Solomon promised to spare Adonijah's life if he proved himself loyal.

One day Adonijah went to Bathsheba asking her to help him to request a favor from the king: "As you know, the kingdom was rightfully mine; all Israel wanted me to be the next king. But the tables were turned, and the kingdom went to my brother instead; for that is the way the Lord wanted it." ". . . Ask him to let me marry Abishag, the girl from Shunem" (1Kings 2:15, 17). Abishag was the very beautiful girl, who looked after King David and took care of him in his old age. But the king had no sexual relations with her.

This request from Adonijah became the straw that broke the camel's back. Read Solomons' reasoning, resolve and action: "Then King Solomon made a vow before the Lord: "May God strike me and even kill me if Adonijah has not sealed his fate with this request. [24] The Lord has confirmed me and placed me on the throne of my father, David; he has established my dynasty as he promised. So as surely as the Lord lives, Adonijah will die this very day!" [25] So King Solomon ordered Benaiah son of Jehoiada to execute him, and Adonijah was put to death." (1Kings 2:23-25 NLT). It may be right to conclude that both lust for power and desire for a woman caused Adonijah's early death.

KING SOLOMON

Solomon was the successor of King David of Israel. God blessed Solomon with "a wise and understanding heart," riches and honor, and a promise that, "If you walk in My ways and keep My statutes and commands just as your father David did, I will give you a long life." (1Kings 3:10-14). And God, being ever faithful to His word, fulfilled His promise to Solomon.

"King Solomon, however, loved many foreign women besides Pharaoh's daughter—Moabites,Ammonites, Edomites, Sidonians and Hittites. [2] They were from nations about which the Lord had told the Israelites, "You must not intermarry with them, because they will surely turn your hearts after their gods." Nevertheless, Solomon held fast to them in love. [3] He had seven hundred wives of royal birth and three hundred concubines, and his wives led him astray." (1Kings 11:1-3 NIV). He tried to please everyone of the wives to the displeasure of God by adopting all the gods that each of the wives brought from her country, and he built a shrine or altar for each of such gods. Solomon's life was turned away from God to idolatry. In spite of his great wisdom, he failed God, and God tore the kingdom of Israel away from him to Jeroboam his servant, leaving only 1/6 (one-sixth) of the kingdom of twelve tribes to Rehoboam, Solomon's son and successor.

In the early 1960s, the headmaster of my elementary school was relieved of his job for putting a pupil in his class in family way. The school was founded and run by a Christian Mission that would not entertain such immoral practice.

A one-time pastor of a fast-growing Church in one of the suburbs of Lagos was asked to resign for indulging in extra marital relations in the church. That job was the pastor's first post-seminary job. And he lost it because of sex-related issues. For a couple of years, he could not get another church to pastor.

Many big political figures in the United States had relationships during their youthful years with young ladies, some of who did not make noise about what happened then. Some of the ladies were playfully touched, kissed, hugged or, on the worst part, groped or taken to bed. But in recent times, as such men began to be known in political circles, and with the growth of the Me-Too-Movement, what these men did with the women (young ladies or girls then) began to hunt the men. The women, especially if they belonged to a different party, came out to accuse the men of taking advantage of them several years ago; the intention of that is to paint the men as unfit for public office.

It sounds incredible that a sitting president of the most powerful nation in the world was abased and humiliated because of sex-related issues! Humiliation, not for losing a battle or war against another nation or failing in some political maneuvers. But because of sex that involved a pretty, young woman, young enough to be his daughter. William Jefferson Clinton (a.k.a. Bill Clinton) served as the 42nd president of the USA from 1993 to 2001. During his second term, he was impeached on December 19, 1998, by the House of Representatives for perjury and obstruction of justice. "Impeachment proceedings were based on allegations that Clinton had illegally lied about, and covered up, his relationship with 22-year-old White House intern (and later Department of Defense) employee Monica Lewinsky"

[107] Although Clinton was not impeached for his affairs with the lady, yet sexual relation was the originator of the perjury and obstruction of justice.

This case of Bill Clinton's impeachment came to the fore again during the first and second impeachment processes of former President Donald John Trump, 45th President of the USA in 2019, being the third US president ever impeached in the over 240 years history of the nation, the first being Andrew Johnson, 17th president (1870 – 1875).

During the proceedings of Trump's impeachment, the news media extensively discussed passed impeachments, and none of such discussions omitted reference to Bill Clinton's impeachment, notwithstanding that Trump's case was not sex-related. Worse still, on January 5, 2020, CNN ran a television documentary of the impeachment trial of Bill Clinton – still alive and kicking just like the (then) young lady that was involved in the case, unlike President Andrew Johnson (1808 to 1875) who had long died and felt no pinch of his name mentioned as many times as possible.

Effectively, former President Bill Clinton was not impeached for having sex with Monica Lewinsky (if he did), but for lying under oath, which would have never arisen without an illicit or suspicious closeness to a lady outside his marriage. Extramarital

---

[107] Bill Clinton. https://en.wikipedia.org/wiki/Bill_Clinton March 7, 2023.

sexual relationship got him into trouble, denting his past image and records. Though he completed his second term of presidency because the Senate did not agree to remove him from office, yet his name has gone down in history of USA Presidency forever as having been impeached. Anytime impeachment is mentioned or discussed Bill Clinton will be mentioned – not for the good things he achieved as president in over ninety-eight percent of his eight years term, but for impeachment which resulted from a relationship that lasted an infinitesimal fraction of the total time, bringing shame and embarrassment to himself, and his family. Thanks to God for his "for-better-for-worse" wife, Hilary Clinton who stood by him till the end. Sex brings down powerful men!

FORMER PRESIDENT DONALD TRUMP

The 45th president of the USA, Mr. Donald J. Trump was on March 30, 2023, indicted by a Manhattan, New York grand jury for his role in a scandal arising from hush money payments made to adult film actress by the name Stormy Daniels, to shut her mouth in view of the 2016 presidential election. By this, Donald Trump became the first ex-president of the USA ever criminally indicted and arraigned in a Manhattan courtroom. Meanwhile, it is said that Trump's offense was not just payment of hush money, but that business records were falsified to cover the real offense close to his presidential election. What concerns us here is that a former topmost (number one) man in America was indicted for an issue that originated from a sexual affair.

The Me-too-movement has emboldened many women who came out recently to openly accuse some US presidential aspirants for past sexual relationships or harassment. Some of such men were accused of rape and, or groping, and forcing them to sign non-disclosure agreement, being such women's employers. But not much was achieved by the women for want of evidence or witnesses, often making it difficult to prove that the sexual relations were not consensual, or ever happened. Not much could be done to such accused men.

PRINCE CHARLES OF THE UNITED KINGDOM

The British Monarchy has not gone without its share of disgrace arising from matters relating to illegal sex. The heir apparent[108] to the throne of the United Kingdom, Prince Charles[109] was said to have been involved with his divorced pre-marriage lover while still married to Princess Diana. That became the immediate cause of the break-up of the marriage and eventual early death of the young woman, Diana in a car crash in France. The prince later got

---

[108] At the time of writing this part of this book, Queen Elizabeth II was still alive, and King Charles III (now) was still a prince and the heir apparent.

[109] Prince Charles was crowned King Charles III on May 6, 2023, before this book was first published in 2025.

remarried to that his lover, Camilla Parker-Bowles in 2005, in spite of the people's objection. That left a dent on the image and name of the prince, especially as he would become head of the Church of England when crowned king of the United Kingdom.

PRINCE ANDREW OF THE UNITED KINGDOM

Worse still is the case of sex assault involving Prince Charles's younger brother, Prince Andrew, who was facing court actions, (even internationally), and stripped of his royal and military titles. In settling the case out-of-court, CNN reported as follows: "Prince Andrew has paid a settlement to sexual abuse accuser Virginia Giuffre, according to her attorney, and a US district judge agreed Tuesday to dismiss her lawsuit against the Duke of York. "The payment was received, the settlement we announced last month has been completed. We are obviously very pleased with the outcome," Giuffre attorney David Boies told CNN.[110]

"Virginia Giuffre v. Prince Andrew" was the lawsuit filed in August 2021 in New York, USA by Virginia L. Giuffre against Prince Andrew, Duke of York and the second son of Queen Elizabeth II. The suit was "filed under New York's Child Victims Act, alleged that she was forced to have several sexual encounters with Andrew in the early 2000s at the age of 17, after being sex

---

[110] "Prince Andrew has paid settlement to Virginia Giuffre, according to her attorney." https://www.cnn.com/2022/03/08/us/prince-andrew-virginia-giuffre-settlement/index.html March 12, 2023

trafficked by the American financier and convicted sex offender Jeffrey Epstein."[111]

With the 'Me-too-movement' making waves in America, more and more men have gotten into trouble because of 'irresponsible sex moves,' which have been termed sexual harassment. Several men have either had to resign their offices or been moved due to related scandals.

A COMPANY VICE PRESIDENT

A one-time promising vice president (V.P.) of a pharmaceutical manufacturing corporation that I am familiar with lost his job unexpectedly due to sex-related issues. His widowed personal assistant desired to bear children, and tactfully talked the man into making concerted efforts to help her get pregnant. The woman and her boss met after office hours in her house as they both monitored her 'fertile period.' That relationship continued for about two years without the expected success. The man began to be concerned that the relationship was deepening beyond expectation and needed to terminate it. But before he did, he observed that the President/CEO had begun to put up some weird attitudes towards

---

[111] Wikipedia: *"Virginia Giuffre v. Prince Andrew"* https://en.wikipedia.org/wiki/Virginia_Giuffre_v._Prince_An drew#:~:text=Prince%20Andrew%20allegations-, June 19, 2025.

him – getting irritated at nearly every action and inaction of the V.P. The VP felt it was getting too much and went to the chairman of the corporation to complain.

The chairman told the VP that the Board of Directors had decided to fire him and asked the CEO to take the action. But because this man had not committed any visible offense that was public knowledge, for which he should be fired, and because of his popularity in the company, the CEO was reluctant to give such information to the VP and rather asked the chairman to do the dirty job. It remained between both of them for several weeks. The chairman also insisted that another V.P. must be relieved of her job if the man must go. Having revealed that secret, the chairman asked the V.P. to see the president for details, who was then comfortable to pass the Board's decision to him. Meanwhile, neither the chairman nor the president told the man the true reason for demanding his retirement. Rather it was taken as part of the on-going reorganization.

About eleven years later, at a Christian gathering far away from home, the preacher, who had the spiritual gift of prophecy, revealed that there was a man present at that meeting, who lost his job as a director in a pharmaceutical company due to sexual relationships with his personal assistant (PA). The preacher described the erstwhile VP's family background – including his parents' family size – and a few other things that helped the VP to recognize without any doubt that he was the one in the picture. It was there and then that it became clear to the ex-VP that it was sex that pulled him down. What he thought was a secret (even to his wife) was known to God, and God delivered to him disciplinary action graciously.

Naturally, it is a man that chases a woman for a relationship, and no matter how a woman looks there must be a man somewhere that gets attracted to her. This is why men who do not strongly and effectively control their instincts and emotions go ahead to any woman that attracts them, and in America today a woman who turns down a man's advances is likely to complain that the man has sexually harassed her. And anything negative might arise from that.

But there are many instances too of women who subtly chase men. If a man complains of sexual harassment from a woman, it often sounds incredible. People were previously of the opinion that it is married women whose husbands do not satisfy financially, who go after other men. But experience has shown that some wives of wealthy men also flirt with other men, especially younger men, just for additional sexual satisfaction. Such women end up spending lots of their money on the men, rather than receive. So, it is not as if only men have been implicated or disgraced for wrongful sex escapades.

MARY KAY

A popular example of women who were disgraced for sexually abusing men is Mary Katherine Letourneau ("Mary Kay" Fualaau) (nee Schmitz).[112] Mary Kay was an American teacher. She in 1997 pleaded guilty to two counts of felony second degree rape of a twelve-year old boy at the time of their first sexual relations, and she was his sixth-grade class teacher in a school in Washington.

While waiting for sentencing by the court, she gave birth to the boy's first child. The state sought a seven-and-a-half-year prison sentence, but she reached a plea deal calling for six months in jail, with three months suspended, and to have no contact with the boy for life. The case received national and international attention.

Not long after Mary Kay had completed three months in jail, the police caught her in a car with the boy. Then a judge revoked her plea agreement and reinstated the prison sentence for the maximum sentence allowed by law - seven and a half years. Eight months after returning to prison, she gave birth to the boy's second child. She was imprisoned from 1998 to 2004 after which she got married to the young man in 2005 and they remained married for fourteen years until they separated in 2019. Mary died an ex-convict in 2020. Sex with a minor!

----

[112] Wikipedia. MARY KAY LETOURNEAU.
https://en.wikipedia.org/wiki/Mary_Kay_Letourneau MARCH 22, 2023.

Between 1776 and 2022 (both years inclusive) about 98 federal elected politicians and officials appointed with the consent of the US Senate have been involved in sex scandals which caused them to have apologized or lost their offices as a consequence (e.g. by resigning, being defeated, or deciding not to run again). Of course, some of the politicians made efforts to deny the accusation. The long list of politicians including their names and brief descriptions of their involvements in Wikipedia under the title "List of federal political sex scandals in the United States"[113] is summarized below by years:

SER. NO.	FROM YEAR	TO YEAR	NO. OF POLITICIANS
1	1776	1899	12
2	1900	1969	9
3	1970	1979	7
4	1980	1989	11
5	1990	1999	15
6	2000	2009	17
7	2010	2019	22
8	2020	2022	5

---

[113] LIST OF FEDERAL POLITICAL SEX SCANDALS IN THE UNITED STATES
https://en.wikipedia.org/wiki/List_of_federal_political_sex_scandals_in_the_United_States#2010%E2%80%932019 March 25, 2023.

5.6 BIBLE TEACHINGS ABOUT SEXUAL RELATIONS

The Holy Bible is a collection of sixty-six books, written by about forty men inspired by the Holy Spirit, over a period of about two thousand years, across many countries of the world. The Bible is in two parts – the Old Testament and New Testament.

The Old Testament consists of thirty-nine books (Genesis to Malachi). The New Testament comprises twenty-seven books (Matthew to Revelation). For persons not familiar with it, the Bible contains books of History, Literature, Law, Prophecies, Philosophy, Architecture, etc.

As old as it is, the Bible addresses, and provides solutions to, issues of this 21st Century and beyond from nearly every discipline just as it did in the first Century A.D... The reason is that it is in the inspired word of GOD. Of itself the Bible says, "All Scripture is inspired by God and is useful to teach us what is true and to make us realize what is wrong in our lives. It corrects us when we are wrong and teaches us to do what is right. [17] God uses it to prepare and equip his people to do every good work." (2 Timothy 3:16-17 NLT).

It is only on the strength of this inspiration that the teachings and regulations of the Bible about sex are confidently reproduced below. Though some people feel the laws and teachings of the Bible are old fashioned, outdated or not modern, following them should help the wise person to lead a life free from the kind of sexual entanglements that lead to trouble and/or destruction.

Exodus 22:19 NKJV "Whoever lies with an animal shall surely be put to death."

Leviticus 18:6-23 NKJV 'None of you shall approach anyone who is near of kin to him, to uncover his nakedness: I am the Lord. [7] The nakedness of your father or the nakedness of your mother you shall not uncover. She is your mother; you shall not uncover her nakedness. [8] The nakedness of your father's wife you shall not uncover; it is your father's nakedness. [9] The nakedness of your sister, the daughter of your father, or the daughter of your mother, whether born at home or elsewhere, their nakedness you shall not uncover. [10] The nakedness of your son's daughter or your daughter's daughter, their nakedness you shall not uncover; for theirs is your own nakedness. [11] The nakedness of your father's wife's daughter, begotten by your father—she is your sister—you shall not uncover her nakedness. [12] You shall not uncover the nakedness of your father's sister; she is near of kin to your father. [13] You shall not uncover the nakedness of your mother's sister, for she is near of kin to your mother. [14] You shall not uncover the nakedness of your father's brother. You shall not approach his wife; she is your aunt. [15] You shall not uncover the nakedness of your daughter-in-law—she is your son's wife—you shall not uncover her nakedness. [16] You shall not uncover the nakedness of your brother's wife; it is your brother's nakedness. [17] You shall not uncover the nakedness of a woman and her daughter, nor shall you take her son's daughter or her daughter's daughter, to uncover her nakedness. They are near of kin to her. It is wickedness. [18] Nor shall you take a woman as a rival to her sister, to uncover her nakedness while the other is alive.

[19] 'Also you shall not approach a woman to uncover her nakedness as long as she is in her customary impurity.

[20] Moreover you shall not lie carnally with your neighbor's wife, to defile yourself with her. [21] And you shall not let any of your descendants pass through the fire to Molech, nor shall you profane the name of your God: I am the Lord. [22] You shall not lie with a male as with a woman. It is an abomination. [23] Nor shall you mate with any animal, to defile yourself with it. Nor shall any woman stand before an animal to mate with it. It is perversion."

Leviticus 20:10, 16, 19 NKJV 'The man who commits adultery with another man's wife, he who commits adultery with his neighbor's wife, the adulterer and the adulteress, shall surely be put to death.

[16] If a woman approaches any animal and mates with it, you shall kill the woman and the animal. They shall surely be put to death. Their blood is upon them.

[19] 'You shall not uncover the nakedness of your mother's sister nor of your father's sister, for that would uncover his near of kin. They shall bear their guilt."

Deuteronomy 5:18 NKJV "You shall not commit adultery."

Deuteronomy 27:21 NKJV "Cursed is the one who lies with any kind of animal.' "And all the people shall say, 'Amen!"

Proverbs 6:32 NKJV "Whoever commits adultery with a woman lacks understanding; He who does so destroys his own soul."

Proverbs 31:3 NKJV "Do not give your strength to women, nor your ways to that which destroys kings."

Matthew 15:19 NKJV "For out of the heart proceed evil thoughts, murders, adulteries, fornications, thefts, false witness, blasphemies."

Mark 7:21-22 NKJV "For from within, out of the heart of men, proceed evil thoughts, adulteries, fornications, murders, [22] thefts, covetousness, wickedness, deceit, lewdness, an evil eye blasphemy, pride, foolishness."

Acts 15:28-29 NKJV "For it seemed good to the Holy Spirit, and to us, to lay upon you no greater burden than these necessary things: [29] that you abstain from things offered to idols, from blood, from things strangled, and from sexual immorality. If you keep yourselves from these, you will do well."

1 Corinthians 5:9 NKJV "I wrote to you in my epistle not to keep company with sexually immoral people. [11] But now I have written to you not to keep company with anyone named a brother, who is sexually immoral, or covetous, or an idolater, or a reviler, or a drunkard, or an extortioner—not even to eat with such a person."
1 Corinthians 6:9-10,13, 18 NKJV [9] Do you not know that the unrighteous will not inherit the kingdom of God? Do not be deceived. Neither fornicators, nor idolaters, nor adulterers, nor homosexuals, nor sodomites, "[10] nor thieves, nor covetous, nor drunkards, nor revilers, nor extortioners will inherit the kingdom of God." [13] Foods for the stomach and the stomach for foods, but God will destroy both it and them. Now the body is not for sexual immorality but for the Lord, and the Lord for the body. [18] Flee sexual immorality. Every sin that a man does is outside the body, but he who commits sexual immorality sins against his own body."
1 Corinthians 7:2 NKJV "Nevertheless, because of sexual immorality, let each man have his own wife, and let each woman have her own husband."
1 Corinthians 10:7-8 NKJV "And do not become idolaters as were some of them. As it is written, "The people sat down to eat and drink, and rose up to play." [8] Nor let us commit sexual immorality, as some of them did, and in one day twenty-three thousand fell;"

2 Corinthians 12:21 NKJV "lest, when I come again, my God will humble me among you, and I shall mourn for many who have sinned before and have not repented of the uncleanness, fornication, and lewdness which they have practiced."

Ephesians 5:3 NKJV "But fornication and all uncleanness or covetousness, let it not even be named among you, as is fitting for saints;"

Colossians 3:5 NKJV "Therefore put to death your members which are on the earth: fornication, uncleanness, passion, evil desire, and covetousness, which is idolatry."

Hebrews 12:14-16 NKJV "Pursue peace with all people, and holiness, without which no one will see the Lord: [15] looking carefully lest anyone fall short of the grace of God; lest any root of bitterness springing up cause trouble, and by this many become defiled; [16] lest there be any fornicator or profane person like Esau, who for one morsel of food sold his birthright."

Hebrews 13:4 NKJV "Marriage is honorable among all, and the bed undefiled; but fornicators and adulterers God will judge."

James 4:4 NKJV "Adulterers and adulteresses! Do you not know that friendship with the world is enmity with God? Whoever therefore wants to be a friend of the world makes himself an enemy of God."

Jude 1:6-7 NKJV "And the angels who did not keep their proper domain, but left their own abode, He has reserved in everlasting chains under darkness for the judgment of the great day; [7] as Sodom and Gomorrah, and the cities around them in a similar manner to these, having given themselves over to sexual immorality and gone after strange flesh, are set forth as an example, suffering the vengeance of eternal fire."

Revelation 2:14, 20, 22 NKJV "[14] But I have a few things against you, because you have there those who hold the doctrine of Balaam, who taught Balak to put a stumbling block before the children of Israel, to eat things sacrificed to idols, and to commit sexual immorality."

"[20] Nevertheless I have a few things against you, because you allow that woman Jezebel, who calls herself a prophetess, to teach and seduce My servants to commit sexual immorality and eat things sacrificed to idols, and to commit sexual immorality.

[22] Indeed I will cast her into a sickbed, and those who commit adultery with her into great tribulation, unless they repent of their deeds."

Revelation 21:8 NKJV "But the cowardly, unbelieving, abominable, murderers, sexually immoral, sorcerers, idolaters, and all liars shall have their part in the lake which burns with fire and brimstone, which is the second death."

Revelation 22:14-15 NKJV "Blessed are those who do His commandments, that they may have the right to the tree of life, and may enter through the gates into the city. [15] But outside are dogs and sorcerers and sexually immoral and murderers and idolaters, and whoever loves and practices a lie."

CHAPTER SIX

RELATIONSHIP BETWEEN MONEY, POWER AND SEX

It has been observed that money and power have an affinity to sex and alcohol. There were times when in some developing countries, owning a car was one of the indices of being, or beginning to be, rich. A man that had no car and went to work by public transport, hardly went anywhere but home after work. He was incapable of giving anybody a ride. But as soon as he acquired a car, he could afford to give rides to people, especially ladies, some of who might end up with him in bed. He could then afford to close from work and visit someone else for one thing or the other before heading for home, and some "respectful" men would give a thousand and one false excuses for returning home late, including traffic.

Many times, men that committed financial fraud to became very rich in money they did not labor for, had been arrested in the home or company of some "free women." One of the ways illegally acquired wealth is spent and wasted is on women – not on a wife! A man of average financial standing may remain faithful to his wife and vice-versa until wealth increases. That becomes the time when every insult is bad enough to make one stay away from home. Things that could be tolerated in times past become too provoking to make him/her stay away from home and, perhaps begin to see another person whose insults are tolerable as jokes. It is observed that many immigrant wives to America, struggle to get employed in the healthcare system as nurses and doctors as those are the major jobs that pay immigrants fairly well. Unfortunately, when the women begin to make money, they abandon respect for their husbands, especially if such husbands do not bring in as much income as they.

In times past, many rich men abused women and got away with it, because such men offered them large sums of money to shut up. On the other hand, because of some power they had over such women, they compelled or persuaded the women to sign some non-disclosure agreement (NDA) to cover traces of their steps. But, unfortunately, with the growth of the MeToo movement,[114] many of such abused women have begun to speak up – some have gone to court to expose the past of those men, bringing the men to disrepute. And because, as Jesus Christ said it, "For nothing is secret that will not be revealed, nor anything hidden that will not be known and come to light" (Luke 8:17 NKJV), the past secret of such wayward men become open, and produces disgrace.

Just like people use money to entice and abuse sex, some use money to acquire power. And often times such persons use that

---

[114] "MeToo is a social movement against sexual abuse, sexual harassment, and rape culture, in which people publicize their experiences of sexual abuse or sexual harassment."
https://en.wikipedia.org/wiki/MeToo movement April 1, 2023.

power to acquire more money. Many instances abound where people that have access to power to amass money to themselves use the money to acquire more power, which if uncontrolled leads them to tyranny.

There are many rich people in power who do not respect the rule of law because they believe they can shut up any opposition with money or authority. Such people like to perpetuate power when they lay hold on it. One of the reasons for such perpetuation is fear. They fear that the evils they have done may be exposed and hunt them. But whatever happens, whether in life or death, the evils that men do live after them, according to William Shakespeare in Julius Caesar.

The other fear that the rich, power-full person entertains is that life may become devalued by the absence of power. Such persons want to die in power or in office, and they do many atrocious things to remain there. This could be one of the disadvantages of monarchy where the king or queen only leaves power, usually, by death.

CHAPTER SEVEN
CONCLUSIONS

In the Bible story of Creation recorded in Genesis 1:1-31, God declared all things He created good. The Bible says, "Then God saw everything that He had made, and indeed it was very good." (Genesis 1:31a).

God made man in His image and gave him the ability to fashion out new things from creation. Money was not one of the items that He created during the Creation Week. As a means of exchange man fashioned out money, which underwent several developmental stages, including trade by barter, commodity money, cowries, metals and metallic objects, gold, silver and copper coins, paper money, and it has not ceased developing. These days, there is money in plastic cards (debit and credit cards), and people talk about crypto currencies. On the other hand, as wealth, it is God that gives people power to get wealth (Deuteronomy 8:18).

In effect, money/wealth in itself is good by God's standards. But there are two things bad here: -

-    The love of money, which is the root of all evils. The apostle Paul said, "Those who want to get rich fall into temptation and a trap and into many foolish and harmful desires that plunge people into ruin and destruction. [10] For the love of money is a root of all kinds of evil. Some people, eager for money, have wandered from the faith and pierced themselves with many griefs." (1Timothy 6:9-10 NIV).

- Worshipping money/wealth rather than the Creator/Giver of it. We read in Romans 1:24-25 (NIV) "Therefore God gave them over in the sinful desires of their hearts to sexual impurity for the degrading of their bodies with one another. [25] They exchanged the truth about God for a lie, and worshiped and served created things rather than the Creator—who is forever praised. Amen."

Money is essential. Money is good for as long as the owner remains in control of it. As soon as one loses control of one's money, pride sets in, followed by evil desires, all of which lead to a fall and subsequent destruction. The more you have it, the more you hunger for more. The wiseman in Proverbs wrote,

"Whoever loves wisdom makes his father rejoice,

But a companion of harlots wastes his wealth" (Proverbs 29:3 NKJV).

Lust for wealth is dangerous and leads to destruction.

In the book of Proverbs Agur wrote,

"Two things I ask of you, Lord; do not refuse me before I die: [8] Keep falsehood and lies far from me; give me neither poverty nor riches, but give me only my daily bread. [9] Otherwise, I may have too much and disown you and say, 'Who is the Lord?' Or I may become poor and steal, and so dishonor the name of my God." (Proverbs 30:7-9 NIV).

Similarly, power is good. All power ultimately belongs to God. Psalm 62:11 reads, "God has spoken once, Twice I have heard this: That power belongs to God."

Jesus Christ also announced to His disciples after His resurrection and shortly before He ascended to heaven, "And Jesus came and spoke to them, saying, "All authority has been given to Me in heaven and on earth." (Matthew 28:18 NKJV).

God gives people power or authority to rule, lead or perform some special functions. Anyone whom God endows with power for any function remains accountable to Him, and the Bible says that it is required of stewards be found faithful (1 Corinthians 4:2). Anyone that determines to serve and please God with the power with which God has endowed him or her stays long in the position, and people led or influenced by that power rejoice, and are at peace. Proverbs 29:2 reads,

"When the righteous are in authority, the people rejoice: but when the wicked beareth rule, the people mourn."

Seeking to please God with/in a position of authority will reflect on the well-being of the people, or otherwise spell misery and woes for the people. People who hold on power need not be boastful, proud or wicked because, like everything else in this world, power is transient. In 1John 2:16-17:

"For all that is in the world, the lust of the flesh, and the lust of the eyes, and the pride of life, is not of the Father, but is of the world. [17] And the world passeth away, and the lust thereof: but he that doeth the will of God abideth for ever."

We also read in 1Corinthians 7:29-31 NKJV, "But this I say, brethren, the time is short, . . . For the form of this world is passing away." You may not know how wicked a man is until he is exposed to, or placed in, a position of power.

In the same vein, sex is one of the great gifts God gave to mankind at creation. In my early years, I had heard people suggest that sex was the forbidden fruit that Adam and Eve ate in the Garden of Eden, which became their sin that brought death to mankind. This argument arose from the thinking that just eating fruit plucked from a certain tree could not have offended God. NO! It was disobedience of God's instruction that displeased Him. And it still displeases Him. God told Adam that they were free to eat of every tree in the Garden except the fruit of one specific tree in the midst of the Garden, which God said they would die if they touched or ate it (Genesis 3:2). And it was exactly the fruit of that very tree that the devil tempted Eve to eat and be wise as God. She and her husband fell into the temptation.

Till today, God does not frown at sexual acts in proper marriages. Sex outside marriage of a man and woman is what is sinful before God – according to several Bible references in this book. God ordained sex to be enjoyed by married male and female partners. But the evil one has used sex as a tool to destroy many men and a couple of women over the centuries. Virtually everyone enjoys legitimate sex. However, people who fall when tempted with sex do so because they lust after it and so, become vulnerable. In James 1:14-15 the Bible says, "But each one is tempted when he is drawn away by his own desires and enticed. [15] Then, when desire has conceived, it gives birth to sin; and sin, when it is full-grown, brings forth death."

This applies to anything lusted after, which opens you up for temptation that could lead to your downfall.

CHAPTER EIGHT

RECOMMENDATIONS

Hosea 4:6 NKJV: "My people are destroyed for lack of knowledge. Because you have rejected knowledge, I also will reject you from being priest for Me; Because you have forgotten the law of your God, I also will forget your children."

Isaiah 5:13 NKJV: "Therefore my people have gone into captivity, Because they have no knowledge; Their honorable men are famished, And their multitude dried up with thirst."

John 8:32 NKJV: "And you shall know the truth, and the truth shall make you free."

When the apostle Paul saw that the whole city of Athens was full of idolatry in that he saw many shrines dedicated to various gods including one dedicated "TO THE UNKNOWN GOD," he told the Athenians, "Truly, these times of ignorance God overlooked, but now commands all men everywhere to repent, [31] because He has appointed a day on which He will judge the world in righteousness by the Man whom He has ordained. He has given assurance of this to all by raising Him from the dead." (Acts 17:30-31 NKJV).

As long as you have your breath, you can right a wrong. You are able to reverse your eternal destination while you are alive, by going to the Lord in repentance for every sin in your life. He will forgive you as we are told in 1John 1:9 – "If we confess our sins, He is faithful and just to forgive us our sins and to cleanse us from all unrighteousness."

We have concluded that neither money (or wealth), power, nor sex is bad in itself, because, according to God, Creator of all things, they were all good. What is bad, dangerous and destructive is the lust for them, which leads to their abuse.

SIGNS OF ABUSE OF MONEY

Know that abuse of money is setting in as soon as the following, which you must avoid in order not to perish become noticeable in your life: -

(1) Getting obsessed with obtaining money and be preoccupied with making money at all times.

(2) Being in denial of the state of things.

(3) Getting involved in dangerous and obscene activities for the purpose of acquiring money.

(4) Tying personal image to money and becoming more disrespectful.

(5) Finding it hard or impossible to change habits related to money.

(6) Becoming stingy in spite of availability of money.

It is often at this point that people begin to find it difficult to offer you advice as such advice might be misconstrued as envy. It, therefore, behooves you to counsel yourself.

SIGNS OF ABUSE OF POWER

Similarly, there are symptoms of abuse of power such as the following: -

(a) Using position to receive favors from subordinates or subjects.

(b) Threatening or manipulating subordinates/subjects.

(c) Using title for self-enrichment rather than for service.

(d) Attachment of self to the most vulnerable in the group.

(e) Demand for absolute loyalty from subordinates/subjects.

(f) Threatening or scandalizing persons that tend to not comply with demands

(g) Making subordinates/subjects totally dependent on him.

(h) Getting violent when not having his way.

(i) Wanting to be in control at all times.

(j) Never taking time off position for fear of being overthrown or replaced.

SIGNS OF SEX ADDICTION WHICH MAY LEAD TO SEX ABUSE

Compulsive sex addiction or hypersexuality disorder, hyper-sexual behavior or nymphomania[115] is both in men and women. Nymphomaniac is a term that was applied only to female that had

---

[115] MENTAL HEALTH. "What Is a Nymphomaniac?" https://www.verywellhealth.com/nymphomania-5209598 April 8, 2023.

excessive desire for sex. But these days it applies to both men and women.

A certain man was described as one that would not allow "anything in skirt" to go past him freely (my apologies for quoting this somewhat derogatory description of people of the female gender). Anybody at this level of enticement/attraction to every woman he meets (or man she meets) is in trouble and needs help. "Signs of a Sex Addict" as reviewed recently by Jennifer Casarella, MD are outlined[116] as follows:

(1) Obsessive Sexual Thoughts – a person dealing with sex addiction may find himself or herself thinking persistently about sex.

(2) Feeling of anxiety, shame, depression or regret, all of which may not still stop the fantasies and uncontrollable desire for sex.

(3) Spending excessive time on attempting to acquire sex, having sex, being sexual, or recovering from sexual experiences.

(4) Having difficulty engaging in other activities such as school work, personal lives as the person may engage in prioritizing sexual behavior over other forms of relaxation or hobbies.

---

[116] Signs of a Sex Addict https://www.webmd.com/mental-health/signs-sex-addict 04/08/2023

(5) Masturbating excessively "during inappropriate times, or even masturbation to the point of causing physical discomfort or pain."

(6) Engaging in risky or inappropriate behaviors which may "include exhibitionism, public sex, sex without protection, and sex with prostitutes."

(7) Cheating on partners. Polygamy does not even cure this.

(8) Committing criminal sex offenses such as "stalking, rape, or child molestation."

At this time the following steps need to be taken as an antidote: -

i)   Pray to God almighty to forgive you of every sin you have committed, including abuse of money, power and sex. Repent, and promise God to change today. Invite Jesus Christ into your heart to be your Savior and Lord. As much as possible, make a restitution to people you have defrauded. Yield control of your life to God, and He will help you by His Holy Spirit to exercise self-control.

ii)   Realize and bear in mind that as it is hard to maintain 'New Year Resolutions,' self-control and humility/meekness are difficult, if not impossible to achieve by your power. ". . . This is the word of the Lord unto Zerubbabel, saying, Not by might, nor by power, but by my spirit, saith the Lord of hosts."

(Zechariah 4:6). Nobody quits sin by will power. You can only do so by trusting in the Lord for help. We also read in Matthew 19:26 that though something may be impossible with men, all things are possible with God. Prophet Jeremiah said the Lord asked, "Behold, I am the Lord, the God of all flesh: is there any thing too hard for me?" (Jeremiah 32:27); and the apostle Paul asserted, "I can do all things through Christ which strengtheneth me." (Philippians 4:13).

So, go to Jesus Christ to help you to overcome your lust. All that you could not achieve by New Year Resolutions are achievable by Christ Jesus. He invites you to Himself in the following words: "Come unto me, all ye that labour and are heavy laden, and I will give you rest.[29] Take my yoke upon you, and learn of me; for I am meek and lowly in heart: and ye shall find rest unto your souls." Matthew 11:28-29).

8.1 REPENTANCE, RESTITUTION AND THE GRACE OF GOD

Jesus Christ spoke a parable to teach a lesson about a foolish rich man that was obsessed with his wealth and himself, without being rich toward God, (Luke 12:13-21).

We see a contrary situation when Jesus Christ encountered Zacchaeus, a very rich tax collector (Publican), and he hosted Jesus Christ in his home. He repented of extortion and offered restitution to all that he had cheated in the cause of his work. Jesus declared that salvation had gotten into Zacchaeus' life and home. Read through Luke 19:1-10 as follows:

"And Jesus entered and passed through Jericho. [2] And, behold, there was a man named Zacchaeus, which was the chief among the publicans, and he was rich. [3] And he sought to see Jesus who he was; and could not for the press, because he was little of stature [4] And he ran before, and climbed up into a sycomore tree to see him: for he was to pass that way. [5] And when Jesus came to the place, he looked up, and saw him, and said unto him, Zacchaeus, make haste, and come down; for to day I must abide at thy house. [6] And he made haste, and came down, and received him joyfully. [7] And when they saw it, they all murmured, saying, That he was gone to be guest with a man that is a sinner. [8] And Zacchaeus stood, and said unto the Lord: Behold, Lord, the half of my goods I give to the poor; and if I have taken any thing from any man by false accusation, I restore him fourfold.

[9] And Jesus said unto him, This day is salvation come to this house, forsomuch as he also is a son of Abraham. [10] For the Son of man is come to seek and to save that which was lost."

8.2 LOVE OF CHRIST VERSUS LOVE OF MONEY

We have concluded that money in and of itself is good and good to have. We have also learnt that the love money is dangerous and should be avoided, because it is the root of all evils, and many people have wondered away from the faith and even pierced themselves with many griefs (1Timothy 6:10).

In view of the above conclusion the apostle Paul advised young Pastor Timothy (and by extension everyone who belongs to the Family of God) to "flee these things; and follow after righteousness, godliness, faith, love, patience, meekness." (1Timothy 6:11). Let's expound this Bible verse a little:

- Pursue Righteousness: No one achieves righteousness by his own strength. Any righteousness acquired by self-effort is worthless before God. The prophet Isaiah wrote, ". . . all our righteousnesses are as filthy rags;" (Isaiah 64:6). It is only the righteousness of Jesus Christ imputed on anyone that believes in Him that is acceptable to God. So, invite Jesus Christ into your heart.

- Pursue Godliness: Vine's Dictionary defines godliness as denoting "that piety which, characterized by a Godward attitude, does that which is well-pleasing to Him."[117]

  An on-line dictionary defines godliness as "the quality or practice of conforming to the laws and wishes of God;

---

[117] Vine's Dictionary, 272.

devoutness and moral uprightness: To be wise in godliness, reflecting the nature of the kingdom of God in the course of everyday life."[118]

The apostle Paul in 1Timothy 6:6 wrote in the Amplified Bible, "But godliness actually is a source of great gain when accompanied by contentment [that contentment which comes from a sense of inner confidence based on the sufficiency of God]." And contentment is the state of being happy and satisfied with what one has.

- Pursue Faith: The Greek word for faith here is πίστις (pistis), which also translates into English as faithfulness amongst other words. Faithfulness is also one of the fruit of the Holy Spirit, which comes in as the Holy Spirit fills you. In Ephesians 5:18 the apostle says, "Do not get drunk on wine, which leads to debauchery. Instead, be filled with the Spirit," In pursuit of faithfulness/faith and all other ('seeds of the') fruit of the Spirit, you have to intentionally pray God daily to fill you. You have to be faithful in service to God, worshipping, praying, Bible study, kindness, helpfulness, etc.

- Pursue Love: Love is an attribute of God. This type of love (Greek ἀγάπη – agape) is for an undeserving person; it is

---

[118] GODLINESS. https://www.dictionary.com/browse/godliness 04/09/2023.

affection for, and benevolence to, someone that cannot repay or is not lovable. Love is the attribute of God, along with His mercy, that caused Him to give 'His only begotten Son, that whosoever believeth in Him should not perish but have eternal life" (John 3:16).

In pursuit of love, it is mandatory to heed the words of Jesus Christ: "A new commandment I give to you, that you love one another; as I have loved you, that you also love one another. [35] By this all will know that you are My disciples, if you have love for one another." (John 13:34-35 NKJV).

Also take note of Mark 12:30-31 (NKJV): "And you shall love the Lord your God with all your heart, with all your soul, with all your mind, and with all your strength.' This is the first commandment. [31] And the second, like it, is this: 'You shall love your neighbor as yourself.' There is no other commandment greater than these."

- <u>Pursue Patience (or Perseverance)</u>: This fruit of the Holy Spirit from the Greek word ὑπομονή (hupomoné) also means steadfastness, patiently waiting for. Patiently wait for God's timing for all your desire. Do not run ahead of God.

- <u>Pursue Meekness (or Gentleness)</u>: This word that also means humility is from the Greek πραότης (praotés) does not mean weakness, rather it implies a low view of oneself – not over-estimating or over-valuing oneself over other people. The Bible says that Moses was the meekest man on the face of the earth (Numbers 12:3), yet he was one of the most consequential persons that walked the earth.

Philippians 2:5-11 (NKJV)

"Let this mind be in you which was also in Christ Jesus, [6] who, being in the form of God, did not consider it robbery to be equal with God, [7] but made Himself of no reputation, taking the form of a bondservant, and coming in the likeness of men. [8] And being found in appearance as a man, He humbled Himself and became obedient to the point of death, even the death of the cross. [9] Therefore God also has highly exalted Him and given Him the name which is above every name, [10] that at the name of Jesus every knee should bow, of those in heaven, and of those on earth, and of those under the earth, [11] and that every tongue should confess that Jesus Christ is Lord, to the glory of God the Father.

The admonition of the Bible to wives is important here:

"For wives, this means submit to your husbands as to the Lord. [23] For a husband is the head of his wife as Christ is the head of the church. He is the Savior of his body, the church. ²⁴ As the church submits to Christ, so you wives should submit <u>to your husbands in everything</u>." (Ephesians 5:22-24 NKJV emphasis added by me). It does not say to submit to your husbands when they are richer than you. These days of Feminist Movement, it takes Christ-like humility for a wife that is richer than her husband, or in a position of power like the late Prime Minister Margaret Thatcher of the United Kingdom, to submit to him in all things.

- We can infer that Jesus Christ, the Author and Perfecter of our faith, Creator of all things (Colossians 1:15-17)[119], was a very humble man. In spite of His qualifications, He humbled and subjected Himself even to death, over which He had authority. Humility was one of the attributes, which we are encouraged to imbibe and practice.

---

[119] Colossians 1:15-17 (NKJV) "He is the image of the invisible God, the firstborn over all creation. [16] For by Him all things were created that are in heaven and that are on earth, visible and invisible, whether thrones or dominions or principalities or powers. All things were created through Him and for Him. [17] And He is before all things, and in Him all things consist."

8.3 SELF CONTROL, POWER OF PRAYER, AND DEPENDENCE ON THE HOLY SPIRIT

Be reminded that power, money and sex are good in themselves. It is the abuse of them that is evil – excessive desire and drive or lust for them. In the light of this, there is need for self-control as a solution to the abuse of money, power and sex.

Lust can be hardly overcome by will power. The apostle Paul wrote, "But the fruit of the Spirit is love, joy, peace, forbearance, kindness, goodness, faithfulness, [23] gentleness and self-control. Against such things there is no law." (Galatians 5:22-23 NIV). Self-control is English translation of the Greek ἐγκράτεια (egkrateia), which Strong's Concordance (1466) also translates as self-mastery, self-restraint, and continence. It's interesting to note that the opposite of self-control includes indiscipline, incontinence, unconstraint, self-indulgence, loss of control, etc.

Exercising self-control encompasses "mastery of all appetites, tempers and passions"[120] such as are listed in Galatians 5:19-21, including enmity, strife – orgies (ESV). As seen earlier, self-control is one of the fruit of the Holy Spirit, which come from the presence of the Hoy Spirit given to people who invite Jesus Christ into their lives and are filled with Him.

---

[120] Expositor's Greek Testament:
Biblehub.com/Commentaries/Galatians5-23.htm

You also need to sustain your self-control and other 'seeds' of the fruit of the Spirit with earnest prayer. Scripture says to pray without ceasing (1Thessalonians 5:17). Since lust cannot be overcome by natural will power but can be overcome just like every other difficult situation or issue by prayer, earnest and sincere prayer is recommended. But you must have the desire and willingness to give up the issue. "Be anxious for nothing, but in everything by prayer and supplication, with thanksgiving, let your requests be made known to God; [7] and the peace of God, which surpasses all understanding, will guard your hearts and minds through Christ Jesus." (Philippians 4:6-7 NKJV).

Put your faith in Jesus Christ and trust Him to help you. He said, "Come to Me, all you who labor and are heavy laden, and I will give you rest." (Matthew 11:28 NKJV). Jesus is faithful to do in your life whatever He promised.

Lust is sin – whether for money, power or sex. If you fail to master it and overcome it, it will destroy you in the end – you lose your soul. Jesus Christ asked in one of His teachings, "For what shall it profit a man, if he shall gain the whole world, and lose his own soul?" (Mark 8:36). Note what God told Cain, the first son of Adam and Eve, who killed his brother Abel, due to envy: "If you do well, will you not be accepted? And if you do not do well, sin lies at the door. And its desire is for you, but you should rule over it." (Genesis 4:7 NKJV). The same message of that time goes to everyone that lusts after anything.

May the Lord give you the grace to find contentment in what you are and have, and bless you to make you channels of blessings. AMEN.

BIBLIOGRAPHY

Bullock, Allan. Hitler. A STUDY IN TYRANNY. New York:
  Harper Collins Publishers, INC, 1962.

Expositor's Greek Testament:
Biblehub.com/Commentaries/Galatians5-23.htm

Harris, Joshua. Sex is not the problem (Lust is): Sexual Purity in
a Lust-saturated
  World. New York: Multnomah Books, 2003.

Hill, Andrew E. and John H. Walton. A SURVEY OF THE
  OLD TESTAMENT 3rd ed. Grand Rapids: Zondervan,
  2009

JOSEPHUS FLAVIUS: William Whiston, A.M. (TR). THE
COMPLETE WORKS.
  Nashville: Thomas Nelson, 1998.

Life Application Study Bible (NIV).

Nwaelene, Daniel Ukadike. "JESUS CHRIST: SAVIOR,
  JUDGE & KING OF THE WORLD. Bloomington, IN:
  WestBow Press, 2017.

Olorunfemi, Fagbemi. THE PERPLEXING AND BRUTAL
  RULE OF GENERAL SAMORI BALCHA – A
  TYRANT.

Thiessen, Henry Clarence. INTRODUCTORY LECTURES IN
  SYSTEMATIC THEOLOGY. Grand Rapids: WM. B.
  Eerdmans Publishing Company, 1949.

Tranquillus, Gaius Suetonius. Robert Graves, TR. THE
TWELVE CAESARS. London:
    Penguin Books, 1957.

Tullock, John H. THE OLD TESTAMENT STORY, 8th

Edition. Upper Saddle River:

    Pearson Prentice Hall, 2009.

Strong, James. KING JAMES NEW STRONG'S

    EXHAUSTIVE CONCORDANCE. Nashville: Thomas

    Nelson Publishers, 1996.

Goodrick, Edward W., John R. Kohlenberger III. THE

    STRONGEST NIV EXHAUSTIVE CONCORDANCE.

    Grand Rapids: Zondervan, 1999.

Vine, W. E. VINE'S COMPLETE EXPOSITORY

    DICTIONARY. Nashville: Thomas Nelso Publishers,

    1996.

Center on Addiction:

    https://www.centeronaddiction.org/addiction/commonly-
    used-illegal-drugs 5/30/2020

Sacred Prostitution.

https://en.wikipedia.org/wiki/Sacred_prostitution June 1, 2020.

    "Managers & Leaders: Warning signs your leader might

    be drunk on power "

https://www.michellegibbings.com/warning-signs-your-leader-
    might-be-drunk-on-power/ February 19, 2022.

Monarchies in Africa:
https://en.wikipedia.org/wiki/Monarchies_in_Africa

"Top 10 Greatest Empires In History"
https://listverse.com/2010/06/22/top-10-greatest-empires-in-history/ 03/31/2022

"British Empire." https://en.wikipedia.org/wiki/British_Empire
03/31/2022.

"2012 ELECTION NEWS." https://www.reuters.com/article/us-usa-campaign-israel/democrats-backpedal-and-change-language-on-jerusalem-idUSBRE8841JC20120906
SEPTEMBER 5, 2012

Pawlowski, A. TODAY: 8 Reasons Why People Cheat.
https://www.today.com/health/infidelity-8-reasons-why-people-cheat-become-unfaithful-t121512 February 5, 2023.

Ellicott's Commentary for English Readers
https://biblehub.com/commentaries/ellicott/ephesians/5.htm

Cleveland Clinic. "5 Benefits of a Healthy Sex Life."
https://health.clevelandclinic.org/benefits-of-sex/
February 25, 2023.

Sexual Health. "What are the Potential Benefits of Having Sex Every Day." https://www.healthline.com/health/healthy-sex/sex-daily February 25, 2023.

PsychCentral. "7 WAYS A PERSON CAN BE ABUSED."
https://psychcentral.com/pro/exhausted-woman/2015/08/7-ways-a-person-can-be-abused#1

https://www.cnn.com/2022/03/08/us/prince-andrew-virginia-giuffre-settlement/index.html

https://en.wikipedia.org/wiki/Mary_Kay_Letourneau

https://en.wikipedia.org/wiki/List_of_federal_political_sex_scandals_in_the_United_States#2010%E2%80%932019 March 25, 2023.
MeToo Movement.
https://en.wikipedia.org/wiki/MeToo_movement

https://www.verywellhealth.com/nymphomania-5209598 April 8, 2023
What Is a Nymphomaniac?

"Signs of a Sex Addict" https://www.webmd.com/mental-health/signs-sex-addict
04/08/2023

Wikipedia: "Virginia Giuffre v. Prince Andrew"

https://en.wikipedia.org/wiki/Virginia_Giuffre_v._Prince_Andrew#:~:text=Prince%20Andrew%20allegations-, June 19, 2025.

General Index

A

Abuse iv, 2, 3, 4, 52, 53, 54, 61, 66, 71, 73, 74, 75, 160, 162, 163, 164, 167, 168, 170, 171, 183, 209, 211, 215, 219, 224, 227, 250, 251, 251, 253, 259, 268, 283

Acquisition 75, 83, 103, 104, 107, 110

Adam 14, 15, 16, 21, 29, 30, 34, 36, 231, 247, 288, 303, 351

Adultery 58, 169, 222, 230, 232, 233, 234, 235, 242, 246, 276, 277, 280, 353

Anti-Semitism 195

Appreciation xiv, 79

Arrogance 76, 183, 216

Authoritarian 191, 196

Authority viii, xii, 3, 4, 34, 35, 36, 62, 94, 95, 97, 98, 99, 100, 110, 112, 114, 115, 120, 127, 132, 136, 161, 162, 168, 174, 181, 193, 215, 217, 218, 220, 228, 284, 287, 301, 352, 353, 354

B

Barons 54

Benevolence 65, 299

Blessings   7, 16, 17, 50, 113, 118, 198, 201, 304

Bloodthirsty   61, 178

Boko Haram   7

C

Clinton   1, 143, 264, 265, 266

Crown   7, 89, 128, 159

Corrupts   3, 95, 352

Chance   226, 227

Christian   vii, x, xv, 2, 7, 21, 45, 48, 65, 84, 115, 141, 158,
                 159, 221, 237, 250, 263, 270, 348, 351, 353, 356

Captivity   16, 125, 129, 132, 133, 155, 201, 213, 290

Confess   4, 13, 30, 225, 233, 291, 300, 354

Contentment   234, 298, 304

Curses   16, 18, 198, 199

Commandment   15, 17, 18, 19, 50, 58, 66, 70, 79, 127, 128, 169,
                 170, 209, 222, 232, 280, 299

Crooked   32, 49, 130, 245, 246, 247

Covetous   60, 148, 241, 278

D

Devil   4, 5, 8, 9, 10, 14, 15, 21, 23, 24, 25, 26, 28, 30, 31,
                 32, 33, 34, 35, 36, 37, 47, 61, 103, 113, 115, 117,
                 118, 219, 288

Divorce   ix, 45, 232, 245, 267

Destiny   xi, 10, 15, 30, 219, 351, 356

Depraved	50
Disobedience	16, 18, 20, 106, 166, 190, 200, 201, 215, 288
Death	iv, 6, 10, 15, 16, 21, 22, 27, 29, 30, 49, 59, 74, 89, 94, 105, 106, 118, 120, 127, 134, 136, 137, 139, 140, 147, 148, 150, 164, 169, 174, 175, 176, 177, 178, 179, 180, 181, 183, 185, 187, 193, 194, 205, 218, 225, 238, 243, 244, 246, 255, 257, 258, 260, 262, 267, 275, 276, 279, 280, 284, 288, 289, 300, 301, 353
Delegation	114
Doubt	9, 165, 211, 271
Darkness	33, 85, 107, 116, 130, 131, 147, 280
Distortion	xii, 160
Downfall	ii, iv, v, viii, xi, 76, 77, 95, 209, 230, 289, 351
Drug	ix, 45, 52, 53, 54, 74, 164, 255

E

Extra-marital	1, 232, 234
Evil	4, 6, 8, 12, 15, 26, 33, 36, 41, 43, 44, 45, 46, 50, 52, 54, 61, 66, 70, 77, 79, 81, 83, 85, 89, 90, 91, 92, 103, 116, 118, 128, 137, 138, 139, 144, 146, 148, 154, 165, 171, 172, 206, 215, 216, 217, 222, 228, 236, 242, 243, 277, 278, 279, 284, 285, 286, 289, 297, 302
Eternal	xi, 10, 12, 19, 22, 29, 147, 280, 290, 299, 351, 352

Eve	14, 15, 16, 37, 231, 247, 288, 303
Exploitation	xi, 59, 73
Election	61, 103, 104, 156, 266, 307

F

Fall	iv, v, viii, x, 4, 6, 7, 14, 20, 24, 30, 39, 43, 76, 79, 84, 85, 88, 95, 118, 162, 183, 184, 186, 200, 209, 216, 218, 249, 256, 279, 285, 286, 289, 349, 351
Fruitful	34, 247
Fellowship	14, 20, 34, 45
Faith	vii, viii, 7, 43, 45, 61, 79, 100, 117, 196, 227, 258, 286, 297, 298, 301, 303, 348, 356
Family	iv, vii, 26, 45, 81, 110, 149, 167, 168, 169, 180, 203, 231, 260, 263, 266, 270, 297
Fornication	58, 77, 169, 230, 234, 235, 236, 237, 238, 240, 24 277, 279
Fear	v, 19, 37, 46, 49, 82, 89, 128, 174, 181, 190, 202, 290, 216, 249, 284, 292, 355
Fraud	50, 51, 117, 282

G

| God | iii, v, vii, x, xiii, xiv, xv, 3, 4, 5, 6, 7, 8, 9, 10, 12, 13, 14, 15, 16, 17, 18, 19, 20, 22, 23, 24, 25, 27, 2 29, 30, 31, 33, 34, 35, 36, 37, 40, 41, 46, 47, 48, 4 50, 55, 60, 62, 64, 65, 66, 67, 68, 69, 70, 71, 72, 7 78, 79, 80, 82, 85, 86, 87, 89, 90, 92, 97, 98, 99, |

                   100, 102, 103, 104, 105, 106, 107, 108, 110, 111,
                   112, 113, 114, 115, 116, 117, 118, 120, 121, 122,
                   123, 124, 129, 130, 131, 132, 133, 134, 136, 141,
                   142, 143, 148, 149, 151, 152, 156, 159, 164, 165,
                   166, 167, 168, 169, 170, 171, 172, 176, 177, 183,
                   184, 185, 199, 200, 201, 203, 209, 210, 211, 213,
                   214, 215, 216, 218, 219, 222, 223, 225, 227, 229,
                   232, 234, 235, 236, 237, 238, 240, 241, 243, 244,
                   247, 248, 256, 257, 258, 259, 260, 262, 263, 266,
                   271, 274, 276, 278, 279, 285, 286, 287, 288, 289,
                   290, 291, 294, 295, 296, 297, 298, 299, 300, 303,
                   348, 349, 350, 351, 352, 353, 354

Government   3, 50, 51, 57, 59, 73, 108, 109, 118, 144, 56, 164,
                   184, 186, 187, 188, 189, 191, 192, 193, 196, 201,
                   203, 353

Godliness   79, 243, 297, 298

Gambling   59, 60

Gay   241

Greed   60, 66, 76, 77, 85, 234, 352

Generosity   78, 190

H

Hell   9, 10, 11, 12, 13, 20, 30, 84, 219, 237, 352

Honorable   157, 279, 290

Heaven   10, 11, 12, 13, 18, 22, 24, 30, 31, 33, 35, 46, 92,
              101, 107, 111, 112, 115, 129, 132, 147, 156, 212,
              213, 214, 223, 225, 287, 300, 352

Hypersexual   292

Husband   16, 36, 62, 63, 71, 156, 168, 169, 222, 146, 248,
              249, 250, 251, 271, 278, 283, 288, 300, 301

Honor   49, 70, 76, 78, 87, 88, 89, 90, 201, 209, 213, 216,
              262

Humility   v, 29, 64, 76, 89, 219, 224, 225, 294, 300, 301, 355

Hardworking   vi, 47

History   xiii, 30, 119, 126, 132, 160, 184, 191, 197, 206,
              256, 265, 266, 274, 307

Harlot   xi, 54, 55, 56, 89, 234, 240, 257, 286

Homosexuality 144, 230, 241, 245

Hoard   92

Heterosexual 241

Heredit   103, 107, 108, 223

I

Immorality   14, 58, 147, 148, 230, 237, 246, 253, 259, 277, 278,
              280

Inheritance   42, 45, 47, 49, 50, 64, 86, 88, 89, 171, 179

Instrumentality 209

Intercourse   56, 230, 232, 233, 234, 235, 237, 238, 241, 244,
              245, 246, 247, 249, 250

Incest   169, 177, 180, 238, 240

Ill-gotten   49, 52, 82

Imputation   103, 110

Identify   160

J

Judgment   7, 10, 79, 82, 91, 104, 115, 137, 147, 148, 168, 169,
                185, 198, 200, 280

Jesus   vii, 8, 9, 10, 11, 13, 19, 20, 21, 23, 24, 25, 26, 27,
                28, 29, 30, 31, 35, 36, 44, 46, 64, 65, 72, 74, 75, 92,
                98, 100, 102, 111, 112, 114, 115, 116, 117, 125,
                134, 135, 136, 137, 138, 139, 140, 143, 150, 157,
                158, 159, 173, 185, 201, 213, 218, 219, 220, 221,
                223, 224, 225, 228, 232, 233, 243, 247, 283, 287,
                294, 295, 296, 297, 299, 300, 301, 302, 303, 305

K

Knowledge   iii, xiii, 9, 15, 16, 36, 49, 95, 103, 104, 113, 114,
                169, 202, 206, 243, 270, 290, 354

L

Loyalty   5, 191, 292

Lust   iv, x, 6, 43, 76, 79, 148, 175, 207, 219, 220, 233,
                234, 242, 243, 244, 252, 253, 262, 286, 288, 289,
                291, 295, 302, 303, 304, 305, 353, 354

Leader	ix, x, xi, xii, 2, 3, 72, 118, 157, 165, 172, 173, 184, 186, 187, 190, 195, 196, 209, 211, 215, 220, 221, 222, 224, 256, 260, 306, 353, 354, 355, 356
Love	xii, 7, 8, 14, 19, 41, 43, 44, 45, 46, 56, 61, 78, 79, 86, 89, 91, 111, 141, 153, 159, 166, 170, 171, 185, 220, 221, 224, 233, 248, 253, 255, 257, 263, 281, 285, 286, 297, 298, 299, 302
Lesbianism	230, 241, 245
Lotteries	59

M

Money	ii, iv, v, viii, ix, xi, xii, xiv, 2, 4, 36, 38, 40, 41, 42, 43, 44, 45, 46, 47, 48, 49, 50, 51, 52, 54, 57, 59, 60 61, 62, 65, 66, 68, 70, 71, 73, 75, 77, 78, 79, 84, 85 86, 87, 88, 91, 92, 95, 118, 163, 172, 178, 190, 193 195, 230, 240, 251, 253, 257, 266, 271, 282, 283, 284, 285, 286, 291, 294, 297, 302, 303, 348, 349, 351, 352, 353, 354, 355, 356
Ministry	21, 23, 112, 114, 157, 185, 192, 211, 348
Mammon	38, 46
Miracle	48, 49, 98, 118, 209
Misuse	xi, 66, 68, 160, 167, 252, 351, 354
Meekness	79, 294, 297, 300
Material	xi, xiii, 36, 38, 77, 118, 132, 352

N

Narcotics	52
Nymphomaniac	292, 308
O	
Oppress	viii, 2, 3, 71, 73, 80, 82, 90, 105, 116, 160, 165, 202, 214, 221, 227, 228
Obedience	17, 29
Ordained	103, 164, 289, 290, 348
Oppression	67, 72, 80, 88, 95, 105, 165, 171, 217
P	
Political	xi, xii, 1, 2, 3, 44, 51, 94, 186, 189, 193, 196, 198, 204, 206, 208, 264, 273, 308, 352, 355
Patience	7, 8, 79, 102, 297, 299
Philanthropic	2, 42
Professional	2, 3, 114, 162, 183, 191, 233, 355
Poverty	39, 40, 41, 43, 75, 89, 182, 251, 286
Power	ii, iii, iv, v, vi, viii, ix, xi, xii, xiii, 2, 3, 4, 25, 30,31,33,35,40,41,43,44,49,60,61,89,90,92,94, 95, 96, 97, 98, 99, 100, 101, 102, 103, 104, 107, 108, 108, 110, 111, 112, 113, 116, 118, 120, , 129, 141, 143,161, 162, 163, 164, 165, 167, 168, 169, 170, 171, 173, 176, 183, 184, 186, 189, 191, 196, 198, 204, 207, 208, 209, 210, , 216, 217,218, 219, 220, 221,222, 224, 225, 227, 230, 243, 244, 251, 253,

	256, 259, 262, 282, 283, 284, 285, 288, 291, 292, 294, 301, 303, 348, 349, 351, 352, 353, 355, 356
Pursue	18, 166, 279, 297, 298, 299, 300
Prayer	9, 16, 116, 176, 223, 227, 302, 303
Pray	v, xiv, 7, 12, 27, 92, 127, 154, 167, 257, 258, 294, 298, 303
Perseverance	299
Prostitute	14, 54, 55, 58, 240, 258, 294
Punishment	73, 74, 82, 127, 142, 146, 162, 169, 172, 177, 200, 226, 257

R

Resist	v, 6,8,9,13,14,103,164,219, 220, 245, 246, 350
Repent	v, 12, 19, 58, 222, 237, 280, 290, 294, 354
Reconciliation	29
Retaliation	318
Repentance	222, 223, 290, 295, 355, 356
Rape	53, 244, 246, 252, 253, 254, 267, 272, 294
Rich	v,ix,2,11,13,22,39,40,41,42,43,44,45,46,47,54,57, 62,64,65,66,67,68,71,72,73,74,75,76,78,79,80,83, 84,85,88,90,113,118,142,157,223,282,283,284,28 296,356
Restitution	142, 222, 223, 294, 295, 296
Ritual	60, 61, 85, 240
Rulers	33,103,108, 110, 116, 126, 135, 136, 165, 218, 22

Robbery   4, 29, 45, 50, 67, 88, 90, 225, 300

S

Sex   ii,iv,v,viii, ix, xi, xii, 2, 4, 16, 57, 58, 164, 230,
                231, 232, 233, 240, 241, 242, 244, 245, 246, 247,
                248, 249, 250, 251, 252, 253, 254, 255, 256, 259,
                264, 265, 266, 267, 268, 269, 271, 272, 273, 274,
                282, 283, 288, 289, 291, 292, 293, 294, 302, 303,
                305, 307, 308, 348, 349, 351, 352, 353, 354, 355,
                356

Sexual   1, 14, 54, 56, 57, 58, 147, 148, 163, 230, 232, 233,
                234, 235, 237, 238, 239, 240, 241, 242, 244, 245,
                246, 247, 248, 249, 250, 251, 252, 253, 254, 255,
                259, 261, 262, 265, 266, 267, 268, 269, 270, 271,
                272, 274, 275, 277, 278, 280, 286, 289, 292, 293,
                305, 307, 353, 354, 355

Sources   47, 103, 118, 351

Spirit   xiii, 6, 14, 22, 23, 24, 25, 27, 33, 37, 58, 76, 81,
                106, 110, 112, 114, 116, 117, 120, 124, 131, 156,
                190, 209, 216, 218, 223, 224, 257, 274, 277, 294,
                298, 299, 302, 303, 354

Salvation   iii, 13, 46, 111, 116, 136, 143, 296

Sentenced   9, 176

Self-control   v, 52, 223, 224, 234, 294, 302, 303, 354

Stealing   50, 51

Sin	xi, 1, 5, 6, 8, 9, 14, 19, 22, 23, 28, 29, 33, 41, 46, 58, 60, 68, 71, 85, 136, 142, 168, 169, 171, 172, 202, 204, 210, 212, 222, 232, 233, 236, 237, 240, 243, 244, 252, 257, 278, 288, 289, 290, 291, 294, 295, 303, 349, 351, 353, 354, 355
Scamming	51
Selfishness	78

T

Temptation	v, x, xi, 4, 5, 6, 7, 8, 9, 10, 14, 20, 23, 25, 27, 29, 34, 35, 36, 43, 60, 79, 220, 249, 285, 288, 289, 348, 349, 350, 351, 353, 354
Tempted	4, 5, 6, 8, 9, 12, 13, 21, 22, 23, 24, 25, 224, 243, 288, 289, 349, 350
Transgression	5, 8, 23, 71
Torment	10, 12

U

Ungodly	7, 47, 115, 149
Usurpation	116, 118, 119

V

Victory	20, 21, 29, 30, 129, 351
Vulgar	181, 231, 232
Vindictive	190

W

Wealth	iv, v, viii, 2, 3, 5, 36, 38, 39, 40, 41, 42, 43, 44, 45, 47, 49, 50, 61, 62, 64, 68, 70, 71, 73, 75, 78, 79, 80, 82, 83, 85, 87, 88, 89, 90, 92, 96, 110, 113, 170, 282, 285, 286, 291, 295, 352, 353, 355
Wife	xiii, 5, 16, 48, 55, 63, 66, 85, 86, 137, 143, 146, 159, 162, 168, 169, 171, 172, 179, 182, 194, 195, 205, 222, 231, 235, 236, 239, 240, 246, 247, 248, 249, 251, 252, 253, 256, 258, 259, 266, 271, 275, 276, 278, 282, 300, 301, 348
World	vii, 13, 15, 19, 24, 25, 26, 29, 30, 31, 32, 33, 34, 35, 36, 41, 47, 51, 52, 54, 57, 60, 61, 62, 74, 111, 112, 115, 125, 133, 134, 140, 160, 184, 186, 191, 195, 200, 201, 205, 208, 221, 243, 244, 247, 252, 253, 264, 274, 279, 288, 290, 303, 305, 355, 356
Warning	85, 201, 227, 306, 352, 353, 354, 355
Whore	54, 240, 241
Whoredom	54
Witnessing	112

Scripture Reference Index

Genesis 1:1-31   285

Genesis 1:28   34, 247

Genesis 1:31a   285

Genesis 2:16-17   15

Genesis 2:19-20   34

Genesis 3:1   15

Genesis 3:1b   9

Genesis 3:1, 14   32

Genesis 3:2   288

Genesis 4:1   231, 247

Genesis 4:7   304

Genesis 4:17a   231

Genesis 13:2   61

Genesis 18:19   62, 104

Genesis 24:35-36   62

Genesis 34:29   39

Genesis 34:31   55, 234

Genesis 36:7   39

Genesis 38:13-18   56

Exodus 3:7-10   105

Exodus 9:14-17   129

Exodus 20:3   170
Exodus 20:13, 14, 17   169
Exodus 20:14   59, 232
Exodus 20:15   50
Exodus 20:15, 17   85
Exodus 20:16-17   66
Exodus 22:18   117
Exodus 22:19   275
Exodus 22:21-23   228

Leviticus 18:6   240
Leviticus 18:6-18   238, 240
Leviticus 18:6-23   275
Leviticus 18:22   147, 231
Leviticus 20:10, 16, 19   276
Leviticus 20:13   147

Numbers 12:3   300
Numbers 23:19   19
Numbers 27:18-20   120
Numbers 32:23   1
Deuteronomy 5:7   170
Deuteronomy 5:18   232, 277
Deuteronomy 5:19   50

Deuteronomy 6:12	79
Deuteronomy 8:11-20	80
Deuteronomy 8:18	41, 49, 85, 92, 113, 285
Deuteronomy 15:7-8	86
Deuteronomy 15:11	86
Deuteronomy 19:14	86
Deuteronomy 21:16	86
Deuteronomy 22:25	244
Deuteronomy 22:28-29	245
Deuteronomy 23:17	240, 241
Deuteronomy 23:19	86
Deuteronomy 23:19-20	86
Deuteronomy 27:21	277
Deuteronomy 28:1-14	16, 17, 198
Deuteronomy 28:15-68	18
Deuteronomy 28:64-65	199
Deuteronomy 29:24-28	199
Deuteronomy 31:1-8, 14-15, 23	120
Joshua 1:1-3	105
Joshua 2:1	56
Judges 11:1	56

Judges chapters 13 to 16   256

Judges 13:1-3   256

Judges 15:15   257

Judges 16:1, 4   56

Judges 16:1-4   257

Judges 16:15-17   257

Judges 16: 24   257

Judges 16:28   258

Judges 14:4   258

Ruth 2:1   62

Ruth 4:3-4   63

Ruth 4:8-10   64

1 Samuel 12:1-2a   106

1 Samuel 13:14   166

1 Samuel 16:1, 13   106

1 Samuel 16:6-13   121

1 Samuel 16:10-13   124

1 Samuel 17:26   122

1 Samuel 17:37-51   124

1 Samuel 23:2-4   167

1 Samuel 23:10-12   167

1 Samuel 24:6   125

1 Samuel 30:8	166
2Samuel 3:9-11	260
2 Samuel 7:16	125
2 Samuel 11:1-12:14	167
2Samuel 11:3-5	259
2 Samuel 11:27b	168
2 Samuel 12:7-12	168
2 Samuel 12:9-13	222
1Kings 1:5	261
1Kings 1:5-8, 49-53	252
1Kings 2:13-27	252
1Kings 2:15-17	252
1Kings 2:23-25	262
1 Kings 2:22-25	252
1Kings 3:10-14	170, 262
1 Kings 3:16	56
1 Kings 10:14-29	68
1 Kings 10:22	69
1 Kings 10:25	69
1 Kings 10:26-11:3	69
1Kings 11:1-3	263
1 Kings 11:1-6	171

1Kings 11:1-10	70
1Kings 11:13	151
1 Kings 16:29-30	171
1 Kings 21:1-16	171
1 Kings 21:7	171
1 Kings 21:20-23	172
2Kings 5:1-19	77
2Kings 19:31	151
2Kings 21:4	151
1 Chronicles 29:12a	39, 49, 87
2 Chronicles 1:12	49
2 Chronicles 6:6	151
2 Chronicles 32:27	39
2 Chronicles 33:4	151
Ezra 1:2	107, 132
Ezra 1:1-3	131
Ezra 1:4	132
Ezra 1:7-11	132
Ezra 6:11	133
Esther 3:1-5	70
Esther 3:2, 12-15	126

Esther 4:16   127

Esther 8:6   128

Esther 8:11, 15-17   128

Job 1:10   38

Psalms 12:3-4   216

Psalms 14:1   209

Psalms 24:1   30, 31

Psalms 37:34-35   216

Psalm 37:1- 2, 9-17, 20, 38   83

Psalm 15:5   87

Psalm 37:21   87

Psalm 39:6   87

Psalm 49:6-7   87

Psalm 49:10   87

Psalm 52:7   87

Psalm 62:10   88

Psalm 62:11   103,216,225, 287

Psalms 75:6-7   211

Psalms 81:11-12   242

Psalms 101:5   216

Psalm 112:5   88

Psalm 112:9   88

Psalms 113:7-8	49
Psalms 125:1	121
Psalms 127:1	157
Psalms 138:6	216
Psalms 147:2	151
Proverbs 1:7	209
Proverbs 6:24-25	242
Proverbs 8:13	216
Proverbs 10:15	39, 43
Proverbs 10:22	47, 88, 113, 118
Proverbs 11:2	216
Proverbs 13:11	83, 88
Proverbs 13:22	42, 50, 88
Proverbs 13:22a	47
Proverbs 15:25	217
Proverbs 16:18	76, 209, 216
Proverbs 18:12	76
Proverbs 15:27	77, 83
Proverbs 11:25-26	78
Proverbs 19:4	40, 41
Proverbs 3:9	88
Proverbs 10:4	88
Proverbs 11:4	88

Proverbs 11:28	88
Proverbs 14:31	89
Proverbs 20:21	89
Proverbs 22:1	89
Proverbs 22:4	89
Proverbs 22:6	x
Proverbs 22:9	89
Proverbs 22:16	80
Proverbs 22:22-23	228
Proverbs 27:24	89
Proverbs 28:22	89
Proverbs 28:25	217
Proverbs 29:2	181,193,217, 287
Proverbs 29:3	89, 286
Proverbs 29:23	209, 216
Proverbs 30:7-9	287
Proverbs 30:8-9	41
Proverbs 31:3	277
Ecclesiastes 4:1	217
Ecclesiastes 5:11	40, 43
Ecclesiastes 5:12	43
Ecclesiastes 5:19	89
Ecclesiastes 5:10	89

Ecclesiastes 5:10-11   44

Ecclesiastes 6:1-2   90

Ecclesiastes 8:4   218

Ecclesiastes 8:8   218

Ecclesiastes 9:11   226

Ecclesiastes 10:19   41, 91

Ecclesiastes 12:13   209

Isaiah 2:11   218

Isaiah 5:13   290

Isaiah 14:4   32

Isaiah 14:12   32

Isaiah 27:1   32

Isaiah 27:13   152

Isaiah 30:19   152

Isaiah 33:20   152

Isaiah 37:32   152

Isaiah 40:9   152

Isaiah 41:27   152

Isaiah 42:8   3, 214

Isaiah 44:26   152

Isaiah 44:28   130, 153

Isaiah 45:1a, 3-5   107

Isaiah 45:1-7, 13   131

Isaiah 52:9   153

Isaiah 53:1-10	141
Isaiah 52:13-14	141
Isaiah 53:6	6
Isaiah 53:9	21
Isaiah 58:6-7	67
Isaiah 64:6	297
Isaiah 65:18-19	153
Isaiah 66:10, 13, 20	153
Jeremiah 2:32	80
Jeremiah 3:17	154
Jeremiah 5:27-28	67
Jeremiah 9:23	90
Jeremiah 17:11	90
Jeremiah 22:15-17	72
Jeremiah 32:27	295
Jeremiah 50:31-32	218
Ezekiel 5:7-12	200
Ezekiel 18:5, 7-9	90
Ezekiel 22:29-31	67
Ezekiel 28:5-7	90
Ezekiel 28:12	32
Ezekiel 28:14	32

Daniel 2:5	211
Daniel 4:25	36
Daniel 4:27	212
Daniel 4:30	212
Daniel 4:31-33	212
Daniel 4:33-34	223
Daniel 4:34	213
Daniel 4:37	213
Daniel 5:1-4	213
Daniel 5:4-25	213
Daniel 5:17-28	214
Daniel 5:25	211
Daniel 8:9-11	32
Daniel 9:24-26a	142
Daniel 9:25	154
Daniel 10:13	32
Daniel 11:32	9
Daniel 5:26-28	210
Joel 2:32	154
Amos 4:1-2	71
Amos 5:10-12	71

Micah 2:1-13   82

Micah 3:11-12   91

Micah 5:12   118

Micah 6:10-13   68

Micah 6:12   72

Zephaniah 2:10   218

Zechariah 2:4   154

Zechariah 4:6   xiii, 218, 295

Zechariah 7:10   228

Zechariah 8:3, 22   154

Zechariah 12:6   155

Zechariah 14:2. 11, 17   155

Malachi 2:1-9   201

Malachi 3:4   155

Malachi 3:5   82

Malachi 3:6   19

Malachi 3:5-7   202

Malachi 3:13-15   202

New Testament

Matthew 2:3-6   135

Matthew 4:1-11   24

Matthew 4:3; 13:39   32

Matthew 5:27-28   233, 242

Matthew 5:32   235

Matthew 6:19-21, 31-33   92

Matthew 6:24   38, 46

Matthew 8:28-34   75

Matthew 7:7   92

Matt. 9:18   97

Matthew 10:1-15   114

Matthew 11:28   303

Matthew 11:28-29   295

Matthew 12:24   32

Matthew 13:38   32

Matthew 15:19   277

Matthew 16:21-23   27

Matt. 17:25   97

Matthew 19:9   232, 235

Matt. 19:26   98

Matthew 20:25   218

Matthew 20:25-27   228

Matt. 21:23   99

Matthew 23:12   213, 219, 225

Matthew 25:41	9, 10, 219
Matthew 26:36-46	28
Matthew 27:24	22
Matthew 27:16-26	137
Matthew 27:57	64, 157
Matthew 27:57-60	157
Matthew 28:11-15	73
Matthew 28:18	30, 115, 287
Matthew 28:1-4	72
Mark 1:11-13	24
Mark 1:13	32
Mark 3:27	40
Mark 5:1-20	75
Mark 7:21-22	277
Mark 7:21-23	77
Mark 8:36	303
Mark 9:35	224
Mark 10:6	97
Mark 10:23-25	46
Mark 10:42-44	228
Mark 12:30-31	299
Mark 15:1-15	138
Mark 15:25-32	28

Mark 15:43   64

Mark 15:43-46   157

Mark 16:15-17   115

Mark 16:15-18   112

Luke 1:30-35   247

Luke 1:32   100

Luke 2:1   134

Luke 4:1-14   25

Luke 4:5-7   32

Luke 4:8-9   36

Luke 8:17   283

Luke 9:43   102

Luke 14:11; 18:14   225

Luke 18:14   219

Luke 19:41-44   150

Luk. 20:20   97

Luke 22:26   97

Luke 11:15   32

Luke 12:13-21   295

Luke 14:13-24   65

Luke 15:12   39

Luke 16:19-31   12

Luke 19:1-10   296

Luke 22:15   242

Luke 22:25-26   229

Luke 23:13-25   136

Luke 23:50   64

Luke 23:50-53   157

Luke 23:51   64

Luke 23:53   157

John 1:3   35

John 1:11-13   111

John 3:1   97

John 3:10-13   11

John 3:16   19

John 3:16-18   111

John 7:1-8   26

John 8:1-11   233

John 8:29   22

John 8:32   290

John 8:41   235

John 8:44   32

John 10:10   33, 36

John 12:31   33

John 13:12-15   224

John 13:34   221

John 13:34-35	299
John 14:6	13
John 14:12	112
John 17:15	33
John 19:4	22
John 19:38-40	157
John 20:21-23	114
John 21:15	221
John 21:16	221
John 21:17	221
Acts 1:8	113, 115
Acts 4:7	98
Acts 4:11-12	111
Acts 8:9-11	116
Acts 10:1-2	64
Acts 13:6-12	117
Acts 13:22	166
Acts 15:20, 20	235
Acts 15:28-29	277
Acts 16:16-20	116
Acts 16:29-31	111
Acts 17:30-31	290
Acts 18:1-2	178

Acts 21:25   235

Acts 26:12   100

Romans 1:24-25   286

Romans 1:26-32   148

Romans 1:27-28   242

Rom. 4:21   99

Romans 5:3-5   8

Romans 3:23   5

Romans 5:12   29

Romans 8:20-22   20

Romans 9:16-17   129

Rom. 9:21   100

Rom. 9:22   99

Romans 10:9-12   13

Romans 12:10, 13   78

Romans 13:1-6   164

1 Corinthians 4:2   287

1 Corinthians 5:1   236

1 Corinthians 5:9   278

1 Corinthians 6:9,13, 18   278

1 Corinthians 6:9-10   60, 148, 241

1 Corinthians 6:13, 18   236

1 Corinthians 6:16-18   14, 58

1 Corinthians 7:2   278

1 Corinthians 7:5   249

1Corinthians 7:29-31   288

1 Corinthians 10:5-6   243

1 Corinthians 10:7-8   278

1 Corinthians 10:12-13 AMP   350

1 Corinthians 11:1   185

1 Corinthians 13:3   40

1 Corinthians   47, 96, 146, 214

2 Corinthians 4:3-4   31, 36

2 Corinthians 4:4   33

2Cor. 4:7   98

2 Corinthians 4:8-12   21

2 Corinthians 5:21   22

2 Corinthians 6:15   33

2 Corinthians 8:11   39

2 Corinthians 11:2-3   37

2 Corinthians 11:3   33

2 Corinthians 11:13-14   37

2 Corinthians 11:14   33

2 Corinthians 12:21   236, 279

Galatians 4:26   155
Galatians 5:19   236
Galatians 5:19-21   234, 238, 302
Galatians 5:22-23   223, 302
Galatians 6:2   78

Ephesians 2:2   33
Eph. 6:10   101
Ephesians 5:3   236, 279
Ephesians 5:18   298
Ephesians 5:22-24   301
Ephesians 5:28-29   248
Ephesians 5:29   248
Ephesians 6:12   33
Ephesians 6:16   33

Philippians 1:23   242
Philippians 2:5-11   30, 225, 300
Philippians 2:8   185
Philippians 4:13   295
Philippians 4:6-7   303

Colossians 1:11   101

Colossians 1:13   33

Colossians 1:15-17   31, 301

Colossians 3:5   236, 279

1 Thessalonians 2:17   242

1 Thessalonians 4:3   236

1Thessalonians 5:17   303

2Thes 1:9   101

2 Thessalonians 2:3   33

2 Thessalonians 3:10   48

1 Timothy 1:8-11   149

1 Timothy 4:1   33

1 Timothy 5:18   59

1Timothy 6:6   298

1 Timothy 6:9   43

1 Timothy 6:9-11   79

1Timothy 6:10   91, 297

1Timothy 6:9-10   286

1Timothy 6:11   297

2 Timothy 2:6-7   vi

2 Timothy 3:16-17   274

Hebrews 4:15	8, 22
Hebrews 7:26	22
Hebrews 9:14	22
Hebrews 9:27	10
Hebrews 12:2	156
Heb. 12:2	100
Hebrews 13:16	78
Heb. 11:19	99
Hebrews 11:23-33	258
Hebrews 12:14-16	279
Hebrews 13:4	279
James 1:2-4	7
James 1:12	7
James 1:13-15	6
James 1:14-15	243, 289
James 2:1-4	44
James 5:1-3	84
James 4:1-2	243
James 4:4	279
James 4:7	14
1 Peter 1:18-19	23

1 Peter 2:21-22   23

1 Peter 3:7   16

1 Peter 4:1-2   244

1 Peter 4:12-19   7

1 Peter 5:2-3   229

1 Peter 5:5-6   219

1 Peter 5:8   33, 37

2Pet. 1:2-4   243

2Pet. 1:16   102

2Pet. 2:11   101

1 John 1:8-9   232

1John 2:16-17   288

1John 1:9   169, 291

1 John 3:2-5   23

1 John 4:3   33

Jude 1: 6-7   280

Revelation 2:14, 20, 22   280

Revelation 2:20-21   237

Revelation 2:20-22   58

Revelation 9:1   33

Revelation 9:11	33
Revelation 9:20-21	237
Revelation 3:12	156
Revelation 12:3	33
Revelation 12:7	34
Revelation 12:9	33
Revelation 12:10	8, 33
Revelation 14:9	34
Rev. 17:13	98
Rev. 20:11a	100
Revelation 21:2, 10	156
Revelation 21:8	59, 238, 280
Revelation 22:14-15	281

About the Author

The author of this book was born of Christian parents. His father was a Baptist schoolteacher and later the pastor of a Baptist church. His wife – the mother of the author – was a stay-at-home mother, the youngest daughter of one of the foremost deacons of Pilgrim Baptist Church in Nigeria.

The author had his primary (or elementary) and secondary (High School) education in Christian (Baptist) schools. He professed faith in Christ at age eleven by the special grace of God. His growth and Christian maturity were gradual, serving the Lord in different capacities in two [other] Nigerian Baptist Convention churches before answering the call to the pastoral ministry.

The author worked briefly as an elementary school teacher, in the Federal Civil Service before switching to the pharmaceutical manufacturing industry, where he rose over a period of over two decades, to the post of Division General Manager. At various levels this man experienced, and encountered people that did experience temptations in areas of money, power and sex.

With a Master of Business Administration (Management), this author went through Baptist Theological Seminary for a four-year Bachelor's degree in Theology (B.Th), followed later in the USA with a Master of Theology (Th.M.) and Doctor of Theology (Th.D.) in Pastoral Theology. He is one of the four ordained ministers (Associate Pastors) in Community Baptist Church, Yonkers, NY, USA., and has previously published three books between 2017 and 2020 (both dates inclusive). He has many videos of sermons on his YouTube channel and other social media.

Prior to relocating to the USA, the author pastored Royal Priesthood Baptist Church, Aseese, Ogun State (near Lagos), Nigeria. He began preaching for YouTube as a means of continuing to propagate the gospel of Christ during the COVID 19 pandemic stay-at-home restriction periods in 2020 and has continued till date even after the restrictions have been lifted.

The author, Rev. Dr. Daniel U. Nwaelene has been married to Patricia for over forty-five years and they have been blessed with children and grandchildren to the glory of God.

In view of the title and message of this book, the author would like, in accord with the apostle Paul, to caution readers of this book that are being tempted to indulge in abuse of power, money or sex as follows:

"Therefore, let the one who thinks he stands firm [immune to temptation, being overconfident and self-righteous], take care that he does not fall [into sin and condemnation]. [13] No temptation [regardless of its source] has overtaken or enticed you that is not common to human experience [nor is any temptation unusual or beyond human resistance]; but God is faithful [to His word—He is compassionate and trustworthy], and He will not let you be tempted beyond your ability [to resist], but along with the temptation He [has in the past and is now and] will [always] provide the way out as well, so that you will be able to endure it [without yielding, and will overcome temptation with joy]. (1 Corinthians 10:12-13 AMP). The Lord will help you to overcome if you trust in Him and call on Him to help you.

MONEY, POWER AND SEX, The Implication of
MONEY, POWER AND SEX, The Implication of

Money, Power and Sex In The Downfall of People
Money, Power and Sex In The Downfall of People

BOOK REVIEW BY STEPHEN DUKE

Rev. Daniel Ukadike Nwaelene's *Money, Power and Sex: The Implication of Money, Power and Sex in the Downfall of People* is an unflinching exploration of three of life's most powerful forces. The book takes subjects often tiptoed around in Christian circles and confronts them directly with biblical truth, pastoral sensitivity, and a clear-eyed awareness of contemporary culture. It is not a simplistic devotional, nor is it dry academic theology; rather, it is a work that blends deep scriptural grounding with practical counsel, historical reflection, and prophetic urgency. Every page reveals the author's conviction that while money, power, and sex are gifts from God, their misuse and abuse have become some of the greatest sources of human downfall.

The book begins by laying a strong theological foundation through an examination of temptation, trials, and eternal destiny. Temptation is carefully defined and distinguished from trials, with James, Job, and Paul providing scriptural lenses. The author explains that temptation itself is not sin but the enticement that leads to it when desire is allowed to mature unchecked. The fall of Adam is contrasted with the victory of Christ, setting the stage for the rest of the book by showing that these struggles are not merely moral but eternal in consequence. The reader is reminded that the stakes of how we handle money, power, and sex are nothing less than heaven or hell, and this gravity anchors the entire work.

The chapter on money is one of the most practical and immediately relevant portions of the book. Rev. Nwaelene treats wealth as morally neutral, a gift that can be stewarded well or abused disastrously. He describes money as a servant rather than a master, citing both Proverbs and Deuteronomy to show that it is God who gives people the ability to create wealth. Personal anecdotes and illustrative stories, including the testimony of "Charlie" who experienced divine provision, keep the discussion grounded in lived reality. The warnings against greed, obsession, and tying identity to material possessions feel especially urgent in today's culture of consumerism. This section succeeds in not only diagnosing the dangers of money but also offering readers a mirror with which to evaluate their own relationship to wealth.

In the chapter on power, the book broadens its scope beyond individual morality to societal and political dynamics. The treatment of power is both theological and historical, drawing on Hebrew and Greek definitions, biblical kings, emperors, modern dictators, and political theorists like Lord Acton. The argument is simple yet profound: all authority is delegated by God, and when human beings forget this, power inevitably corrupts. Examples of monarchs who clung to their thrones until death, politicians who engineered coups to retain influence, and clergy who abused their pastoral authority demonstrate the universality of this temptation. This section gives the book a global resonance, speaking not only to Christians in pews but also to leaders in government, business, and church administration who need the reminder that leadership is stewardship, not ownership.

The chapter on sex is written with remarkable balance and courage. The author is frank about the destructive consequences of sexual sin, whether adultery, prostitution, infidelity, or abuse, yet he avoids sensationalism. Instead, he consistently grounds his arguments in biblical teaching, affirming that God created sex for marriage and blessing while warning that lust perverts it into a force of ruin. Stories like Samson and Delilah, Solomon's wives, and modern scandals from the #MeToo movement are cited together, showing how timeless this struggle is. James 1:14–15 serves as a theological anchor, warning that desire unchecked leads to sin and death. What makes this chapter especially powerful is its tone of compassion; it is not written to condemn but to warn, offering readers both clarity and hope for redemption. One of the most insightful contributions of the book is the discussion of how money, power, and sex interrelate. Rev. Nwaelene demonstrates that these forces rarely operate in isolation. Wealth buys influence, influence creates opportunities for sexual compromise, and scandals then expose corruption, leading to disgrace. This triangular cycle of temptation has toppled kings, ruined businesses, fractured churches, and destroyed families. The recognition of this interconnection makes the book especially timely in an age when leaders are regularly undone by exactly this combination of forces.

The conclusion of the book brings together theology and practical counsel. Money, power, and sex are all affirmed as good, essential, and God-given, but their misuse through lust and idolatry transforms them into destructive masters. The recommendations offered are both spiritual and practical: repent while there is still time, confess sins openly, cultivate biblical knowledge, rely on the Holy Spirit, and embrace accountability and self-control. Particularly helpful is the author's list of signs of abuse in money, power, and sex. These serve as diagnostic tools for readers, helping them recognize warning signs before they spiral into collapse. The practical orientation of the final chapter ensures that the book does not end in theory but in lived application.

As a writer, Rev. Nwaelene demonstrates a style that is both pastoral and technical. His pages are saturated with Scripture, often quoted in full from multiple translations, giving the text both authority and richness. He defines terms clearly, structures arguments logically, and repeats key ideas for emphasis, making the book accessible to lay readers while still suitable for theological study. His tone is compassionate but firm, addressing sensitive topics like sexual sin and political corruption without fear but also without sensationalism. His use of historical, biblical, and contemporary examples broadens the reach of the book, ensuring its relevance across cultures and contexts.

The impact of this book is profound. In a world marked by financial scandals, political corruption, moral collapse, and the commodification of sex, its message is both prophetic and practical. It serves as a preventive manual for those who aspire to leadership and wealth, a mirror for those already in positions of influence, and a restorative guide for those who have stumbled and seek repentance. Church leaders, young professionals, married couples, policymakers, and students alike will find themselves addressed in these pages.

Ultimately, *Money, Power and Sex* is a must-read. It combines biblical depth, pastoral sensitivity, and practical application in a way that very few books do. It is more than a warning; it is a roadmap. It exposes the traps of money, power, and sex, but it also points toward the freedom found in Christ through repentance, humility, and stewardship. The book deserves to be read widely in churches, seminaries,

leadership seminars, and personal study groups. Rev. Nwaelene has written not just a book, but a lasting resource for navigating some of the greatest challenges of human existence with integrity, faith, and hope.

Verdict:A must-read for anyone who desires to live faithfully in a world where money, power, and sex constantly threaten to derail destiny. This book deserves a place not only on Christian bookshelves but also in leadership seminars, marriage counseling programs,and academic theological study.

*Money, Power, and Sex*is a significant contribution to contemporary Christian thought. It is theologically solid, pastorally sensitive, and prophetically urgent. Rev. Nwaelene demonstrates both courage and care, addressing topics that many shy away from yet doing so with balance, clarity, and deep biblical grounding.

His writing style, rich in Scripture, clear in argument, and practical in application, ensures that the book will remain a resource for years to come. It is at once a mirrorthat exposes personal compromise and a mapthat points the way toward repentance, integrity, and divine blessing.